GOODNIGHT, L.A.

GOODNIGHT, L.A.

The Rise and Fall of Classic Rock—
The Untold Story from Inside the
Legendary Recording Studios

Kent Hartman

DA CAPO PRESS

Da Capo Press
Hachette Book Group
1290 Avenue of the Americas, New York, NY 10104
dacapopress.com

Printed in the United States of America

First Edition: September 2017
Published by Da Capo Press, an imprint of Perseus Books, LLC, a subsidiary of Hachette Book Group, Inc.
The Hachette Speakers Bureau provides a wide range of authors for speaking events. To find out more, go to www.hachettespeakersbureau.com or call (866) 376-6591.
The publisher is not responsible for websites (or their content) that are not owned by the publisher.

Print book interior design by Linda Mark

Library of Congress Cataloging-in-Publication Data
Names: Hartman, Kent.
Title: Goodnight, L.A.: the rise and fall of classic rock-the untold story from inside the legendary recording studios / Kent Hartman.
Description: Boston, MA: Da Capo Press, [2017] | Includes index. |
Identifiers: LCCN 2017012443 (print) | LCCN 2017013995 (ebook) |
ISBN 9780306824388 | ISBN 9780306824371 (hardcover)
Subjects: LCSH: Rock music—United States—1961–1970—History and criticism. | Rock music—United States—1971–1980—History and criticism. | Rock Music—Production and direction—United States—History—20th century.
Classification: LCC ML3534.3 (ebook) | LCC ML3534.3 .H38 2017 (print) | DDC
781.660973—dc23
LC record available at https://lccn.loc.gov/2017012443

ISBNs: 978-0-306-82437-1 (hardcover), 978-0-306-82438-8 (e-book)

LSC-C

10 9 8 7 6 5 4 3 2 1

For my late father, George Hartman,
the finest man I have ever known

CONTENTS

Contents

PROLOGUE

WHILE ROLLING DOWN THE STREET ON A CITY BUS IN PORT-land, Oregon, with my best friend back in early 1976, the idea suddenly dawned on us: Why not open a record store of our own? We had just turned sixteen and were completely obsessed with music, album rock in particular. If we weren't playing our latest 33⅓-RPM vinyl acquisitions, we were talking about them. And when it came to Saturdays (or most any day in the summer), all bets were off: we were headed to the nearest retailer to load up on more.

From Everybody's Records, owned by the great Tom Keenan, to Longhair Music, to Django's—sometimes even across town at the always-mesmerizing Music Millennium (still open to this day and owned by Oregon music legend Terry Currier)—Jim and I were constantly on the prowl for our latest LP fix. Taste-wise, while he went a little more toward the prog-rock end of the spectrum with bands such as Yes, Starcastle (remember them?), and Emerson, Lake & Palmer, we nevertheless met in the middle on a slew of fantastic acts, especially Chicago, Loggins and Messina (our first unchaperoned concert), Wings, Tower of Power, and too many others to even list.

Naming our joint venture the 'Lectric Grape Record Company after the punch line to a silly joke making the rounds at the time, we were off and running. We then got a business license and established a purchasing arrangement with soggy Portland's biggest record wholesaler, an outfit fittingly called Raintree Distributing. After setting up shop inside the student store of our high school, we had the enthusiasm of the faculty on our side and an instant clientele of over sixteen hundred record-hungry teens.

Though we sold our share of albums, we also tended to use up the profits pretty fast in order to buy more for ourselves, now at wholesale prices. But we learned a lot, had fun, and would have likely continued indefinitely had it not been for the nastiness of the owner of a new nearby record store that raised heck with the principal and subsequently the school board over us somehow being unfair competition (lack of overhead, I guess).

Unfortunately, instead of supporting two budding young entrepreneurs, the powers-that-be ultimately caved and sided with the store-owner, closing us down after about a year in existence. Naturally, the guy who complained ended up shuttering his shop around six months later. But by then it was too late; Jim and I were civilians once more, back to buying our albums at retail prices until the bands we loved eventually faded away.

Except that as life moved along, the rush of the music from that era never left either of us, providing inspiration in different ways. Jim went on to become an accomplished pianist among his other pursuits, including currently owning a thriving microbrewery. And I somehow ended up in the music business, putting in close to twenty years of being near the thing I've always loved most.

So *Goodnight, L.A.* is an ode to the music of that long-ago, finite time. Yes, it is also a follow-up of sorts to my first book, *The Wrecking Crew*, in that it traces what really happened behind the scenes in the recording studios in Los Angeles during the seventies and eighties—until the combined forces of disco, punk, new wave, MTV, hair metal, rap, and finally grunge put an end to all the merriment, that is.

In terms of carrying the narrative, *Goodnight, L.A.*'s two main characters are Keith Olsen, a music producer, and Waddy Wachtel, a studio and touring guitarist. They, as much or more than anyone, were at the center of it all in the L.A. studios during what was undoubtedly rock's apex. Both were also stars in their own right, even if much of the public never had any awareness. Perhaps you've heard of them; if not, just check out the liner notes and credits inside and/or on the backs of dozens of your old classic rock album covers. You'll be in for a surprise.

Though the hits have long since dried up, many if not most of the same album-rock artists from those days are still around, appearing nightly before thousands. Though I wish them well in their current endeavors, mostly I am unendingly glad to have been there the first time around, to have experienced the pleasure of their music as it was originally happening. And I am equally happy now to share the massive number of stories I've culled from those very musicians and producers. If I could somehow beam myself back, I probably would. It really was that cool. But until the technology of time travel catches up with my dreams, permit me the joy of showing you within the pages of *Goodnight, L.A.* what it was all like.

one

TALK, TALK

Get the hell off my stage.

—JANIS JOPLIN

WHEN CHARLES MANSON SQUEEZED OFF THE FIRST ROUND from his .38 automatic inside the Sound City Recording Studio in Van Nuys, California, no one knew what to do. But one bullet was all it took. Before the future serial killer could even think about firing a second shot, everyone in the place dove for cover.

It was early 1969, over six months before the grizzly Tate-LaBianca murders for which Manson and his "family" would forever be associated, when the diminutive ex-con was simply known to most as "Charlie." A lifelong petty thief, Manson had migrated to California during the mid-sixties, in part to try his hand at a career in music. As a self-taught singer-songwriter with an acoustic guitar ever at the ready, Manson had written a number of songs by the time he hooked up with the Beach Boys' cofounder and drummer, Dennis Wilson.

Wilson, a ruggedly handsome, naïve, fun-loving character with an eye for the ladies (and they for him), came across a couple of Manson's female followers one day as they hitchhiked along the Pacific Coast Highway in Malibu. After giving Patricia Krenwinkel and Ella Jo Bailey a ride back to his palatial home on Sunset Boulevard, the young women quickly dropped their clothes and made themselves available to Wilson in any way he wanted, an opportunity the free-spirited musician could not resist. From there the girls invited their beloved Charlie, along with a busload of his other followers, to move right on in with them. And for a time it seemed like one big party to Wilson. He had sex with any and all of the girls whenever he pleased, no questions asked and no condoms required; it was his own private Gomorrah.

But after Wilson talked his friend, the record producer Terry Melcher (and Doris Day's son), into giving Manson a tryout in the studio, things went downhill in a hurry. Melcher disliked Manson's singing even more than he disliked his personality and declined to offer him a recording contract. In turn, an infuriated Manson came down hard on Wilson, demanding that he make good on his alleged promise to help him become a star.

Not knowing what else to do and growing more fearful by the day in the face of Manson's increasingly menacing ways, Wilson finally told Manson he would pay for him to cut some songs at Sound City in Van Nuys, out in the San Fernando Valley, which was a new studio Wilson had heard about that apparently wasn't too expensive. Which all went as planned until afterward, when Wilson neglected to pay the bill for the recording time. Accordingly, the studio chose to hold onto Manson's master tapes until the money appeared, as per industry custom.

And that's when the gunplay began.

"Give me my fucking tapes," a wild-eyed Manson snarled, waving his Smith & Wesson as he stepped inside the studio's front door.

The petrified sound engineer and receptionist on duty that day didn't have to be asked twice. Manson got his tapes and Sound City ended up with a nice bullet hole in a metal cabinet for its trouble.

Which, on many levels, was the perfect metaphor for the rapidly changing American music business itself in the sixties.

BY MID-1969 THE SIMPLE, HAPPY-GO-LUCKY WORLD OF 45-RPM singles and Top Forty AM radio in America was beginning a slow, inexorable decline toward irrelevancy. Once the twin titans of delivering hit songs to the public, 45s and AM were gradually being supplanted in popularity by vinyl LPs and the newly created "underground" free-form radio found on the high-fidelity FM stereo bandwidth.

Album-wise, the seeds of sonic change came two years prior with the release of *Sgt. Pepper's Lonely Hearts Club Band* by the Beatles in 1967. The first true rock-and-roll concept album (though some would argue that *Pet Sounds* in 1966 by the Beach Boys got there first or even the Beatles' own *Revolver*), the artistically adventurous *Sgt. Pepper's* astonished listeners in countless ways, perhaps chief among them because every song on the LP was good. As in, really good.

While other successful rock-and-roll acts of the day such as Gary Lewis and the Playboys, the Buckinghams, and the Grass Roots remained perfectly content with the status quo of putting out a new album every six months that contained a couple of hoped-for hits and eight or ten unremarkable "filler" tracks, the Beatles would have none of it. They raised the bar for one and all with *Sgt. Pepper's* by making every tune matter. The melody, the lyrics, the instrumentation, the arrangement, the cohesion, the sequencing, the message, the cover art—it was all inextricably entwined. Albums were now to be listened to from beginning to end. No more cherry-picking among the cuts just to hear the latest hit song from the radio. The record labels, of course, still tried to pick the hits via 45-RPM releases to AM radio, but the public increasingly wanted the entire album to matter. Listening had become a full-blown, immersive, even communal experience. Accordingly, new LP releases were alternately ogled, examined, discussed, dissected, deconstructed, reconstructed, criticized, embraced, rejected, cherished, and generally played until the grooves wore out.

Dozens of popular albums released in the late sixties, including such classics as *Everybody Knows This Is Nowhere* by Neil Young with Crazy Horse, *To Our Children's Children's Children* by the Moody Blues, and *Volunteers* by Jefferson Airplane, became virtual manifestos among American youth yet contained exactly zero Top Forty hits. Times were changing fast, at least in terms of music consumption. Record buyers now expected more.

As a consequence, rock and roll was growing up in a hurry, getting bigger, badder, and more sophisticated—not to mention more thought provoking—almost by the day. With all apologies to the Archies and the Partridge Family, the prevailing national mood in America at the dawn of the seventies, at least among those under the age of thirty, had very little to do with sugary-sweet love songs and virtually everything to do with a reexamination of the nation's direction. The still-raging Vietnam War along with rampant poverty, political corruption, and long-festering civil rights issues made peppy pop ditties like "Sugar, Sugar" and "I Think I Love You" almost laughable to anyone not in elementary school.

And with these changing times came a new breed of Los Angeles–based musicians, producers, engineers, and recording studio owners all intent on achieving a similar goal. They aimed to take popular music to places their forebears—pioneers such as Chuck Berry, Little Richard, and Jerry Lee Lewis—could never have imagined.

As soon as Keith Olsen crashed to the ground in the fall of 1963, he knew he was hurt. Bad. A five-foot-seven, 135-pound freshman trying out for wide receiver for the University of Minnesota's frosh football team, Olsen—on paper anyway—had no business even being in the same zip code as the rest of the Golden Gophers' gridiron goliaths. He was a boy in a man's world, a very big man's world. But the will to impress the opposite sex can sometimes make an adolescent do head-scratching things, including obliterating a much-needed finger.

A standout musician and natural-born electronics whiz from Sioux Falls, South Dakota, Olsen came to campus out of high school to study cello, hardly the ideal background for catching footballs at the collegiate level. Yet there he was, on the third day of practice, arms outstretched, gamely getting pulverized all over again. Only this time around things were different.

At the conclusion of one particularly ill-fated slant route, a defender's sharp cleats inadvertently ground Olsen's right hand into what looked like a mass of uncooked hamburger. As he lay on the turf writhing in pain at the sight of what previously had been a perfectly healthy middle finger, Olsen instantly knew his season was done. Probably his football career too, such as it was. A wide receiver needs all ten digits, especially if he is the size of the team's water boy.

After the Minnesota team doctor examined Olsen's mangled hand and declared that he would need to spend the rest of the season on the team's injured list, Olsen was actually elated. With being cut from the squad likely to occur anyway before the regular season opener, he had hit the jackpot. Guys on injured reserve got letterman's sweaters. And guys with letterman's sweaters got the girls.

With extra time available while his finger healed and in between going to classes and dating one of the cheerleaders (the letterman sweater had paid off handsomely), Olsen, a talented all-around musician, one day found himself being asked by an acquaintance if he could help put a band together as support for Jimmie Rodgers, the pop singing star best known for the 1957 Top Ten smash "Honeycomb." Though Rodgers hadn't had a hit record in some years, it was still an opportunity that the ambitious, cherubic-faced Olsen wouldn't have passed up for the world, blurting out "Yes-I-can" so fast it sounded like all one word.

While getting ready to hit the road as part of an upper Midwest hootenanny tour, Rodgers needed some locals to play along with him for a stretch of dates. Along with various musician possibilities from around town, the quick-thinking Olsen, now that he could at least bend his finger, offered up his own services on bass, an instrument he had also been playing for years. And it proved to be a shrewd move. Six months of touring with Jimmie Rodgers later, after feeling like he had learned more about the music business than he ever could have in school, Keith Olsen officially dropped out of college for good in order to embark on what would become the musical adventure of a lifetime.

WHEN FIVE-YEAR-OLD BOBBY WACHTEL SAW A GUITAR IN A NEW York City store window one day in 1952, he instinctively knew then and there what he wanted to do with the rest of his life. Walking along with his mom, Wachtel happened to spot through the glass a man on the screen of a small, flickering black-and-white television set holding a hollow-body, jazz-style Gibson L-5 electric guitar. To the wide-eyed youngster it seemed as if the instrument had come straight from outer space.

"What is *that*?" Wachtel cried out, pointing.

"A guitar" came his mother's reply.

"I want one."

And that was all it took. The notion of owning and playing a guitar—no matter that at the time he had no obvious musical talent or any kind of know-how—became the fixated and persistent Wachtel's unrelenting mantra for the next four years, even after his beloved mother passed away from lung cancer not long after his sixth birthday.

Finally, at the age of nine the redheaded, pint-sized Wachtel's fondest dream came true. His father, in an effort to silence his son once and for all, bought Wachtel a cheap Kamico archtop acoustic guitar for Christmas. Though Jewish by origin, the Wachtel family's holiday orientation proved to be a rather mixed bag, with presents being opened on the morning of December 25 every year just like their Christian counterparts, yet always in the shadow of Hanukah lights on display throughout the house. But whatever the occasion, little Bobby Wachtel at long last had a guitar of his own. And from that moment forward he jammed on his new axe like his life depended on it, quickly learning to play virtually any song by ear.

But being a naturally gifted musician and having a viable future can often be two different things. A miserable truant from the age of ten, the opinionated, four-letter-word-spewing Wachtel hated school with a passion. For him it felt like a prison with no useful purpose. How was geometry or geography or, worst of all, PE going to help him become a better guitarist? Wachtel learned to lie his way through his first three years at tough Newtown High School in Queens in regard to his attendance (or lack thereof), only barely staying ahead of mandatory expulsion and, worse yet, narrowly avoiding the wrath of his suspicious father. Eventually the suggestion came from the administration that it might be in everyone's best interest if Wachtel perhaps found another, more suitable school.

Wachtel ended up transferring for his senior year to Quintano's School for Young Professionals in Manhattan, a last refuge for the artistically talented and behaviorally free-spirited. A place from which virtually everyone graduated. Or at least so it seemed. On the last day of class, when handed the final exam he needed to pass in order to get his diploma, Wachtel simply stared at the pages before him. He had no earthly idea how to answer the questions. Being able to reel off a blistering fifth-position, minor-pentatonic solo on his Les Paul electric guitar faster than most people could blink was of no help. The permanent label of "high school dropout" seemed assured. But good fortune came to Wachtel's rescue at the last moment.

"Just answer what you can," the sympathetic teacher said with a knowing look, "and I'll mark you only on what you get right."

By this time Bobby Wachtel's first name had also been supplanted by the bizarre-sounding mash-up nickname of "Waddy," courtesy of a fellow band member who could take no more of Wachtel's bossy ways. "What's the matter, *Waaadddy?*" the exasperated musician whined in a child-like voice one day during band rehearsal. Though Wachtel hated it at first, the new appellation stuck anyway, giving him a hard-to-forget name to match his equally hard-to-forget small size and red hair.

From his near brush with flunking out of Quintano's, it was immediately off to Newport, Rhode Island, for the self-admitted "fuck everything" rebel Wachtel in order to play with his band, the Orphans, a tight little rock-and-roll outfit that had been gaining a bit of a weekend following throughout New England. But it wasn't meant to last. With the Orphans splintering several months later in the wake of several members leaving for college to avoid the draft, a depressed, broke Wachtel formed a new band out of the remnants, called it Twice Nicely, and hoped for the best. Music was all he knew. It was all he wanted to know. It somehow would have to see him through.

WHILE RIDING ALONG IN AN OLD GREYHOUND-STYLE TOUR BUS
on an interstate highway somewhere deep in America's Heartland,
Keith Olsen shook his prized shoebox one more time. Yep, they were
all still in there. The container's contents, much to his satisfaction,
comprised a large and growing collection of motel room keys with the
names and phone numbers taped on them of all the groupies he had
managed to "befriend" while crisscrossing the country as the bass
player for a new band called the Music Machine. It was December of
1966, and the group had a hit record in heavy rotation on AM radio
called "Talk Talk." A nasty, raspy, attitudinal affair, the song person-
ified sixties garage rock at its most potent, a proto-punk precursor to
the Ramones, the Sex Pistols, and even Green Day. And that was saying a lot when fluffy pop fare such as "I'm a Believer" by the Monkees
and "Snoopy vs. the Red Baron" by the Royal Guardsmen held the top
two spots on the Billboard Hot 100 the same week "Talk Talk" hit its
peak at number fifteen in early January of 1967.

With jet-black hair, equally black clothes, and a single black leather
glove (more than a decade before Michael Jackson sported a similar af-
fectation), the Music Machine looked like they sounded—dangerous.
The Lovin' Spoonful or Herman's Hermits they were not. Which also
proved to be their eventual undoing. The Music Machine's uniqueness
made them interesting to the point of almost immediate obsolescence.
The unavoidable economic truth remained that most teenage music
listeners during the mid-sixties still preferred their music sunny-side
up, not dark and foreboding.

By mid-1967, after a good six months on the road squeezing every
last dollar and round of applause out of their one and only hit, the
Music Machine decided to call it quits. Creative differences between

Keith Olsen and the band's lead singer (and main songwriter), Sean Bonniwell, along with a mysteriously disproportionate split of revenue among the members, became too much to overcome.

But not before one evening in Newport, Rhode Island, when Olsen met a guitarist backstage after a Music Machine show who would become central to his and many other's as-yet-unimagined futures in the music business.

"Man, you guys are good," the guitar player enthused.

"Thanks," Olsen replied, turning to see a weird-looking twenty-year-old kid with long, frizzy red hair staring at him. It was Waddy Wachtel.

As Olsen and Wachtel chatted for a few minutes they realized they had the same musical sensibilities.

"I've got a band too. Can we go somewhere and talk?" Wachtel asked. He burned to know what it was like to have a record deal and a nationwide hit. After they shared dinner and Olsen had the chance to watch Wachtel's band play the next day, Olsen couldn't believe what he had seen.

"So who the hell *is* this guy 'Waddy'?" an incredulous Olsen asked the concert's local promoter. The answer came back simple and to the point:

"He's our Clapton."

WITHIN SECONDS AFTER THE MOMENT KEITH OLSEN FIRST SAW Stevie Nicks and Lindsey Buckingham open their mouths and begin harmonizing together onstage, he knew he had stumbled upon something special. Something so special, in fact, that he instinctively knew he could turn them into a hit-making act if given half a chance. The only question would be how fast he could get the pair out of their band and into a recording studio.

It was 1971, and following the dissolution of the Music Machine several years earlier, Olsen had spent his time working his way up the studio ranks in Hollywood. The knowledge he had gained about the recording side of the music business from being a member of a popular band, even if only for a short time, had served him well. He realized he wasn't a good enough singer or songwriter to strike out on his own or to even front a band, yet he was equally certain of something else: Olsen felt he knew exactly how to put together a hit record.

Accordingly, Olsen hooked on as an independent staff producer for a stretch at Columbia Records on Sunset Boulevard in Hollywood, then joined a small label nearby called Together Records so he could continue working alongside his old college friend, Curt Boettcher, an established talent who had produced Top Ten singles for the Association ("Along Comes Mary") and Tommy Roe ("Sweet Pea" and "Hooray for Hazel"). When Boettcher decided to move on after several months, Olsen elected to do the same: it was time for him to finally go out on his own.

Having cut a few demos over time at Sound City for various projects that never really happened, Olsen found that he liked the acoustics of the place, especially for drums. Though the tracking room inside Sound City's Studio A was nothing more than a generic-looking giant box (it previously had been a warehouse space and a Vox amplifier showroom), the enclosure somehow helped snares, tom-toms, and bass drums come alive like no other studio in town. It could make even a basic four-piece kit, if properly mic'd, sound huge. Notably, the band Spirit, featuring Mark Andes, Randy California, and Jay Ferguson (later of "Thunder Island" fame), made great use of the studio's unique sound qualities when recording their classic 1970 LP, *Twelve Dreams of Dr. Sardonicus*. Also, with scant business, the lightly used Sound City would be a perfect musical laboratory within which Olsen could conduct his ambitious music production experiments with little interruption. To that end, he managed to work out a deal with Joe Gottfried, Sound City's genial yet perpetually broke owner-founder, that gave Olsen a one-third stake in the facility as well as unlimited free studio use in exchange for an immediate and desperately needed $4,000 cash infusion to pay off an outstanding IRS lien.

With plenty of recording time now at his disposal, Olsen began actively searching for promising acts he could sign and produce. Anybody who had a tip on a hot band knew whom to call. Olsen would give a listen to anyone and everyone, from rock to blues to R&B, as long as they were good at what they did. Amateurs need not apply. From there, he figured, it would just be a matter of cutting a strong demo and then shopping it around town to the scores of hungry record labels who were always looking for the next chart topper. With combined 1970 US retail LP and tape sales coming in at an eye-popping $1.7 billion (a 9 percent increase over the year before), label heads wanted more. Lots more.

For their part, Stevie Nicks and Lindsey Buckingham had been toiling away within the Bay Area's club and fair circuit for the better part of four years as members of a popular five-piece band called Fritz. Jokingly named after a former classmate of theirs from Menlo-Atherton High School (it originally had been the Fritz Rabyne Memorial Band), the group played an eclectic mix of covers, self-penned ballads, and rockers while often appearing as the opening act for a series of big-time artists such as Jimi Hendrix, the Moody Blues, Leon Russell, Steve Miller, Chicago—and, on July 12, 1970, at the Santa Clara County Fairgrounds—a brilliant-yet-temperamental singer by the name of Janis Joplin.

On tour with her new backing band, Full Tilt Boogie, the hard-drinking, hard-drugging Joplin seemed agitated from the start. To compound matters, the show had begun late, causing Fritz to run past their agreed-upon cut-off time—a big no-no for an opening act. Joplin, who was watching from just offstage, didn't take kindly to being made to wait her turn, especially from some punk-ass local band she had never heard of. As the minutes ticked by, the recent Woodstock headliner became ever more vocal about her displeasure, demanding that Fritz end their set *now*.

"What the fuck are you assholes doing?" Joplin yelled while staring daggers at a horrified Nicks, who was in midperformance.

"Get the hell off my stage."

At the end of the song a frightened Fritz did just that. After saying a quick thank you to the audience and grabbing their gear, the band members scrambled out of sight as fast as they could. But not Nicks. Despite the caustic tongue lashing she had just received, she stayed behind to watch. This was her chance to see the biggest female rock-and-roll artist in the world do her thing. And Janis didn't disappoint.

Hitting the stage in silky purple bell-bottom pants, a frilly white blouse, and Native American jewelry along with a trademark set of feathers haphazardly placed in her hair, Joplin proved to be mesmerizing. Her scratchy, plaintive vocals were heartfelt, aching even, with the reality of an unhappy life painfully evident in every note. The woman who had been screaming at Nicks only minutes before was now Stevie's hero.

Though Joplin was hardly a conventional physical beauty, in that moment she nonetheless became beautiful to Nicks by making such a powerful and deeply emotional connection with the audience—something Nicks longed to bring to her own stage work. That single performance on that day by a woman who would live less than three more months (Joplin died of a heroin overdose on October 4, 1970, just days after recording "Me and Bobby McGee") inspired Stevie Nicks like no other. It stirred her to find her own voice and style, no matter what it might take or where it might take her.

Which proved to be perfect timing for Keith Olsen.

Having learned about Fritz through their manager, who had been dialing every producer in Los Angeles in an attempt to stir up at least some kind of recording interest in the band, Olsen agreed to fly up to San Francisco on their dollar to check them out. After being picked up at the San Francisco airport by a scruffy, twenty-two-year-old Lindsey Buckingham and the group's drummer in their beat-up instrument-filled van, Olsen rode along with them to that evening's concert at a private girl's high school, where he gamely helped load in the gear.

Then, ten minutes before showtime Stevie Nicks walked through the door. And roughly eleven minutes after that, Olsen knew all he needed to know. Buckingham and Nicks were standouts. Their talent and chemistry were obvious, not to mention they both looked and acted like rock stars. They had presence. And Olsen had been around long enough to know the difference. He had to sign them. Immediately following the show he made his pitch.

"Let's get together at my studio. Can you do it next week?"

Fritz didn't need to be asked twice. The band members were exultant. A chance for success beyond the confines of the Bay Area finally seemed possible.

A couple of days later, on a Sunday morning, the fivesome drove five hours south to Van Nuys and set about cutting a demo with Olsen at Sound City. As they labored all day on just one song, Olsen's creative instincts had not changed regarding the individual members of the band. He felt the same way he did when he saw them play live. Only two of them had star potential—Buckingham and Nicks. The rest were ordinary at best. Now came the hard part. Stepping out of the studio with Buckingham and Nicks at the end of the day's marathon twelve-hour recording session, Olsen decided to lay it on the line. He knew his bluntness would likely sting.

"You two are good, but the rest of the band is going to hold you back."

So there it was. Olsen was willing to move forward with them as a duo but not with their existing bandmates in any capacity. He would need to bring in musicians of his own choosing if the three of them were to record anything more. The song they had cut that day sounded to Olsen like any other garage band—it simply wasn't worth shopping around. The uniqueness of the Buckingham-Nicks vocal blend was nowhere to be found. They needed to be spotlighted, not buried. Even Sound City's vaunted drum sound couldn't put the production over the top.

Understandably, Olsen's words hurt Stevie and Lindsey. The other three in Fritz were their friends. How could they just ditch them? They had all been working long and hard to make it. This was to be the band's big break. The two told Olsen they would think about it. The group then drove back up the coast to ponder their career direction.

In the meantime little did Buckingham and Nicks know that the decision about their professional future was about to be made for them. It would come as if from the heavens by way of a bizarre combination of events involving a British drummer named Mick Fleetwood, a bad case of mononucleosis, and the help of guitarist Waddy Wachtel.

two

COLOUR MY WORLD

What the fuck is a Cowsill?

—WADDY WACHTEL

ONE DAY IN MID-1967, AFTER AVIDLY LISTENING TO EVERY song several times over on the Beatles' new *Sgt. Pepper's Lonely Hearts Club Band* album, James Pankow, the trombonist for a Chicago-based band called the Big Thing, realized there was only one thing left for him to do: throw his bottle of Vitalis hair tonic in the trash.

Working a nightclub circuit throughout the upper Midwest, the Big Thing had been almost exclusively playing the Top Forty radio hits of the day during countless shows from Milwaukee to Sioux Falls, Peoria to Des Moines, along with dozens of smaller cities and towns across the region. Familiar favorites such as "Soul Man," "Got to Get You into My Life," and "I Got You (I Feel Good)" got the crowd dancing and singing, all right. Which naturally pleased the club owners, as happy patrons drank more and therefore spent more. But other than paying the bills, performing covers of other people's records every night meant little to a seven-piece group of highly skilled musicians intent on creating their own songs and sound—not to mention jettisoning their buttoned-down stage attire of cheap suits and slicked-back hair.

In August of 1967, during the height of the Summer of Love, while playing a weeklong residency at a club in the small town of Niles, Michigan, the Big Thing's fortunes began to change. There they caught up with a college friend from Chicago named James Guercio, who had come to see them play after a heads-up phone call from the band's saxophonist/flautist, Walter Parazaider. Guercio, a supremely confident, charismatic, classically trained musician, had recently achieved major success on the other side of the studio glass as the Los Angeles–based, million-selling producer of fellow Chicagoans, the Buckinghams ("Kind of a Drag," "Don't You Care," "Hey Baby"). And he liked what he saw from his old pals in the Big Thing.

"You're the best band I've heard in a long time," Guercio enthused at the end of his visit. "It may take a while, but I want to get you guys out to L.A."

In the interim, by mid-1968, having changed their live set list to include an array of original compositions and now wearing whatever clothes they felt like on stage, the Big Thing's members were finally staying true to their musical instincts, despite being frequently fired by irate club owners who were less than thrilled with the band's new, non–Top Forty direction. Featuring the unusual presence of three equally capable lead singers—Robert Lamm (tenor/baritone), Terry Kath (deep baritone), and Peter Cetera (high tenor)—each with his own distinctive phrasing, timbre, and range, along with a crackerjack three-piece horn section led by Pankow, little by little the Big Thing was actually becoming a big thing, at least regionally. Unlike their competition, they played rock, jazz, blues, and R&B with equal facility, sometimes all in the same song and often with a set of provocative, socially conscious lyrics to match.

Within a year of James Guercio's promise to whisk the members of the Big Thing to sunny Southern California, the twenty-three-year-old wunderkind producer was as good as his word. After signing them to an all-encompassing contract that made him both their manager and producer as well as a co-owner of their song publishing rights, Guercio paid for the band to move to Hollywood, where he promptly rechristened them Chicago Transit Authority (or CTA) after the real Windy City bus and train system.

Guercio put the group up in a cramped, rundown, three-bedroom rental house underneath the busy 101 Freeway and let them have at it. Though not much to look at and filled with the buzz of nearby traffic, the group's new domicile nevertheless served its intended purpose. Pankow, for one, staked his claim to the bungalow's tiny dining room, turning it into a makeshift bedroom and trombone practice area with an old blanket hung as a room divider. Others crashed where they could, even in the bathtub.

Despite taking advantage of their fair share of what Hollywood had to offer young rock-and-rollers on the rise, including plenty of girls, pot, and the occasional harder substance, the members of CTA were nothing if not disciplined. The minimum of eight hours a day they spent for months on end woodshedding while holed up in their almost laughably small living room yielded a slew of new self-penned tunes.

After playing a short run of West Coast club dates in order to test out their new name and material, they then auditioned for the famed Whisky a Go Go on the Sunset Strip and quickly became that storied venue's house band on Sunday and Monday nights. Celebrities such as Jimi Hendrix, Joey Heatherton, and Steve McQueen were regular attendees, with a bowled-over Hendrix even telling Parazaider one evening, "You guys got a horn section that sounds like one set of lungs and a guitar player [Terry Kath] that's better than me." Shortly thereafter, at Hendrix's specific request, CTA became the opening act for a couple of dozen shows on his late-spring 1969 American tour.

After securing a deal for Chicago Transit Authority with Columbia Records, based on some demos of the songs they had painstakingly worked up while sitting cheek-by-jowl in their home, Guercio flew with the band to New York City to cut their first LP. Over a whirlwind five-day period inside Columbia's smallish sixteen-track sixth-floor Studio E on East 52nd Street, the band completely let loose. The music, fueled by years of pent-up dreams, ambitions, and just plain dues paying, came pouring out of them in a torrent of notes and passion, enough to unexpectedly create a double album.

Their hip, one-of-a-kind rock-meets-horns sound leveled a sonic heaviness and lyrical maturity at listeners that perfectly fit the tenor of the times. With powerful tracks such as "Someday" (with the famous "the whole world is watching" crowd chant from the 1968 Democratic Convention police riot), "Listen," and "Questions 67 and 68," CTA had become the Big Thing on steroids, with a desire for social change to match. In a year that would feature youthful rebellion as its moral centerpiece—from Woodstock to antiwar protests to John and Yoko's bed-ins for peace—Chicago Transit Authority had joined the revolution. Straight-laced Columbia Records executives, if a bit wary of what they might have on their hands, were nonetheless blown away by the band's profit potential.

Three months later, in April of 1969, the album, simply titled *Chicago Transit Authority*, hit the streets to widespread critical acclaim and steady sales. Six months after that, by the end of the year, the seven members of CTA—despite having a strong first LP release—had not so much as dented the upper half of the Billboard Hot 100 singles chart, which based its rankings on a combination of retail sales of 45s and Top Forty airplay.

Conversely, underground FM programmers loved CTA. The counterculture embraced the band. College radio played their music incessantly. But hit-song-driven AM radio, where a successful career could happen virtually overnight with the right set of spins by the right disc jockeys in the right cities, gave CTA a collective shrug. The marketing, promotion, and A&R people at Columbia Records did what they could to help break the band among the mainstream, but the program directors at the big AM Top Forty stations in places like New York, Los Angeles, and Dallas always came back with the same question: "Where are the singles?"

Which left a disappointed Chicago Transit Authority searching to find an answer. They wanted hits, but they also played only what they felt. And what they felt generally turned out to be seven-minute-plus message songs, far too long for the average pop radio listener who mostly just wanted something catchy to sing along with. More so, nationwide radio shows such as Casey Kasem's *American Top Forty*, while hardly hip, delivered a weekly countdown of "the biggest hits in the land" to millions of avid listeners. Something that could provide unprecedented exposure *if* a song met Casey's stringent length and content requirements, which, in turn, were based on the all-powerful Billboard Hot 100 singles chart.

Fortunately for Chicago Transit Authority, record labels at the turn of the seventies were surprisingly patient—in today's terms—with their acts regarding chart success and sales, so Columbia wasn't likely to drop them, at least not yet. But earning a prominent enough position in the label's music-talent pecking order was another story. With superstars such as Bob Dylan, Simon & Garfunkel, Janis Joplin, Barbra Streisand, and the suddenly white-hot Blood, Sweat &

Tears—Columbia's *other* horn-based band—already on the roster, a newbie, hitless outfit like CTA had to fight for their place at the table. There were only so many marketing and promotion dollars to go around, let alone time available among those who made the corporate-level decisions about how to spend that money, which meant that being a favored act mattered greatly. A major record label might sign twenty or more new artists in a given year and then only focus their resources to any meaningful degree on just two or three.

So the big issue remained: How can a band that is determined to share its political and social philosophies in songs that are at least twice as long as almost anything else on the Top Forty still find a way to achieve widespread popularity?

For Chicago Transit Authority the answer would come soon enough from between two beds inside a Holiday Inn motel room somewhere in middle America.

AS THE FATHER OF SIX PRECOCIOUS PERFORMING CHILDREN FROM Newport, Rhode Island, Richard "Bud" Cowsill ran a family consisting of equal parts musical brilliance and violent dysfunction. During 1967 his kids, known simply as the Cowsills, had burst on the national music scene with their debut single, "The Rain, the Park, and Other Things," which made it all the way to number three. At first the media dismissed them as just another novelty act. With the band originally consisting of four boys (soon to be five, plus one girl) in various stages of pre-through-post pubescence, along with, eventually, their ever-present, pint-sized singing mother, Barbara (affectionately known as "Mini-Mom"), it was easy to make that mistake.

However, it quickly became clear that the Cowsills—the future template for ABC's *Partridge Family* television series—were anything but a bunch of featherweight one-hit wonders. Skilled singers and musicians, even if a couple of them were still in elementary school, they were tight and talented. This was especially true of the oldest of the siblings, Bill, who was the band's familial equivalent of Brian Wilson of the Beach Boys in terms of his brilliant musicianship. Bill Cowsill knew how to sing, play guitar, create a memorable melody line, and write compelling lyrics with remarkable polish. He was also the Cowsills' unquestioned in-studio leader and all-around musical guiding light, revered by everyone in his family—everyone, that is, except his father.

There is no other way to describe Bud Cowsill than to say that he was an angry, jealous, depraved man. Growing up in unimaginably seedy circumstances as the child of a broken-down prostitute and a smalltime boxing promoter, the underside of life was all he knew. Joining the Navy while still in high school to escape the fractiousness and poverty of his home, the military provided Cowsill with the only example of any real discipline he had ever known. And he made sure to put those same unyielding, heavy-handed techniques to good use on the tender flesh and bones of his own flesh and blood.

Beaten senseless over the slightest of infractions, the Cowsill children were regularly ordered to meet as a group in the living room where, with great theatricality, Bud would move the furniture out of the way, as if creating a giant boxing ring. The quaking kids would then be forced to line up in a row and have the daylights punched out of them, one at a time. If anybody resisted or dared to talk back, they were hit again and again. Some were struck multiple times simply because Bud didn't like the look on their faces. While lips were being fattened and eyes were being blackened, the children would hear their dad solemnly repeat over and over, "You've got to pay the fiddler," as if his deranged flurry of unwarranted fisticuffs was somehow an important teaching moment.

Worse yet, the usually drunk-out-of-his-mind Bud Cowsill took to making illicit late-night visits to his young daughter's bedroom. Long petrified of hearing her father's footsteps coming down the hall and knowing that yet another round of sexual abuse was about to occur, Susan Cowsill eventually managed to summon the courage to turn the tables one evening at the age of twelve, bloodying her loaded father's face and knocking him to the ground. From then on, she lived with one of her older brothers, Paul, usually the only one to fight back against Bud's beatings, who had moved to his own place following his eighteenth birthday.

But the flip side of the Cowsills' family journey was the music—always the music. It was their only escape from the living hell of their home life. It was also their undeniable gift. In addition to "The Rain, the Park, and Other Things," the band's late-sixties Top Forty entries included "We Can Fly," "Indian Lake," and, most prominently, the number-two-charting cover of the theme song from the musical *Hair*. Despite his unpardonable sins against his children behind closed doors and without any meaningful managerial direction on his part (an agency booked all their appearances and MGM handled the recording end of things), the ambitious Bud Cowsill nevertheless ended up with a very public hit act on his hands. Something he never ceased to crow about ("I'm the band's manager—everything goes through me," he reminded people). The clean-cut mom-and-kids Cowsills septet starred on network TV variety shows. They appeared in milk ads. They became the fresh-scrubbed darlings of leading teen 'zines, such as *16* and *Tiger Beat*. Most of all, the Cowsills did whatever their old man told them to. Or else.

Though lacking any kind of musical talent and having no business experience, the monetary success Bud Cowsill began to experience through his children only encouraged him, by early 1968, to try his hand at adding to his "stable" of artists. Maybe he couldn't strum a guitar or decipher a recording contract, but the functionally illiterate Cowsill knew one thing if he knew his own name: more was always better than less.

Which is the precise philosophy that led him, inebriated as usual, to start visiting a nearby club in order to check out a band called the Orphans.

WHILE NOODLING AROUND ON A FENDER RHODES ELECTRIC PI-ano in the middle of the night inside a guestroom at a Holiday Inn in early 1970 while on tour with Chicago Transit Authority, a simple chord progression suddenly caught James Pankow's ear. Having lately been immersing himself in the Brandenburg Concertos by Bach, the German composer's style of layering melody lines was very much on Pankow's mind as he played a three-note ascending and then a three-note descending Fmajor7 arpeggio: *Bah-dah-dah, Dah-dah-dah, Bah-dah-dah, Dah-dah-dah.* As he then changed the lead note in the arpeggio in relation to the arpeggio before it, the hypnotic, up-one-side-and-down-the-other chord pattern turned into a round, eventually ending up back at Fmajor7.

Excited by what he had come up with, Pankow began humming an even simpler yet lilting contrapuntal melody over the top as he went along: *Dah-dah-dah-dah, Dah-dah-dah-dah.* Immediately recognizing the melodic sound he had in his head to be that of a flute, Pankow leapt to his feet from his playing position sandwiched between the two beds in his room and dashed down the hall. Banging for nearly a minute on flautist Walt Parazaider's door, Pankow was not to be turned away.

"Dude, what time is it?" is all that a half-asleep Parazaider could muster.

"I don't know—three-thirty, I guess," the out-of-breath Pankow huffed. "Quick, get your flute."

An initially hesitant Parazaider, the founder of the band, did as he was told. He had seen that kind of fever in Pankow before and knew it usually meant something good was about to happen. After throwing on some clothes, Parazaider grabbed his instrument and headed down the hall to Pankow's room. There the two began running through Pankow's new composition, with the classically trained Parazaider adding the melody line just as his bandmate and friend had written it. The sound of Pankow's arpeggiated keyboard chord changes in combination with the sublime elegance of Parazaider's flute were a thing of beauty, even better than Pankow had imagined. After they finished playing the short, less-than-three-minute instrumental, the two sat in silence, reveling in the magic. Finally, however, Pankow needed to know if his intuition was right.

"Tell me the truth, man. Is this any good?"

"Any good?" a wide-eyed Parazaider replied, breaking into a huge smile. "This song is going to make me famous, motherfucker!"

A few days following their late-night hotel room jam, Pankow came up with a set of simple romantic lyrics to match his instrumental piece. With the trombonist being a firm believer that the biggest hits on the planet have always been love songs—that love is the most powerful of human emotions—he called his new composition "Colour My World." And to put the song over the top, he opted to go with the husky-voiced, preternaturally soulful Terry Kath on lead vocal, a decision that paid immediate dividends. The instant Kath opened his mouth in the recording studio and began to croon the words, "As time goes on . . . " Pankow felt himself get goose bumps. He still wasn't sure the song would be a success with the public, but he knew then and there it was the best damn thing he had ever written.

As nineteen-year-old Waddy Wachtel stood on stage playing his electric guitar with his band, the Orphans, before the usual Izod-and-Topsiders-wearing crowd inside Dorian's nightclub in Newport, Rhode Island—home of the famed America's Cup yacht race—he did a double take. There at a table with a big shit-eating grin on his face was the same heckling drunk who had been giving him trouble for the better part of a week.

"Play us some real music for once," the middle-aged lush bellowed, obviously pleased with himself, especially after getting a couple of chuckles from fellow patrons.

A by-now fed-up Wachtel gamely played on, doing his best to temporarily ignore the distraction. At the end of his band's set he motioned for the club's manager to come over.

"See that guy over there? I want you to throw him out," Wachtel said angrily. "He's driving me crazy."

"I guess you don't know who he is then," the manager replied.

"No, and I don't care."

"You should. He's the Cowsills' father."

A puzzled Wachtel looked as if some kind of space alien had just spoken to him.

"What the fuck is a Cowsill?"

During March of 1970, as James Pankow cruised along with the top down in his used Mercedes 450 SEL convertible on Santa Monica Boulevard in Hollywood, glorying in the kind of gorgeous warm weather seldom experienced at that time of year back home in Chicago, he decided to flip on the car's radio. While idly punching through the various preset buttons on the dashboard, the trombonist and songwriter happened to land on 93 KHJ-AM, the Southland's premier Top Forty radio station. Figuring it might be a good chance to check out what the competition was up to, Pankow cranked the volume. But instead of hearing the latest single release from the Beatles or the Doors or the Rolling Stones, what he heard was . . . himself.

After almost slamming into the car in front of him out of surprise, Pankow, his head spinning, pulled to the side of the road. "Make Me Smile," the song now on the radio, was but a small part of an almost thirteen-minute suite of interconnected songs he had composed called "Ballet for a Girl in Buchannon." Taking up almost the entirety of side two of his group's second album, simply titled *Chicago*, "Ballet" recently had been recorded partly in Hollywood this time around, just down the street inside Columbia Record's cavernous Studio A. Written as an ode to a girlfriend who had gone off to college in West Virginia and broken Pankow's heart, no part of "Ballet"—which also included "Colour My World"—was ever intended to be a single, certainly not in the stand-alone, truncated form he had just heard. Yet there it was, front and center, on the most important music station in all of Los Angeles, maybe even the country. Pankow guessed that James Guercio or somebody at the label—probably both—had taken it upon themselves to edit "Make Me Smile" right out of the suite and down to AM-friendly size.

Though unsure on one level about how he felt hearing his prized artistic work hacked up for public consumption, Pankow was far from taking umbrage. In fact, he was thrilled. Pankow instinctively knew what the moment meant. He and his band finally had a hit single to call their own—they were on their way. The mighty KHJ was not in the business of playing random songs that had no future. If a record made the station's playlist, it was almost surely bound to be a hit.

What Pankow found out next pleased him even more. "Make Me Smile" made it to number nine on the Billboard Hot 100 just a few weeks later. Chicago Transit Authority (now officially known as just "Chicago" for its simplicity, *not* due to any threatened legal action from the real mass transit folks as some have speculated) finally had their big AM hit. More so, they were about to have two of them from the same album. Sung by Peter Cetera, the Robert Lamm–written "25 or 6 to 4"—a song about writing a song—became a virtual AM anthem during the summer of 1970, leaping to number four on Billboard through the strength of its mesmeric, machine-gun-like—and now-classic—descending chord progression along with a gnarly, rollicking, wah-wah-infused one-minute-plus electric guitar solo.

From there the audiotape editing floodgates burst open at Columbia Records. Viewed as found money, nothing makes a record label happier than discovering possible gold in an artist's back catalog. With razor blades and cutting blocks poised, three more songs, this time from the band's *first* LP—"Questions 67 and 68," "Beginnings," and "Does Anybody Really Know What Time It Is?"—were also promptly trimmed down to a suitable AM radio length, culminating in yet more Top Forty smashes for the group, all within barely over a year. Further, "Colour My World," snipped from "Ballet" just like its sister song, "Make Me Smile," became a Top Ten single too, in the process making Walt Parazaider's indelible flute solo world famous, just as he predicted.

An avalanche of popular success, it represented the kind of mass appeal that most bands never experience. However, it proved to be only the beginning for Chicago. Soon thereafter, as the early seventies moved forward, they would become one of the biggest bands in the world. But their much-coveted fame and fortune would also take a dark turn. The seven members would pay an unbearably heavy toll for their runaway success, especially their guitarist and lead singer, Terry Kath.

three

CRYING IN THE NIGHT

You're the only one in that band.
You know that, right?

—DAVID CROSBY

AFTER SEVERAL MORE ABRASIVE ENCOUNTERS BETWEEN
Waddy Wachtel and Bud Cowsill at Dorian's over the next few
months and after Wachtel had attended a nearby Cowsills concert to
see what the buzz was all about, Bud upped his ante. Liking what he
had been hearing, he approached Wachtel about becoming the Orphans' manager. He was sure he could get them a record deal, maybe
even an opening-act slot on a nationwide tour. A disgusted Wachtel,
however, still wanted nothing to do with the persistent barfly who
kept buzzing around him.

In desperation, after a flurry of futile attempts to get Wachtel to
change his mind, a typically pickled-to-the-gills Cowsill stammered,
"If I get a million dollars, will you sign with me then?"

"Yeah, sure. Whatever," Wachtel replied, quickly dismissing the ridiculous idea that the town drunk could ever possibly have that kind of wherewithal.

Mostly Wachtel just wanted the silly one-sided courtship to end. He then had Cowsill immediately thrown out of Dorian's for the umpteenth time. There were more important things for him to worry about anyway. Like how he was possibly going to make a living with his current gig just days from ending.

By the beginning of 1968, after his run at Dorian's had concluded, Waddy Wachtel's music career was virtually over. With the Orphans having recently disbanded and with no other offers coming in, Wachtel reluctantly accepted an invitation to play the winter snow season at the Sugarbush Resort in Vermont with his new, hastily assembled five-piece band, Twice Nicely. Taking the stage on a nightly basis to provide après ski entertainment for a bunch of sweater-clad, hot-buttered-rum-sipping Jean Claude Killy wannabes was better than starving, of course. But there existed little future or musical satisfaction in it either. Playing in the tiny, picturesque town of Warren, while a perfectly pleasant place, might as well have been Antarctica as far as Wachtel was concerned. He yearned to cut an album of his own or maybe become a respected session guitarist, and that meant returning to actual civilization. The mountains of Vermont were hardly a hotbed of name-brand musical activity.

Wachtel wanted to either go back to New York City and hook up with a major producer of some kind or maybe travel west to Los Angeles and stake his claim there. Though his notions were vague as to how to go about achieving either of these aims, he knew those were the places where everything was happening in rock and roll. New, chart-topping hard-rock acts like Steppenwolf ("Born to be Wild"), Iron Butterfly ("In-A-Gadda-Da-Vida"), and Vanilla Fudge ("You

Keep Me Hanging On"), featuring guitarists far less talented than Wachtel, were suddenly making it big while Waddy toiled away in snowbound obscurity—a truth in no way lost on him.

Finally, just as the morose Wachtel was about to break up Twice Nicely and do the unthinkable by slinking back home to live with his dad and brother in Brooklyn, the guitarist's salvation unexpectedly appeared one day before a show at Sugarbush. It was the ever-caustic Bud Cowsill, who had tracked down Wachtel in Vermont and had come to sign his man.

"I got the million dollars, asshole," Cowsill said by way of greeting.

"What?"

"You said you'd sign with me if I could come up with a million. And I have it."

With MGM Records having recently signed the Cowsills to a lucrative multirecord deal, Bud Cowsill was feeling flush. And he had an empire to build.

A worn-down Wachtel, though still suspicious of the boozed-up character in front of him, ultimately surrendered. He simply had no other options.

"Okay, fine," he said. "You're my manager. Now get me the fuck out of here."

IN EARLY 1969, WHEN WADDY WACHTEL SPOTTED DAVID CROSBY dining a mere three tables away in a Hollywood restaurant, he froze. Having recently moved to Los Angeles with his new manager, Bud Cowsill, and the rest of the Cowsills, along with the other four members of Twice Nicely, Wachtel couldn't believe his eyes. The notoriously outspoken Crosby was his idol.

Rising from his seat, Wachtel shyly approached the former Byrd and soon-to-be-star of Crosby, Stills & Nash.

"Excuse me," Wachtel said earnestly. "I'm sorry to bother you. But I just arrived here from the East Coast, and I've got a band I'd love for you to hear. My manager is Bud Cowsill of the Cowsills."

Crosby almost spit out his food.

"Ew, god," he said with obvious disgust.

A miscalculating Wachtel quickly backpedaled. He couldn't have chosen a lamer band-name calling card in the eyes of the too-cool-for-school Crosby if he had tried.

"I know, I know. I've got nothing to do with them," Wachtel said, attempting to show solidarity. "Just their manager."

After the two chatted for a couple more minutes, the remarkably accommodating midmeal Crosby agreed to come check out Wachtel's band. Maybe they were somebody he would want to produce, he indicated. Wachtel left the restaurant in euphoric disbelief.

FOR KEITH OLSEN MUSIC WAS ALWAYS SUPPOSED TO BE ABOUT the sandbox. To him "working" music was in no way the same as "playing" music. And playing music was akin to exploring and creating as an adult in an aural version of a child's sandbox. It was the freedom that mattered. Success would flow from there, he was sure of that. Though Olsen had yet to come up with anything close to a breakout hit as a producer, chasing dollars and musical trends was a prescription for failure, that much he knew. Olsen had seen many in the music business try and fail doing that. A uniqueness and clarity of vision were the keys, along with just plain hard work. To thine own muse be true. Additionally, nothing delighted Olsen more than finding new, talented musicians willing to join him in his indoor recording "sandbox" at Sound City, a welcome mat that would soon extend to a guitarist by the name of Waddy Wachtel.

Wachtel's first recording job in Los Angeles ironically turned out to be on a session for Bill Cowsill, son of the drunken Bud. Having recently been thrown out of the family band by his father after a violent brawl between the two in the lounge of the Flamingo Hotel in Las Vegas, where a bitter, jilted-feeling Bud had criticized his son's continued association with "that ungrateful, pot-smoking Wachtel," Bill had struck out on his own to cut a solo album. Needing some exceptional lead guitar work, he called on his old friend Waddy, who was happy to oblige.

Following the Bill Cowsill gig via a recommendation from a friend, Wachtel ended up playing guitar on a few sessions for the seemingly ubiquitous producer Curt Boettcher, which in turn led Waddy right back to none other than Keith Olsen, Boettcher's friend and occasional producing partner—the same guy Wachtel had met five years before in Rhode Island. After getting over the surprise of running into each other after so long and in such a "hey, small world" fashion, Olsen began hiring Waddy to play on many of his personal producing projects. He considered the still-unknown Wachtel to easily be one of the best guitarists in Hollywood and delightedly added him to his Sound City sandbox of first-call players.

Not long after, in the middle of a period spent working on some new Twice Nicely tunes with Keith Olsen at Sound City that the two hoped might turn around that band's fortunes, Wachtel received a phone call one day from David Crosby.

"Waddy, look, I've got to tell you something," Crosby said, sounding concerned. Having stopped by some months before at the Coldwater Canyon rental house Wachtel shared with the rest of the band (on Bud Cowsill's dime) to watch them rehearse, Crosby and Wachtel had subsequently formed a friendship. And the more Crosby saw of Wachtel's situation, the more he hated to see his new pal wasting his time.

"What's up?" Wachtel said.

Crosby, as was his way, didn't mince words.

"You're the only one in that band. You know that, right?"

Though meant as both a compliment and friendly career advice, those were the exact words that Wachtel didn't want to hear. He may have been the group's standout musician, but he was also loyal. At least to a point.

"Oh, man . . . thanks, David, I appreciate it. But I just can't leave my group. We're sounding really good right now."

But after the phone conversation Crosby's words stayed on Wachtel's mind. What if he was right? Other than making a little bread by playing guitar on the Cowsill's poor-selling, early 1970 album, *II x II*, Wachtel had little else going on. Aside from whatever work Olsen could throw at him, Wachtel needed to get his name out there if he was going to become a session regular around town. Bud Cowsill hadn't been able to land Twice Nicely a record deal either. After blowing opportunities for the band with Atlantic, Columbia, and other labels that had shown serious interest, the hot-tempered, self-aggrandizing Cowsill was now both a liability and an irrelevancy. And with the rest of Wachtel's bandmates—excluding Judi Pulver, his girlfriend and cosongwriter in the group—constantly complaining about their lack of success yet doing nothing about it, an increasingly resentful Wachtel gradually came to the conclusion that the sacrifice on his part was no longer worth it.

Setting up a mandatory group meeting, a newly determined Wachtel bluntly told the other three guys in Twice Nicely, "I'm not quitting—you're fired. There's a difference." And that was that. From there Wachtel called Bud Cowsill and relieved him of his managerial duties too. No more hangers-on and no more drunken buffoons. If

Wachtel was going to make it in the music business in L.A., which was still a very big *if*, he was going to do it his way. Or no way at all.

WHILE KEITH OLSEN DILIGENTLY WORKED THROUGH THE BETTER part of 1973 on countless songs in the studio for lots of little-known singer-songwriters and fledgling rock bands who were all trying to make it big but never would, the producer finally had an important recording opportunity come his way, something he was willing to stake his career on. It was the return of Lindsey Buckingham and Stevie Nicks.

Having spent most of the past year lying in bed with a debilitating case of mononucleosis, Buckingham, with his now-girlfriend Nicks's devoted nursing help and encouragement, had transformed himself from primarily a bass player into a world-class guitarist. Flat on his back with barely enough energy to even move his arms, Buckingham would struggle to hold onto his guitar while ever so gently fingerpicking various notes and chord patterns (as opposed to using a guitarist's more traditional plastic flat pick, which would have required too much movement and effort). By repeating these exercises ad infinitum for months on end, through sheer determination and a clear case of talent, Buckingham developed a uniquely percussive style and sound—exactly the kind of thing Keith Olsen valued most in a musician. He only wanted to work with the best, those who were not only committed to their craft but who also had something different to offer. For the nascent producer, different was where hit records came from.

With Olsen continuing to check in on Buckingham and Nicks over the phone every couple of months while Lindsey slowly regained his health, the pair would in turn play Olsen bits and pieces of what they had been working on. Much to Olsen's relief, the magical blend of their voices was still there, maybe even more so. Further, the two had been writing and demoing songs together on a small, four-track reel-to-reel tape recorder whenever Buckingham felt up to it. Good songs too, Olsen thought. And as an added bonus, given Buckingham's lengthy illness, he and Nicks never did have to decide whether to officially quit their band, Fritz, in order to move to Los Angeles to work with Olsen—the mono diagnosis made the decision for them. With Buckingham out of commission and Nicks by his side, the other members of Fritz had gone their own ways.

Finally arriving in L.A. with a stack of demo reels containing a bunch of completed songs along with their trusty four-track tape recorder, a small mixer, and several suitcases and guitar cases all loaded into their little Toyota, Lindsey Buckingham and Stevie Nicks made a beeline for Olsen's place in Coldwater Canyon. From inside a small guesthouse up a long, leafy, winding driveway, Olsen ambled out the front door to greet them.

"You made it," he said brightly, giving them each a hug.

After ushering the couple inside and getting them suitably settled to stay in his tiny basement for the near future at least, Olsen dutifully sat down and put on a pair of Koss headphones. Buckingham and Nicks could simply wait no longer for him to hear their material. After powering up their reel-to-reel recorder and pressing *play*, the two then intently scrutinized even the slightest movements on Olsen's face as their new producer carefully analyzed each song, such as early versions of "Crying in the Night," "Crystal," and "Lola (My Love)." At the end of the impromptu listening session a solemn-looking Olsen slowly removed his ear cans and then turned toward the pair.

"Well . . . " he said, pausing for effect, "I love it."

And so did the record label.

But not the first one Olsen shopped the songs to. And not the second, third, or fourth either. After bringing the Buckingham and Nicks demo material into the studio at Sound City and giving it an artful editing and mix-down job to improve the overall sonic quality, Olsen took tape copies of the songs to every label in town, big and small. Receiving the same "thanks, but no thanks" wherever he went—if even that much—an increasingly concerned Olsen finally approached tiny Anthem Records, which had a distribution deal with industry giant Polydor. There the executives saw it his way. They agreed to a deal with Olsen on the spot. With singer-songwriters such as James Taylor, Carly Simon, Carole King, and many others currently all the rage, Buckingham and Nicks were just the kind of act the label was looking for, even if the duo had a tendency to rock more than they played folk.

Trying to build his company's roster, Olsen then took the opportunity to pitch the eager label men on the two other acts he had recently signed to production deals, a couple of musicians about whose work he felt strongly. Much to Olsen's surprise, Anthem went for them both too. The first was a soft-spoken, Puerto Rican–born singer, songwriter, and multi-instrumentalist by the name of Jorge Calderón who had a funky, groove-laden style. The other was Waddy Wachtel.

ON JULY 3, 1974, KEITH OLSEN'S LONG-HELD PRECIOUS COLLECtion of hotel room keys from his days with the Music Machine melted into a big bright glob of plastic and metal. By the next morning, on the Fourth of July, Olsen was still living with Lindsey Buckingham and Stevie Nicks, all right, but he was now occupying *their* basement.

Returning home with his beloved dog, Pogologo, after buying a shirt, Olsen first noticed a billow of smoke in his neighborhood and wondered what was up. He then saw fire hoses running up his drive-way with water running down and knew it couldn't be good. After navigating his way up the steep incline on foot, Olsen saw that the small, two-bedroom, one-bath guesthouse he rented had not only caught fire; it had burned to the ground. Thanks to some neighbor-hood kids and their fireworks, there was nothing left but the cement foundation, a bunch of charred rubble, and the metal harp from the innards of his grand piano.

Left homeless and possessionless with two shirts to his name (the one on his back and the one he just bought), Olsen turned to his friends and clients, Lindsey and Stevie, for help. They gladly took him in, giving Olsen a place to crash in the small basement of their new rental in Studio City.

With all three coming down fast from the high of recently seeing the *Buckingham Nicks* LP released to retail, only to then sell virtually no copies, the house fire, while tragic, somehow almost seemed the lesser of the two dramatic life events. Having employed the services of Jerry Scheff (bass) and Ronnie Tutt (drums) from Elvis's TCB band, along with Waddy Wachtel and several other strong local musicians, the album, cut in a mere five weeks at Sound City, had initially ap-peared on the verge of major success, especially with standout radio-ready tracks such as "Crystal" and "Crying in the Night." With a racy black-and-white cover shot of Buckingham and Nicks posing nude from the waist up along with a clutch of well-crafted songs and stellar vocals by them both, the record had everything going for it—except for marketing and promotion.

For reasons that would forever remain unclear, Polydor chose to put almost no time, effort, or money into letting the world know about *Buckingham Nicks*. After a pressing of only thirty-five thou-sand copies and precious little PR, the label inexplicably moved on, leaving Buckingham, Nicks, and Olsen devastated. Other than being breakout stars in Birmingham, Alabama, of all places (a random FM station there fell in love with the album), Lindsey and Stevie were right back where they started: unknown.

As a tearful Richard Dashut sat on the front steps of Crystal Sound Recording Studios in Hollywood, he knew he was on the verge of doing something drastic. Having worked as the janitor/gofer/brass-railing polisher at the popular recording studio for several months in mid-1971, the mounting abuse the sensitive Dashut felt he had experienced at the hands of the studio's manager had finally taken its toll.

Co-owned by Andrew Berliner, a driven businessman with an exceptional aptitude for all things audio and electronic, and John Fischbach, a gifted young producer, Crystal catered in particular to the needs of a cadre of up-and-coming singer-songwriters such as Jackson Browne, Stevie Wonder, and, on her first solo album (immediately prior to *Tapestry*), Carole King. Further, with an exceptional mastering room and lathe (used for cutting an audio-signal-modulated groove into the surface of a special lacquer-coated blank disc or "acetate" right in the studio), producers such as Keith Olsen regularly took advantage of Crystal's facilities when in need of burning demos of their work. Yet it was another singer and occasional songwriter, Bobby Darin, who unexpectedly stepped forward to offer the weeping Dashut a measure of comfort.

Far more ambitious than wanting to be remembered only as the one-time teen idol, then pop crooner, then folk singer who had huge hits in the fifties and sixties with "Splish Splash," "Mack the Knife," and "If I Were a Carpenter," Darin, now in his mid-thirties, had recently signed a deal with Motown Records to pursue an R&B

direction. A master of reinvention and a restless soul with mortality on his mind (he had a damaged heart valve from a childhood case of rheumatic fever that would soon kill him), Darin had come to Crystal Sound to lay down some tracks for his upcoming album, *Bobby Darin*.

"What's wrong, man?" Darin asked, taking a seat.

A shocked Dashut couldn't believe who was talking to him. Yet he couldn't stop his feelings from suddenly pouring out either.

"I've just been screamed at again, for what I don't know. I can't take this anymore. I'm going to quit the business."

Darin nodded and then offered a bit of hard-earned advice.

"I've been there. But if you leave now, they win. Above all else, you've got to believe in yourself. If you really love music, just hang in there. It'll get better, I promise."

As Dashut then watched Bobby Darin stand up and head back inside, he thought about what the legendary singer had just said. Maybe Darin was right. Maybe something good would happen if he could somehow manage to stick it out a little while longer. Relationships were the key to everything in the music business—Dashut knew that much. And a great place to forge them was inside a recording studio. With that, he rose, wiped his eyes, blew his nose, and walked back inside too.

four

FROZEN LOVE

Nobody wants to hear a song about
an old rotten apple core.

—CAROLE KING

O N THE DAY AFTER KEITH OLSEN'S HOUSE BURNED DOWN, THE dispirited young producer unexpectedly received a piece of advice that would forever change the way he approached his career.

After the *Buckingham Nicks* flop Olsen wasn't sure what to do next. He had invested his heart, soul, and bank account into that project, only to see it die a quick death. With no commercially viable recording project on the horizon and now no home either, Olsen wondered whether he should even stay in the music business. There had to be an easier way to make a living. Plenty of his producing contemporaries, such as James Guercio with Chicago, Ted Templeman with the Doobie Brothers, and Gus Dudgeon with Elton John were well on their way, scoring hit after hit. Olsen wondered whether they were really better at what they did or maybe they just had better

47

songs and acts coming their way. At any rate, he knew something needed to change.

In order to clear his head, Olsen decided to accept a last-minute invitation from a friend to attend a big Fourth of July bash in Malibu at the singer-songwriter Carole King's beach house. By the summer of 1974 King was a bona fide superstar, with six Top Forty hit singles in the past three years alone and a seventh about to chart ("Jazzman"). This was all in addition to her 1971 LP, *Tapestry*, which was the biggest-selling album to date in music history.

Further, King, who wrote or cowrote almost all of her own material, was the author (with her ex-husband, Gerry Goffin) of countless hits for other artists during the early to mid-sixties. Working out of the famed Brill Building near New York City's Times Square (and its sister building across the street at 1650 Broadway) as one of the many in-house songwriting teams for various publishing companies, the Goffin-King combo had come up with such classics as "The Locomotion," "Up on the Roof," and "Will You Love Me Tomorrow." There was no doubt in anyone's mind as to Carole King's ability to compose a hit song. In that regard, the thirty-three-year-old was a virtual living legend. Now relocated to the L.A. area and always willing to help a fellow musician, the tiny, curly-haired King decided to share some of her hard-won wisdom with the obviously down-and-out Olsen.

"Keith, as you go through life, you have your daily experiences," King explained as she and Olsen strolled along the beach after stepping away midparty. "You put those experiences into an imaginary bag on your shoulder."

Though Olsen wasn't quite sure where the world-famous musician was going with her soliloquy, he found himself hanging on every word.

"Whenever you sit down to write a song," King continued, "you reach into this bag and pull out something that is a part of your soul."

She then stopped, staring straight at Olsen.

"But whatever you do, *never* get too comfortable."

Olsen froze. This was the four-time Grammy-winning Carole King talking, after all. He had to know why.

"Because when you get too comfortable," King replied, "you stop putting things in. You just take things out. And one day you'll reach into the bag, rummage around, and pull out an old rotten apple core."

With a wry smile, she then added the payoff.

"And, Keith, nobody wants to hear a song about an old rotten apple core."

Olsen felt chills run through his body. No one had ever explained the craft of songwriting to him that way. It was as if he had just been presented with the record industry's version of the Dead Sea Scrolls. King was making it clear that, for a song to be successful, it was all about the quality of the storytelling. And life experiences were the key. They fueled the telling of the story both lyrically and melodically, making the combination of words and music relatable.

Leaving the party later that night, Olsen felt renewed hope and a refined sense of purpose. Okay, so maybe the *Buckingham Nicks* LP hadn't been a hit. And maybe his house had burned down. Yes, they were both devastating events. But they were life experiences too, weren't they? The kind everyone has. Something, for better or worse, to put into the imaginary bag on his shoulder yet available to pull out at the right time to help shape a batch of songs for an album that *would* be a hit.

With Carole King's words running through his mind on what seemed like an infinite loop, Olsen realized he just needed to keep the faith and remain open to whatever life had to offer, both in and out of the studio. Sooner or later a recording artist with some truly special stories to tell would come his way. And he would be ready.

WHILE BARELY HANGING ON SEVERAL MONTHS LONGER AT CRYStal Sound after his chance encounter with Bobby Darin, Richard Dashut finally received his inevitable walking papers. Though instead of being in trouble for anything specific this time around, the manager of the place simply dismissed Dashut without explanation. After spending the next couple of weeks in bed alternately crying and wondering about his future employability now that he had actually gotten fired for apparently no reason at all, Dashut received a phone call one day that couldn't have come at a better time. On the line was Dave DeVore, Keith Olsen's first engineer and protégé over at Sound City. DeVore wanted to know if Dashut might have interest in coming to work for the two of them. Having gotten to know both DeVore and Olsen through the pair's use of the mastering room and lathe equipment at Crystal, a thrilled Dashut accepted on the spot.

For Dashut, however, Olsen was not the easiest guy to get to know. Nor could he believe his plain dumb good luck in being asked to work for him. Between Olsen's direct manner and high IQ, the ultrafocused producer could be intimidating for those like Dashut, who looked up to him. More so, the confident Olsen was who the insecure Dashut secretly wanted to be.

On Richard Dashut's first day at Sound City, however, instead of learning about the functioning of the various pieces of electronic equipment, he was assigned, along with several others, to the ignominious task of painting the walls and ceiling of the giant tracking room inside Studio A. Grateful to be there—or anywhere, for that matter—

Dashut threw himself into the project. If painting a room would help him learn to make records, then so be it.

"Here, let me help you with that," Dashut said at one point, gently taking a roller from a young blonde-haired woman who had more paint on her than on the ceiling.

"My name's Richard, by the way," the always-friendly Dashut offered.

"Hi, I'm Stevie. That's my boyfriend, Lindsey, over there," she said, pointing. And from that moment forward the three were inseparable. Within minutes of meeting, Buckingham and Dashut were smoking a fat joint together in the studio's maintenance room while listening to the playback of the latest Buckingham Nicks material.

By the end of the day, after painting most of the room, the threesome had even decided to get an apartment together. Keith Olsen had recently gotten his own place after bunking with Buckingham and Nicks for a while after the house fire, which left the pair in need of finding more affordable accommodations. As a further by-product of the unexpected friendship with Buckingham and Nicks, born instantly of shared interests and circumstances, in the not-so-distant future Dashut would also end up taking on a major position in the music business that he neither wanted nor felt remotely qualified for.

DURING THE FALL OF 1974, WHEN THE STRINGY-HAIRED, RAIL-thin, six-foot-six-inch Mick Fleetwood strode through the front door of Sound City, Keith Olsen at first had no idea who he was. Working on editing a song in Studio B, Olsen invited Fleetwood, who quickly introduced himself as the leader of the band Fleetwood Mac, into the much larger Studio A to check out the sound of the place. With his group gearing up to record their next album, Mick was looking for a new studio, a fresh vibe. Through an acquaintance Fleetwood had been told about the amazing acoustics inside Sound City, particularly for drums. Being Fleetwood Mac's drummer extraordinaire and therefore knowing firsthand how important a solid bottom end is to any good rock-and-roll recording, Fleetwood decided to drive out to Van Nuys and give the place a listen.

After spooling up a reel of two-inch, twenty-four-track tape on the Studer deck, Olsen sat bolt upright before Studio A's massive, custom Neve 8078 mixing console like Leonard Bernstein in front of the New York Philharmonic with baton raised. No ordinary mixer, the hugely expensive (more than $70,000), hand-wired, British-made, eighty-channel Neve (which Olsen had talked Joe Gottfried and Sound City's new third partner, businessman Tom Skeeter, into purchasing) added an exquisite yet subtle musicality to virtually any recording. It was also something no other studio in town had, which gave Olsen and Sound City a unique and valuable production draw.

With the master volume faders on the console raised, the song Olsen had chosen to demo for Fleetwood was "Frozen Love" from the recent *Buckingham Nicks* album, which Olsen thought would showcase the studio's acoustics to its best advantage. As the music burst forth through the high-end control room monitors, Fleetwood instantly began nodding his head and tapping his foot in time. It was clear the well-seasoned drummer liked what he heard, sonically and otherwise.

Formed in London in the summer of 1967 by Peter Green (lead guitar), Mick Fleetwood (drums), Jeremy Spencer (slide guitar), and Bob Brunning (bass), the blues-oriented, London-based Fleetwood Mac would go through many personnel changes over the course of the next several years. Only weeks after launching, an on-again-off-again John McVie became a permanent member on bass, replacing Brunning. At Green's request, a third guitarist, Danny Kirwan, joined in

1969. (Green had suggested the name "Fleetwood Mac" based on Fleetwood's and McVie's last names when the three left John Mayall's Bluesbreakers together to form their new band.)

A few years later, by the dawn of the seventies, the acclaimed yet mentally unstable Green, nicknamed "The Green God" by his adoring fans for his guitar prowess, left Fleetwood Mac not long after taking LSD at a Munich party, which had exacerbated his decline. The troubled Spencer departed soon after as well, abruptly running off one day to join a mysterious religious cult known as the Children of God. With Fleetwood and McVie desperately trying to keep the band alive through all the turmoil (drummers and bass players can't very well go it alone), they brought aboard an attractive, velvety-voiced keyboardist and singer named Christine Perfect, who would soon become McVie's wife (and change her last name). In 1971, while searching for Spencer's replacement, the group added American guitarist and Los Angeles native Bob Welch, who was also an accomplished rock-and-roll singer and songwriter.

With Fleetwood Mac's roster of musicians more or less stable by the early seventies, with the exception of an additional guitarist and singer combo who swiftly came and went, the core lineup of Fleetwood, McVie, McVie, and Welch participated in putting out five albums to increasing popularity in the United States. Their catalog of songs included such FM favorites as "Show Me a Little of Your Love," "Bare Trees," and "Hypnotized."

But all good bands must eventually come to an end, perhaps especially in the case of Fleetwood Mac. In the fall of 1974, having moved to the United States at the behest of a homesick Welch, the quartet cut the *Heroes Are Hard to Find* LP in Los Angeles (the first time they had done so), which climbed to number thirty-four on the Billboard Top 200 album chart, making it the band's best showing yet. Despite the success, Welch, who had grown tired of the group's nonstop touring as well as the endless legal battles they endured regarding a fake Fleetwood Mac that had been floating around, decided to quit. A shocked Fleetwood tried to talk him out of it, but Welch wouldn't budge, leaving the band with only three members and no guitarist, lead or otherwise. And that's when Mick Fleetwood decided to get in touch with Keith Olsen.

After Olsen had played "Frozen Love" for Fleetwood in the studio that day at Sound City, the drummer couldn't get the sound and quality of not only the studio but also Olsen's engineering out of his mind. Fleetwood felt the combination might be a perfect fit for recording Fleetwood Mac's next album, a six-week project to commence in February of 1975. Of course, though there were lots of other places to record in town, from the Record Plant to the Sound Factory to American Recording, where earlier in the decade Three Dog Night had recorded fistfuls of monstrous hits under the guidance of their gifted producer (and the studio's owner) Richie Podolor. But Mick Fleetwood was sold on Sound City.

Following a call from Fleetwood, an elated Olsen was on board. With the words of Carole King still on his mind from the previous summer, Olsen felt this might be the moment he had been waiting for—a way to step beyond the failure of the *Buckingham Nicks* album and employ his unique in-studio artistry on behalf of a name-brand band. He was ready to reach into that imaginary bag on his shoulder and pull out some magic.

Further, Mick Fleetwood was unable to get the guitarist who played on "Frozen Love" out of his mind. Not knowing who it was but loving the rhythmic style and needing a replacement for Welch as soon as humanly possible after striking out with several other possibilities, an anxious Fleetwood subsequently got a hold of Olsen on New Year's Eve to ask about hiring the guy he had heard. But what Fleetwood found out gave him pause. Olsen explained that the guitarist had a steady, live-in girlfriend. What's more, they were a musical duo and came as a package. Plus, the two were signed to an exclusive production contract with Olsen. If Fleetwood wanted Lindsey, he would have to take Stevie—and Keith too, as not just engineer but coproducer as well.

"I think you'll find that part to be nonnegotiable," Olsen added.

For Buckingham and Nicks the past several months after their album tanked had not only been rough spiritually but financially too. While Buckingham busily worked out guitar lines and arrangements for their next batch of songs, Nicks waitressed at a Roaring Twenties–style eatery in Hollywood called Clementine's so they could pay the rent. But they were still a team, artistically and romantically. Nothing could break that.

Going back to his bandmates with Olsen's information, Fleetwood and the McVies then debated the pros and cons of adding *two* new members, including another female singer, along with Olsen as coproducer. With a brand-new Warner Bros. recording contract in hand, they needed to get busy on their first album for their new label. After concluding that both Buckingham and Nicks would make a solid—if different-than-expected—kind of fit and with the McVies' blessing, Fleetwood asked Olsen to see whether Lindsey and Stevie might be interested.

Though it was the biggest party night of the year, Olsen knew he needed to immediately get in touch with Lindsey and Stevie. Not only was Fleetwood's interest something that could ignite their careers; it was also likely the only way Olsen was going to keep the six-week booking with Fleetwood Mac at Sound City. With Bob Welch gone and Mick Fleetwood in a predicament, it was either help find the band a new guitarist or possibly say goodbye to the album project. And with precious little money in the bank, Olsen was desperately counting on the income.

With his New Year's date by his side, Olsen hopped in his car and sped south over the Hollywood Hills to the apartment Buckingham and Nicks had moved into with their friend Richard Dashut near L.A.'s Fairfax District. After a surprised Buckingham and Nicks, who were throwing a small party, ushered Olsen and his date inside, the foursome adjourned to one of the bedrooms so Olsen could share the good news. He was sure it would generate an automatic "yes." A floored Buckingham, however, demurred, lamenting that he "could never play in the shadow of Peter Green." Nor did he want to be hemmed in by playing in someone else's band. He and Stevie had come too far.

But Olsen wasn't going to let this one go. Such an opportunity, he made plain, could break things wide open for all of them. Fleetwood Mac had a record deal and a recognizable name. Buckingham, Nicks, and Olsen did not.

Several exhausting hours later, with Olsen noting that if Buckingham didn't like it, he could always quit, the guitarist seemed on the verge of agreeing to try the whole thing on for size for one month. But he wanted to discuss it with Nicks in private.

"Can you give us a little time to talk it over?"

Olsen said Fleetwood needed to know soon; he would give the drummer Buckingham's phone number, and the two of them could take it from there.

Throughout the next couple of days Lindsey batted the idea around with Stevie, who, after running out to the store and buying several Fleetwood Mac albums to listen to, thought they actually could add something to the band. Buckingham still wasn't so sure. Fleetwood Mac and the duo of Buckingham Nicks were very different musical animals, at least on paper. One was steeped in British blues, the other in California-style pop/rock. Buckingham's main influences were groups like the Beach Boys and the Kingston Trio; he loved their intricate vocal harmonizing and instantly recognizable riffs. Though aware of Fleetwood Mac, mainly because of Peter Green's legendary guitar work and through FM radio favorites such as "Albatross" and "Oh, Well," the band was certainly not one of Buckingham's favorites. But he knew they were good at what they did. He also knew he needed some further advice. That's when he made a call of his own— to Waddy Wachtel.

Having been introduced to Buckingham and Nicks by Keith Olsen, Wachtel had played his 1960 Les Paul sunburst guitar all over the *Buckingham Nicks* LP, in the process becoming the duo's close friend and confidant. It also didn't hurt their burgeoning relationship that Wachtel, like Buckingham, simply idolized the work of Brian Wilson. The three had even done some acoustic dates together around town, along with Jorge Calderón on bass and occasionally Gary "Hoppy" Hodges on drums, playing clubs such as the well-known Troubadour. But for now Buckingham was in a veritable quandary and very much needed his friend's hopefully sage advice.

"What should I tell Mick, man? I'm not sure I want to do it," Buckingham asked.

Ever pragmatic, Wachtel was dumbfounded. It all made perfect sense to him.

"Okay, well, right now you're making two mistakes," he said. "One of them is you're on the phone with me instead of calling Fleetwood back and saying yes right now. The other is that you didn't ask if I could join them too."

After Buckingham finished laughing and the conversation ended, he thought about what Wachtel had said. Joining Fleetwood Mac didn't have to be a lifetime proposition, after all. He and Stevie could always leave if it didn't work out. And maybe, just maybe, it would.

five

ONLY LOVE IS REAL

This doesn't sound anything close to a blues band.

—John McVie

I N THE FALL OF 1973, SOMEWHERE IN THE SKIES OVER RURAL Indiana, as Helen Reddy's manicured fingernails dug deep into the leather armrests of her airplane seat, the stylish Australian-born pop chanteuse best known for the number-one hit single "I Am Woman" began to silently pray. For along with her husband/manager, Jeff Wald, and the rest of her band and crew, Reddy was preparing to die.

Having leased a Learjet at the last minute following Reddy's final concert date on the current tour in order to cut down on travel fatigue going back home to California, the trip was expected to be nothing more than a simple, luxurious power-hop over America's heartland. An exhausted Reddy had been gamely grinding out gig after gig up and down the East Coast, singing her growing list of Top Forty hits before an adoring public, including "I Don't Know How to Love Him," "Delta Dawn," and "Leave Me Alone (Ruby Red Dress)."

By the last night of the tour a private plane ride sounded like just the antidote to what had been a grueling stretch of appearances.

But that was before the massive thunderstorm hit.

At first all seemed tranquil onboard the opulent aircraft. Reddy played Scrabble with some of her band members. A small bar cart made its way down the aisle. Spirits were high. It had been a successful tour, and the close-knit group of travelers was finally homeward bound, ready for some much-needed downtime. Family and friends would be eagerly waiting for them at the airport. Reddy, for one, couldn't wait to see her ten-year-old daughter and toddler son.

Then, somewhere over Indiana, things began to change. Out of nowhere the Learjet lurched, followed by a huge shudder, as if trying to shake off the misdirection. A quick drop and a series of increasingly alarming bumps came next—enough movement to cause drinks to spill and nerves to fray. The board game was quickly stashed and seatbelts were fastened. Seasoned road veterans all, Reddy and her entourage had experienced their share of rough rides before; all bands had—it unfortunately came with the job. But this somehow seemed different. And they were right.

After a second shudder, the plane suddenly tilted nose first, heading into free-fall. A violent downdraft inside a thunderhead had rendered the pilots unable to maintain rudder and wing-flap control, causing the loss of all stabilization. With fuel down to virtual fumes after a valiant fight by the pilots to keep the airliner aloft, the two overworked General Electric turbo engines soon failed as well. The powerless jet was now at the mercy of the huge storm, being tossed about as if nothing more than a child's tin toy.

As the aircraft spiraled downward at an ever-increasing rate, the passengers and crew quickly found themselves plummeting toward earth at a face-stretching, lung-compressing, hypersonic speed of Mach 6—over forty-five hundred miles per hour. Reddy, like everyone else on board, was helplessly pinned to her seat from the crushing effects of the G-force. Potentially deadly luggage and cabin debris flew everywhere. The bulkheads rolled up like sardine can lids, and the windows popped out into the ether. Oxygen masks dropped from the ceiling. Some passengers screamed. A few hastily confessed past sins to anyone who would listen. Others, like Reddy, were deep in prayer.

Miraculously, the pilots pulled the plane out of its nosedive just in time. After the Learjet finally crash-landed in the middle of a Moline, Illinois cornfield and came to a rumbling, thumping, bouncing stop, there was nothing but an eerie silence. No one moved. No one could see. No one even knew for sure if they were dead or alive.

On this flight was Reddy's tour manager, Paul Cowsill, who was nothing if not a practiced survivor after the unbelievable physical abuse he had endured as a youth. Cowsill, after clawing his way out of his now-mangled seat, immediately yelled out to ask if everyone was okay. He then began helping the stunned passengers out of the crumpled fuselage as quickly as possible, observing with wonder that minor scratches and bruises were all anyone had suffered. Soon a series of fire trucks and other emergency rescue vehicles arrived, followed shortly thereafter by a van to ferry everyone to a local Moline hotel. Not even a hospital visit was needed. But the shock remained.

Within minutes after an exhausted Cowsill checked everybody in at the front desk then flopped face first on his own bed, his room's phone rang. It was Reddy and Wald. They wanted him to come to their suite right away. Worrying that there might be a health problem or perhaps the two were somehow angry with him over the plane crash, Cowsill went straight there. Upon arrival, however, he could see that the pair was anything but upset. In fact, they were downright welcoming.

After a quick round of "are you okays," Reddy gave Cowsill a big hug. Though he at first wasn't sure what was up, the pair seemed to him to be simply concerned about his well-being, which he appreciated. Nevertheless, Cowsill felt like chewing them both out. Renting the Learjet from a company with whom none of them had ever done business had been a rushed, last-minute arrangement necessitated by Reddy and Wald's sudden decision to opt out of taking their regularly scheduled commercial flight the next morning. Being the tour manager and also cautious by nature, Cowsill much preferred having more time when making travel arrangements for everyone. He was against the idea from the beginning. No Learjet, no crash. Yet recognizing his employer's genuine sincerity, Cowsill merely thanked them for reaching out to him with such kindness and then returned to his room.

But that wasn't to be the last act of generosity on his employers' part. Within a little over a year Paul Cowsill would receive from them nothing less than a second, all-expenses-paid shot at the big time and end up working with Keith Olsen and Waddy Wachtel in the process.

BY 1970 JIM MESSINA SIMPLY COULD TAKE NO MORE. HAVING spent the past couple of years as one of the founding members of the groundbreaking country-rock group Poco along with being the band's producer, the rigors of touring and the growing personality conflicts between group members had become too much for the twenty-four-year-old to handle. With a professional music pedigree dating back to the mid-sixties, first as a studio engineer and then as a band member and producer with/for the final incarnation of the original Buffalo Springfield—alongside future superstars Stephen Stills and Neil Young—Messina was an accomplished singer, songwriter, guitarist, and bassist.

Then, of course, there were Jim Messina's technical skills. Having engineered the second and third Buffalo Springfield albums while also producing the latter, he found that sitting behind the mixing console helping to shape the sound of musicians in a studio to be a perfect fit. The compactly built, ever-precise Southern California native loved nothing more than taking other people's musical ideas and making them better. Which is why the young producer decided to get in touch with Clive Davis, the powerful head of CBS Records.

Four years into his position, Davis was a legend in the making. Though an attorney by trade, the music-obsessed executive also had what is known in the business as "ears"—that is, he could often deftly recognize on both an artistic and commercial level exactly which elements within a given song were likely (or not) going to help it become a hit. The avuncular Davis also had a shrewd eye for the talent behind those songs.

Having become the president of CBS Records in 1967, the parent of subsidiary labels Columbia and Epic, Davis would make his mark over the ensuing years by signing a slew of new rock-and-roll artists to his company's traditionally easy-listening-heavy roster, including several little-known acts who would soon become household names: Janis Joplin; Santana; Blood, Sweat & Tears; Chicago; Billy Joel; Earth, Wind & Fire; Aerosmith; and Bruce Springsteen. But it was another signee, the band Poco, about which Davis had agreed to an in-person meeting with Jim Messina.

"To be honest, I've had it, Clive," the inwardly intense yet outwardly low-key Messina said during their short get-together. "All the touring and band problems are wearing me down. I really just want to produce."

Messina assured his surprised boss, however, that he fully intended to honor his commitments by finishing the second Poco album, currently in progress. He owed it to both the band and the label to see it through. But that would be the end of his run.

Knowing the quality of Messina's production work for both Buffalo Springfield and Poco, including the rare, disciplined ability to come in at or under budget on a recording project, Davis felt like he had a winner on his hands. Labels needed skilled, conscientious, in-house staff producers who could deliver the goods in a timely and economical manner. They were the backbone of the business, not to mention hard to find. It would be better to sign the multitalented Messina to a straight production deal than to lose his services altogether. The kid was a revenue generator.

"You know, that all sounds like a good plan," Davis replied, smiling. "Let's start thinking about some people for you to work with."

BY EARLY 1975, AFTER THE FIZZLE OF THE *BUCKINGHAM NICKS* LP and with his friends Lindsey and Stevie now firmly in place (but not him) as the newest members of Fleetwood Mac, Waddy Wachtel found himself back in his usual position: hustling for work. Some weeks he had paying guitar gigs; some weeks he didn't. Nothing if not devoted to his chosen career path, Wachtel took whatever came his way—demos, jingles, anything to keep the cash coming in and his name in the game.

But by mid-year, having been recommended by a friend to add guitar to some tracks for the actor/singer Tim Curry (*Rocky Horror Picture Show*) on his new album, Wachtel's luck began to change. During the recording sessions he unknowingly impressed Curry's tough-to-please producer, the legendary Lou Adler (Jan and Dean, the Mamas and the Papas, Cheech and Chong) enough to be asked to play on the next album for Adler's biggest client, Carole King.

After finishing the soundtrack for a made-for-TV animated children's special called *Really Rosie* in the summer of 1975, King turned her attention to cutting her next studio album. To be titled *Thoroughbred* and a return of sorts to her Brill Building tunesmith roots, several of the songs earmarked for the LP were cowritten by King and her former cubicle partner, ex-husband Gerry Goffin, including what would become the album's lone hit, "Only Love Is Real."

On the first day of recording in August, as Wachtel, guitar case in hand, headed down the hallway inside the venerable Tudor-style A&M Records facility on La Brea Avenue in West Hollywood where the session would take place, he suddenly stopped. There, coming toward him, was a woman who could pass for his twin. Short in stature, with cascading ringlets of shoulder-length reddish-brown hair and the same facial features, the similarities between the two were remarkable. Almost like Lucille Ball looking in the mirror to see "herself" played by Harpo Marx on the classic *I Love Lucy* episode (which reprised the even more famous Groucho and Harpo mirror-image movie bit from the Marx Brothers' *Duck Soup*), Wachtel and his hall mate, none other than Carole King herself, couldn't help but stare.

"Who are *you*?" King asked.

"I'm Waddy."

A smiling King looked him up and down.

"Are you my brother or something?"

From that moment on, the two musicians got along as if they actually were real-life siblings. So well, in fact, that upon the album's completion Lou Adler made Wachtel an offer he couldn't refuse: an invitation to go on tour as part of King's highly paid band, which included Danny Kortchmar (guitar), Russell Kunkel (drums), and Leland Sklar (bass). Wachtel knew the high-profile Kunkel and Sklar in passing from seeing them around town on other recording sessions. Both were premier, first-call players with no shortage of work portunities. Wachtel, however, had no familiarity with Kortchmar. However, Wachtel would soon end up knowing the guitarist everyone called "Kootch" better than he could have ever imagined.

IN EARLY JANUARY OF 1975, MUCH TO THE UTTER RELIEF AND joy of both Keith Olsen and Mick Fleetwood, the duo of Stevie Nicks and Lindsey Buckingham officially accepted Fleetwood's invitation to join Fleetwood Mac. After having dinner together at a local Mexican restaurant right after New Year's, the three Brits and two Americans found that they got along better than expected. And after several rehearsals they all realized that the merging of their musical styles, while questionable in the abstract, was magical in the execution.

Fleetwood and the two McVies provided the kind of solid, blues-based, locked-in rhythm section that Buckingham and Nicks had always dreamed of singing and playing with. In return, Buckingham and Nicks provided a California-style pop sensibility and degree of songcraft that had seemingly endless potential. Maybe the best part of all was the vocal blend. Stevie, Lindsey, and Christine complemented each other's lead vocals with a variety of sophisticated, interwoven high harmonies that sounded as if the three had been singing together for years. After several weeks of refining their sound, by the end of January the five finally felt ready to hit the studio and lay it all down on tape.

For Olsen, coproducing and engineering Fleetwood Mac's self-titled album during February and March of 1975 would turn out to be both incredibly difficult and, at times, incredibly easy. With several compositions already in recording-ready form from the now-abandoned second Buckingham Nicks album project, including "Monday Morning," "I'm So Afraid," and "Rhiannon," Buckingham and Nicks came well equipped to contribute their share to the songwriting load. Further, with "Say You Love Me" and "Over My Head" by Christine McVie, a delighted Olsen found himself with a wealth of standout material with which to work.

However, while McVie's lush, straightforward love ballads were a relative breeze for Olsen to record, not so with Nicks's "Rhiannon." In particular, the drum pattern proved to be almost impossible for Fleetwood to nail down. A premier percussionist by trade, Fleetwood played from the heart and from the gut. His blues-born technique and unbridled, almost maniacal passion behind the kit had always been central to the overall Fleetwood Mac sound. His hands and feet were the band's engine. The only thing Fleetwood lacked was formal training. Drum-obsessed since his youth, he had dropped out of school for good by the age of fifteen and had been pounding the skins for a living ever since. There had been no lessons, no specialized education along the way to better prepare him for playing unusual passages.

Being the shaper-in-chief of Nicks's songs in the studio, Buckingham envisioned a particular drumming style on "Rhiannon" that differed from the typical blues/rock method of striking the snare drum on the two and four beats on each measure. Buckingham wanted to mix it up, to employ syncopation and different textures, along with little or no reliance either on tapping out a standard eighth-note pattern on the hi-hat. To a veteran blues practitioner like Fleetwood, this was foreign territory. Nonetheless, as always the drummer gave it his best effort. Yet after countless takes over a two-day period, Olsen could see that what Buckingham wanted in terms of a backbeat was only going to happen through some major editing. Taking the first two recorded takes of the song and isolating just the drum track on each, Olsen got to work.

An imaginary tale about a witch-like celestial being, loosely based on a character from a novel called *Triad: A Novel of the Supernatural* by Mary Leader that Nicks had read a couple of years prior, "Rhiannon" required a deceptively complex rhythmic combination featuring alternating snare and tom-tom strikes on either the two or four beat, depending on the verse or chorus and also where it happened to be within the song. With razor blade in hand, like a surgeon's scalpel, Olsen sat down for the better part of a day and carefully cut out a multitude of snippets from the two-inch magnetic recording tape that contained the specific drum sounds/strikes he wanted. He then Scotch-taped all the little pieces together in a precise, groove-laden order, creating a perfectly rendered "Mick Fleetwood" drum loop in the process. This infinite drumming pattern subsequently played over and over underneath the rest of the instruments and voices as the song ran through its four-minute, twelve-second length.

On a different occasion not too many months before, Olsen had unwittingly encouraged the creation of another important song for the new Fleetwood Mac album. Stevie Nicks had arrived at Olsen's house late one evening in tears from yet another squabble with Buckingham. The pair's relationship, while caring, was also rocky. The constant shortage of money and lack of career prospects in the wake of the *Buckingham Nicks* failure had taken a toll on the couple, with Nicks even contemplating possibly going back to college and leaving Buckingham for good.

Looking for a sympathetic ear, Nicks turned to her friend, Olsen, who was happy to listen and console. However, with a recording date scheduled for early the next morning and needing to get some sleep, Olsen suggested that she take his guitar into the spare bedroom and write a song about her troubles. After all, channeling her feelings into musical form is what Nicks did best. Perhaps it would be cathartic, he offered; at least it might make her feel a little better. So Nicks did. The resulting composition turned out to be the rough basis for "Landslide," which she then finished soon thereafter in the mountains of

Colorado while accompanying Buckingham on his brief touring stint as lead guitarist for Don Everly.

After the basic instrumental tracking had been completed on *Fleetwood Mac* by the end of February, it came time to add the vocals. Between Nicks's unique vibrato and innate storytelling ability, Buckingham's three-octave-plus range and lead-singer-like instincts, and Christine McVie's languid, breathy style, Olsen could not have been more pleased. To have one good singer on an album project was a relief, to have two was a welcomed rarity, but to have three pro-quality vocalists—and songwriters—all in one band and all at the top of their games was nothing short of a bonanza.

When it finally came time to sit down behind Sound City's state-of-the-art Neve console in Studio A alongside Fleetwood and Buckingham to mix the record, Olsen immediately knew it was special, maybe even more than that. Though he had yet to produce a hit record, he had certainly been involved with them. And *Fleetwood Mac* by Fleetwood Mac was maybe the best thing he had ever heard. It met all three of Olsen's production requirements, in order of importance: first, the songwriting was superb; second, the vocal and instrumental performances were inspired; and third, the sonic quality was stellar. Though given the blues-based sound Fleetwood Mac had long been known for, the new record, at least at first, didn't quite appeal to everyone in the group.

"You know, we used to be a blues band," the no-nonsense, chain-smoking John McVie grumbled between puffs one evening during playback. "This doesn't sound anything close to a blues band."

Recognizing a possible gold record when he heard one, Olsen, who was sitting at the console manning the controls, couldn't let the comment slide. Not with an album like this sitting in their mutual laps.

"It may be pretty far away from the blues, John," a smiling Olsen replied, "but it's a lot closer to the bank."

FOR AS LONG AS KENNY LOGGINS COULD REMEMBER, BECOMING a professional musician was all he ever really wanted to do. Other than somehow making it to the NBA, which wasn't very likely (though he did play on his high school's varsity team), nothing had remotely seized the interest and passion of the Alhambra, California–raised Loggins like writing songs and then performing them for anyone who would listen. Born with a deceptively fierce determination hidden beneath a friendly, laid-back, almost shy exterior, the lanky, handsome Loggins was also blessed with the kind of shape-shifting voice that allowed him to sing a variety of musical styles and sing them all well, from country to folk to rock and roll.

After playing in several local bands during and after high school all the way up through a two-year stint at nearby Pasadena Community College, Loggins finally hooked on, in 1968 at the age of twenty, as a staff songwriter with ABC/Wingate publishing in Hollywood. Though a low-paying position at only a hundred bucks a week (Loggins split the rent with his girlfriend on a tiny, roach-infested apartment in a rough area of East L.A.), the job did allow him to see what professional songwriting was like from the inside out. It also gave Loggins the opportunity to pitch a few of his tunes to the up-and-coming, country-flavored Nitty Gritty Dirt Band, with one even scoring a Hot 100 hit for that group ("House at Pooh Corner," number fifty-three, 1970).

But the ambitious Loggins wanted more—*he* wanted to be the one singing his stuff on the Billboard charts. He knew that no one could get inside his songs like he could—there just needed to be a point of entry in getting exposure. Fortunately for Loggins, at the same time during the turn of the decade his older brother, Dan, who managed a record store, passed along a rough demo tape of some of Kenny's songs to Don Ellis, a former record store friend. Ellis, who had recently been hired in the A&R department by Clive Davis at CBS Records, dutifully gave it a listen, then handed it off to his boss. When Davis heard the tape he immediately flipped. He loved Loggins's voice and felt that maybe he had found his next hit act. The key, however, would be to assign the right producer to Loggins, someone who could take his batch of folkie tunes and give them some mainstream appeal. After reflection Davis decided he knew just the man for the job: Jim Messina.

However, when Messina received a call from Ellis about working with the unknown Loggins, the ex-Poco producer/guitarist was considerably less than enthused. He wanted a musician with a rock-and-roll background to be his first production client for Clive, not some folkie—that genre was dead and buried. Who even cared anymore about people like Glenn Yarborough or the Kingston Trio or fucking Trini Lopez? Even folk's eventual hybrid cousin, folk-rock, had come and gone in terms of popularity by the late sixties, with bands such as the Byrds, the Mamas and the Papas, and Messina's old outfit, Buffalo Springfield, being prime examples.

Nor did Jim Messina want to do any kind of country-rock. He had been there and done that with Poco. In fact, Messina didn't want any more "hybrids" at all. For that very reason he had recently turned down potentially lucrative opportunities to work with the easy-listening crooner star Andy Williams as well as with a brand-new, country-rock-leaning Dan Fogelberg, both Columbia Records acts. Messina just wanted to produce some killer rock and roll. To him there was a simple reason why contemporary rockers such as the Rolling Stones, Santana, Creedence Clearwater Revival, Three Dog Night, the Guess Who, and Grand Funk Railroad dominated the airwaves and the records charts: that's the kind of music people wanted to hear. Nobody was clamoring for folk.

"Tell you what, the best thing would be to have him stop by my house with some tapes. and maybe he can have dinner with my wife and me," Messina told Ellis about Loggins. "It'll give me a chance to see if he and I might be musically compatible."

A few days later a longhaired, bearded Kenny Loggins ambled up the steps of Messina's Hollywood two-story duplex and knocked on the door.

"Hey, man. Welcome," Messina said brightly, ushering Loggins inside.

After the two exchanged pleasantries and Messina introduced his wife to his possible client, Messina noticed that Loggins had nothing with him.

"Did you bring your tapes?" Messina asked.

"Actually I don't have any."

For Messina this was not a good sign. To him, being unprepared showed a lack of professionalism. And he was in no way interested in wasting his time on some amateur.

"Okay, so do you want to just play and sing some of your tunes for me then?"

"Uh, well, that's going to be a problem too," Loggins said, turning red. "I don't own a guitar."

Messina didn't know whether to laugh or cry. Mostly he just wanted to wring Don Ellis's neck for putting him in such a lame, awkward situation.

"I'll tell you what—I've got a little Sony two-track recorder and an old nylon-string guitar you can use."

Expecting the worst, Messina then set up the machine's two microphones on a coffee table in front of Loggins, handed his guest the guitar, and plopped into a nearby chair, ready to say "thanks but no thanks" as fast as he could. But when Loggins started singing and strumming, a funny thing happened: Messina liked it. Unpolished though the performance was, Loggins had some solid material, despite his folk leanings. Further, his unique-sounding tenor voice radiated warmth and sincerity. He was believable; Loggins knew how to sell a song. Messina had been around long enough to know that being relatable was a rare and valuable quality. That's what made hit records.

After Loggins left, Messina sat down with his wife to talk things over. The lack of tapes and guitar were a cause for concern, as were all the folk songs.

"I just don't know how ambitious he is," Messina said, his worry evident. "Also, it would take a tremendous amount of work to get Kenny up to speed, to be more rock and roll."

Messina paused.

"But you know, I like his voice. I think maybe I could work with him."

six

THE TIME HAS COME

They told me not to talk to you.

—STEVIE NICKS

KEITH OLSEN'S INSTINCTS ABOUT THE NEW FLEETWOOD MAC album proved to be spot on. The album did go gold, then platinum, then more. But it was a slow build in getting there.

When *Fleetwood Mac* made its retail debut the first week of July in 1975, the record-buying public did what they had done for virtually every other Fleetwood Mac album release over the previous seven years: they bought a few. Despite what Keith Olsen, the band, and even an impressed Reprise Records (the Warner Bros. Records subsidiary to which they were signed) felt about the quality of the new LP, it was also a different sound. Way different.

Gone was Bob Welch and his sophisticated, FM-friendly touch. In were Stevie Nicks and Lindsey Buckingham, giving the band a new, sexier image and a more pop-like direction. The public was going to have to be educated all over again as to just what exactly Fleetwood

Mac was. Some old fans would undoubtedly drop out. And there would hopefully be some new ones. Most of all the band just wanted the opportunity to make its case. So the fivesome, along with their tour manager, John Courage, and their new live-sound man, Richard Dashut, hit the road.

With just a big enough residual name to headline the college circuit and also appear as the opener for more prominent acts such as Rod Stewart, Jefferson Starship, and Ten Years After, Fleetwood Mac toured relentlessly in support of their album over the next year and more. In the meantime *Fleetwood Mac*—buoyed by three Top Twenty hit singles ("Over My Head," "Rhiannon," and "Say You Love Me") that were endlessly pushed to radio around the country by an independent promotion man cannily hired by Warner Bros.—steadily, stealthily kept creeping its way up the charts. Finally, in September of 1976, almost fifteen months after its release, the LP made it all the way to the number-one spot on the Billboard Top 200, in the process setting a record for taking the longest number of weeks to get there.

Overjoyed with their hard-won, chart-topping success and new status as a burgeoning headliner, by the fall of 1976 the five members of Fleetwood Mac eagerly began planning their next album. They wanted it to be even stronger and better than the last, something that would resonate with listeners and put the newly red-hot band over the top among the public.

After thinking things over, the new LP would also need to be coproduced, the band had decided, by someone other than Keith Olsen. Despite their current level of never-before-experienced success with Olsen at the helm—and at the risk of jeopardizing it all by suddenly making such a bold, chemistry-changing move—the lure of going forward with a new producer more likely to agree with their ideas proved to be an irresistible, if dangerous, draw.

ONCE OUT ON TOUR WITH CAROLE KING, EVERYTHING FELL INTO place for Waddy Wachtel. Playing with a contemporary, first-tier act (unlike his previous touring work with the by-then-passé Everly Brothers), Wachtel melded into King's band like he had known them all his life. Known as "The Section," Kortchmar, Kunkel, and Sklar (along with their usual keyboardist, Craig Doerge, whom the piano-playing King did not need) were a well-oiled machine. Successors to the vaunted Los Angeles–based Wrecking Crew studio musicians who had played most or all of the instruments, often in secret, on dozens upon dozens of hit records throughout the sixties, the Section members, by the mid-seventies, were racking up an enviable list of their own accomplishments.

Various combinations (and often all four) of Doerge, Kortchmar, Kunkel, and Sklar played on "California Sound" classics such as "Doctor My Eyes" by Jackson Browne, "Fire and Rain" by James Taylor, and "I Feel the Earth Move" by King herself. Though the foursome, sometimes also referred to as the "Mellow Mafia," was far from the only group of studio musicians in town, for a while they seemed to be listed among the credits on nearly every album of consequence coming out of Los Angeles. And though each had found his own way into the business and into playing with Carole King, it was Danny Kortchmar who had known and played with her the longest.

Born and raised in Westchester County, New York, to a wealthy screw machine manufacturer and his novelist wife, Kortchmar moved to Manhattan soon after high school, where he began playing guitar in a variety of local bands, including by late 1966 the Flying Machine, featuring an eighteen-year-old James Taylor. After Taylor left for England in 1968 to sign with the Beatles' new record label, Apple,

Kortchmar hooked on with the satirical rock band the Fugs for a time, then accepted an offer to move to Los Angeles with the Fugs' bassist, Charles Larkey, to seek their musical fortunes. From there the two joined forces with Carole King, an old friend of Larkey's—and Larkey's soon-to-be wife—in order to form a short-lived trio called the City.

Though produced by Lou Adler and with seemingly everything going for it in terms of label backing, the City's one and only album, *Now That Everything's Been Said*, failed to make a dent and they disbanded. Without a group to call his own, Kortchmar instead began to focus on working his way up the sideman food chain by playing guitar on lots of album sessions around town, including, within a couple of years, those for *Sweet Baby James*, the breakthrough release by his old friend Taylor, and on King's *Tapestry*. Remaining on good terms with her even after her eventual divorce from Larkey, Kortchmar continued to play on all of King's albums through the mid-seventies.

On the 1976 tour with Wachtel, however, Kortchmar's long-held position as an integral part of Carole King's band—and, for that matter, his very life—nearly came to an end at the hands of her latest boyfriend/husband-to-be. Following King's split from Larkey (and after her walk-and-talk with Keith Olsen on the beach in Malibu), King surprised many by choosing to adopt a back-to-nature lifestyle as a resident of rural Idaho. She and her new boyfriend, Rick Evers, a volatile, heavy-drug-using, self-styled mountain man lived much of the time there on a sprawling, primitively appointed ranch high in the Sawtooth Mountains north of Sun Valley.

Fancying himself to be a talented, as-yet undiscovered singer and songwriter in his own right, Evers immediately insinuated himself into the all-too-blinded-by-love King's musical affairs, so much so that his simmering jealousies toward any men in her life came to a full boil one evening, just as King and her bandmates made their way backstage after their first encore before a cheering crowd of thousands.

As an amped-up Danny Kortchmar bounded backstage, he exhorted, "That was fuckin' great!" And that was also all it took.

Bam.

Evers, who had been lurking just out of sight, punched Kortchmar square in the face, knocking him flat. A wide-eyed Waddy Wachtel, having just grabbed a seat for a short breather on a nearby equipment case, watched in horror as his new bandmate dropped to the floor like a bag of cement. Without thinking, the slightly built Wachtel then stood up to his full, unimposing height on top of his perch, puffed out his chest, and, like some kind of comically ill-conceived combination of Raggedy Andy and Superman, dove through the air and landed on top of Evers, fists flying.

As the outmatched Wachtel quickly began to realize his error in judgment in taking on his much larger and much meaner opponent, King's well-muscled drummer, Russ Kunkel, joined the fracas along with several roadies. With the vicious, snarling, animal-like Evers finally subdued, the band, along with a woozy Kortchmar, slowly made their way back onstage to a waiting crowd and a bewildered King, who had somehow missed all the action.

Once offstage for good after the second and final encore, which featured a rousing, sing-along version of "(You Make Me Feel Like) A Natural Woman," Kortchmar made straight for Wachtel.

"Man, I don't know who you are, but you and I are brothers—forever."

A LITTLE OVER A YEAR AFTER NARROWLY ESCAPING DEATH IN THE plane crash with Helen Reddy in the Illinois cornfield, Paul Cowsill began to seriously reexamine his existence. Maybe working as a tour manager wasn't the best way to be raising a family after all. He and his wife had two small children, and Cowsill wanted to be there for them as much as possible. He yearned to be everything his own father had not been: caring, nurturing, available. But being on the road for weeks at a time had already caused him to miss so much of their young lives—not to mention it was a great way to get killed. That's one reason why he decided to accept something he never dreamed would come his way again: a recording contract.

With the Cowsills having dissolved a couple of years into the seventies, Paul Cowsill had subsequently built a successful career behind the scenes first as a live sound engineer, then a tour manager. From an occupational perspective, he liked what he did. He got to be involved in music without the worry of trying to stay on top, to be the star. The heartache of the professional ups and downs he had experienced with his family and their band had left him disillusioned with the fickle performing end of the business.

Yet when Jeff Wald, Helen Reddy's husband and manager, came to him with an offer to step back out front, Cowsill was at first dismissive, then skeptical, and finally, slowly intrigued.

"This is going to be your year," Wald enthused to Cowsill one day as they sat in the Sydney Airport while on tour in Australia.

"Why is this my year?"

"Because I'm going to get you a record deal."

"A *what*?"

Cowsill was both stunned and confused. Going back in the studio was the last thing on his mind. He worked for others now. His days as a pop musician were long gone. The Cowsills had disbanded—hadn't Wald heard?

"The contract is gonna be for you alone," Reddy's husband added. "You can do whatever you want."

As Wald talked it up over the next several days, Cowsill decided to let the idea marinate. Who knew where it might lead. His old performing juices began to flow.

Whether Wald was making the offer out of gratitude to Cowsill for a long run of solid service or was using him as a way to make life unpleasant for Al Coury, the head of A&R at Capitol Records, Cowsill couldn't be sure. Wald planned to demand that if his wife re-signed with Capitol when her existing deal soon expired, Coury had to sign Cowsill too. Given that Cowsill had absolutely no track record as either the leader of a band or as a solo artist, it was far-fetched to think that either Coury or anyone else at Capitol would want the former child star within a hundred yards of their current artist roster. Which, of course, they didn't. Except that, in Cowsill's estimation, Wald despised Coury so much that he probably wanted to stick the label exec with an albatross of a contract just because he could. If Coury wanted the red-hot Reddy, he would have to take the ice-cold Cowsill along with her. That was the deal, pally—take it or leave it.

With a string of hits to her credit by this point, including her most recent number-one smash, "Angie Baby," Reddy was a veritable gold-record machine. And with Capitol's most famous and lucrative cash cows, the Beatles and the Beach Boys, far in the rearview mirror (the Beatles had disbanded in 1970, with the Beach Boys jumping ship for Warner/Reprise the same year), the label desperately needed Reddy's hefty revenue stream. Which left Cowsill with a brand-new, $30,000 record deal on his hands and an even bigger dilemma: Who the heck was he going to find to help him pull this thing off?

While driving through North Hollywood not long after the signing, with the thought swirling in his mind of how best to go about making the new record, Paul Cowsill suddenly couldn't believe his eyes: there, wandering down the sidewalk in his bare feet and wearing a pair of dirty, torn blue jeans, was his oldest brother, Bill, the one-time musical mastermind behind the Cowsills' sound and success. Pulling up next to him, Cowsill rolled down his window.

"Billy!"

A squinting, obviously wasted Bill Cowsill peered inside the vehicle, trying to make the connection.

"Pauly, hey. What's happening, baby?" he finally managed to stammer to his younger brother, who then pushed open the passenger-side door.

"Get in the car, man. I've got good news."

As soon as Paul Cowsill heard the words come out of his mouth, he knew he had made a mistake. Cowsill wanted more than anything to do his new album project his way. No matter Jeff Wald's exact intention in making the deal happen, he had nevertheless done Cowsill a huge favor. This would be a chance—for once, Cowsill felt—to get things done right, without anybody interfering. The Cowsills might still be going strong had his father not fucked things up. It was also an opportunity for Cowsill to make a name by himself, to really test his limits as a musician away from his family. A late bloomer, he was a belated addition to the already established, hit-making Cowsills when he joined up, along with his mom and sister, in 1968. Now, though, it was his chance to shine.

Yet through it all Bill remained a larger-than-life presence in Paul Cowsill's eyes, despite Bill's currently wobbly condition. He was thought of as the family's Brian Wilson, after all. Maybe if Billy got his act together, he could help coproduce. What could be better?

But brother Bill didn't get his act together. Not even close. After calling in the best session musicians in town, including stalwarts such as Russ Kunkel, Lee Sklar, and longtime family friend Waddy Wachtel (plus other brother Barry Cowsill, one of the original four Cowsill boys), Paul Cowsill found himself to be the captain of a rapidly sinking musical ship. If Bill showed up for rehearsals or recording sessions, it was a minor miracle—that is, if he could be found in the first place. And when he did make an appearance, Bill's rampant drug and alcohol consumption, combined with what many suspected to be a growing mental illness, often rendered him incoherent at best and incapacitated at worst. With no other choice and with a heavy heart, Paul Cowsill finally had to ban his brother from the studio altogether.

For the disillusioned Cowsill, the low point came one evening at Sound City in late 1974 (around the same time Mick Fleetwood made his fateful visit there to discover the guitar work of Lindsey Buckingham). Having recently hired Keith Olsen at Wachtel's suggestion to record and produce a few songs Bill had written, Cowsill had stopped by to listen to the playback of what they had cut so far. Olsen, Wachtel, and Cowsill, now the three leaders of the project, wanted to sit down together to determine whether there was something—anything—that might be usable.

About halfway through the listening session, however, with the music blaring and all three in deep concentration, Studio A's control room door suddenly burst open. Before anyone could react, in stumbled a drunk, belligerent Bill Cowsill with a half-empty vodka bottle in his hand and mayhem on his mind. Making straight for the twenty-four-track tape machine, he tore the still-moving take-up reel off the unit with his free hand and flung it across the room. As the brown, two-inch magnetic tape unspooled in great slithery strands all over the floor, Paul Cowsill leapt from his seat, whirled in the air like the second coming of Bruce Lee, and karate-kicked his brother as hard as he could, sending him sprawling.

As Bill Cowsill landed with a thud, blood simultaneously began spewing everywhere from Paul Cowsill's sandal-clad foot, which had been badly cut midkick on the now-shattered vodka bottle. Though staggered and clearly out of his mind, Bill Cowsill refused to give up, however. If he couldn't have "his" tape with "his" songs on it, then no one could. Crawling to the unspooled pile nearby, he grabbed a length of tape and began gnawing it in half. An irate, bleeding Paul Cowsill then dove on top of him, putting his crazed brother in a headlock. A furious Olsen immediately stood up and called a halt to the session, throwing everyone out. And that was that. The two Cowsills' professional involvement with not only Keith Olsen and Sound City but also with each other was over.

Bill Cowsill, whom Paul had told in no uncertain terms after the incident that "this town isn't big enough for the both of us," fled to Canada, never to return. As for the Capitol Records project, Paul Cowsill and Waddy Wachtel briefly regrouped shortly after the brouhaha as a duo named Bridey Murphy (which Bill Cowsill coined before his ouster) and managed to record one song together, with Cowsill on vocals and Wachtel playing all the instruments. Written by Judi Pulver, Wachtel's by-now ex-girlfriend, "The Time Has Come," recorded in Capitol's Studio B, came out as a single at the tail end of 1974 and promptly sank without a trace after being ignored by the label's marketing and promotions team.

As for Paul Cowsill, he would turn his back on the music business for many years and instead become involved in the construction industry, his tolerance for bad behavior having reached an end. But working with the Cowsills was in no way the last time Waddy Wachtel would find himself involved with a difficult, substance-abusing musician. Against his better judgment, the guitarist would soon end up as the cowriter and coproducer of a world-famous song with yet another out-of-control talent by the name of Warren Zevon.

ON SATURDAY, SEPTEMBER 4, 1976, THE VERY DAY *FLEETWOOD Mac* finally reached number one on Billboard's Top 200 album chart,

Keith Olsen received a check in the mail for $5,000. Not from Warner/ Reprise, the album's record label and the entity that distributed royalties, but, oddly, from the band Fleetwood Mac themselves.

With Olsen having signed a deal with Mick and the band to coproduce and engineer the album along with allowing his (Olsen's) clients, Buckingham and Nicks, to participate on it, Olsen had also agreed to the insisted-upon proviso by Fleetwood Mac that he would only start receiving his roughly two-percentage-point share of the gross retail sales (against a $10,000 advance) *after* 220,000 units had sold. This total represented the average number of albums Fleetwood Mac had been selling each time out in recent years before hooking up with Olsen. Which all seemed fair to the producer; he was there, after all, to assist in taking them to the next level; they didn't need him to help keep the status quo. Their recording efforts had been generally good to the tune of almost a quarter-million copies sold no matter what they had put out, from *Bare Trees* to *Mystery to Me* to *Heroes Are Hard to Find*. The inside joke had always been that, year in and year out, although far from a superstar act, Fleetwood Mac at least always dependably covered Warner Bros. Records' light bill. And Olsen certainly wasn't looking for any handouts either. A proud man, he wanted to make his own way.

But what gave Keith Olsen pause that Saturday morning had to do with the language on the back of the check. After turning it over, he noticed that it said, "Endorsement of this check relinquishes all rights and privileges for Reprise album number K54043." As the words jumped out at him, a stunned Olsen sat back in his chair. He immediately knew what the carefully crafted little sentence really meant: Fleetwood Mac was dumping him. Moreover, they were trying to do it without paying him the rest of what he was owed. With *Fleetwood Mac* now selling a ridiculous 250,000 units a *week*, the timing of his "severance" check, to Olsen, seemed highly suspicious.

After repeatedly attempting to get through to anyone he could from the group, including, finally, a sheepish yet ever-honest Nicks who confessed, "They told me not to talk to you," Olsen felt he had no recourse but to file a multimillion-dollar lawsuit against the five musicians. Spending tens of thousands he didn't have on high-powered attorneys, Olsen subsequently reached a settlement with Fleetwood Mac's legal team on the steps of the Beverly Hills Courthouse minutes before the trial was set to begin.

And that was it.

After all the handholding, cajoling, and utter dedication on behalf of Buckingham and Nicks for the better part of four years, Keith Olsen was out. Not only was he no longer working with Fleetwood Mac—after doing plenty to help turn that group into a household name via their first number-one album—but gone too were his prized discoveries, Stevie and Lindsey.

For Olsen that part hurt the most. They were not just his clients; they were his friends. The three had all hit the big time together after years of mutual struggle and sacrifice. It seemed they were destined to work alongside each other for many projects to come. *Welcome to the music business*, Olsen had to remind himself. Greed prevails. The lessons of his up-and-down days with the Music Machine came flooding back: take nothing for granted; no matter what success may be currently going on, circumstances can change in the record industry, for better or worse, with little or no warning.

Which, for Olsen, is exactly what happened next. Following the heartbreaking split with Fleetwood Mac, he would soon receive an out-of-the-blue call from one of the biggest powerbrokers of them all, someone who would change his life: Clive Davis.

seven

THAT'LL BE THE DAY

This isn't going on *my* record.

—LINDA RONSTADT

I N EARLY 1976 RICHARD DASHUT WALKED THROUGH THE WALLY Heider Studios parking lot in Hollywood with Mick Fleetwood late one evening after having auditioned yet another possible producer for the next Fleetwood Mac album. With so much at stake, the young sound engineer worried about what Mick and the band were going to do.

With Dashut's former boss, Keith Olsen, no longer on board, Fleetwood Mac had been searching in vain for a suitable replacement, someone with fresh ideas who could hopefully help them make an even better album than the platinum, still-selling *Fleetwood Mac*. Bursting with creative energy and a feeling of momentum after scoring three Top Twenty hits in the past year, the five musicians were hungry to take things to the next level.

By the mid-seventies almost all the biggest rock acts had world-class producers to guide them—or at least rein them in, as the case may be. The Eagles first employed the legendary London-based Glyn Johns (Rolling Stones, Led Zeppelin, the Who) on their first couple of albums, then brought in fellow American Bill Szymczyk (B. B. King, James Gang, J. Geils Band) and realized even greater success. The hit-making juggernaut Chicago had been with James William Guercio for what seemed like forever. And everyone knew the Doobie Brothers never made a move without Ted Templeman on the other side of the glass. But so far Fleetwood Mac had come up empty-handed.

With the multitalented Lindsey Buckingham as the band's do-everything arranger and de facto producer anyway, the role of an outside producer necessitated a unique set of qualities. It required the services of a relatively ego-less person who could slide into place at the mixing console as a complimentary yet independent-thinking presence—someone blessed with a great musical ear, excellent record-making instincts, and, perhaps as much or more than anything, the ability to get along. With five strong-willed personalities, the members of Fleetwood Mac could be a lot for anyone to handle.

As Richard Dashut got to his car the towering Fleetwood put his arm around his foot-shorter friend.

"Well, Dashut, it looks like you're our coproducer now," Fleetwood said matter-of-factly.

A confused Dashut at first thought Fleetwood was kidding—the drummer was well known for his dry sense of humor. But even if he wasn't joshing around, surely Fleetwood knew that Dashut had only been working as the band's live sound engineer for a little over a year. More so, Dashut had never produced anything for anyone.

"Mick, you can't be serious," Dashut said, hoping it was all a joke. "I don't know how to be a producer. I'm an engineer, and barely that."

Fleetwood, the ever-so-British son of a decorated World War II RAF pilot, would have none of it. Where he came from, when duty called, men stepped forward, no questions asked. A stiff upper lip and all that.

"Shut up, Dashut," Fleetwood replied. "Quit sniveling. You start tomorrow."

IN THE EARLY FALL OF 1967, AS THE SINGER LINDA RONSTADT and her two bandmates in the Stone Poneys, Kenny Edwards and Bobby Kimmel, drove up La Brea Avenue in their beat-up car on the way to a meeting at Capitol Records, they suddenly heard a loud, shrieking, metal-on-metal sound. Looking out the window, thinking something might have happened nearby, the three soon realized the problem was on their end as the vehicle began to slow of its own accord. After they finally rolled to a halt several blocks later, the trio climbed out into the blazing Southern California sun and began pushing the automobile to a nearby gas station.

Once there they received the bad news: the motor had frozen, with the mechanic recommending that the heap simply be towed to a junkyard and forgotten. For Ronstadt it was a pivotal moment. With precious little money and barely a toehold in the music business to that point, despite the Stone Poneys having a record deal with Capitol, perhaps her L.A. gambit wasn't going to pan out after all. After arriving a couple of years earlier from Tucson full of passion and hope, she and the other Stone Poneys members, with whom Ronstadt became acquainted at the Troubadour, had yet to see any real success. Barely eking out a living playing local coffee houses and small clubs, their first album had not sold well. Their second, *Evergreen, Volume 2*, had recently been released and looked to be heading toward a similar fate. With no cash, they couldn't have fixed their car had they wanted to. Things looked bleaker than ever. And that's when Ronstadt overheard a song playing on the gas station's radio.

It was "Different Drum," one of the cuts from the Stone Poneys' latest album, a track that, ironically, the producer chose to rerecord (over Ronstadt's objections) with the Wrecking Crew playing all the instruments the second time around in place of Ronstadt and her band. It was also a song Ronstadt figured she would probably never hear again anyway, especially given its new, less appealing (to her) sound. Nevertheless, there it was, coming over the airwaves, big as life. Something neither she nor Edwards and Kimmel had ever experienced. It was almost like a dream. Further, "Different Drum" was being played on 93 KHJ-AM, the biggest Top Forty station in the Los Angeles area.

Whooping with delight, Ronstadt and her fellow car-less bandmates momentarily forgot about being stranded and celebrated their achievement with a series of hugs, then all too quickly fell back into reality and called someone to pick them up. Shortly thereafter "Different Drum" went all the way to number twelve on the Billboard charts, establishing Ronstadt—with her powerful soprano voice—as a singer to watch. Which is precisely what those in the music industry did for the better part of the next seven years. They watched. And then watched some more.

With the Stone Poneys dissolving not long after their lone hit, Ronstadt had immediately gone solo, staying with Capitol. Experiencing a level of up and (mostly) down success over the next few years, her only charting effort came with the number-twenty-five single "Long, Long Time" in 1970, confounding those who followed her career. With the part-Mexican Ronstadt's sexy looks and world-class singing ability, she should have been a star.

Which is when John Boylan decided to step in.

Boylan, the Brooklyn-born, Buffalo-raised, Bard-educated son of a physician, could empathize with Ronstadt's plight. As a handsome theater major, he had moved to New York City after college to try his hand at acting. When no roles of consequence materialized, Boylan instead fell into working for a music publisher, which then brought him into the orbit of the singing star Rick Nelson. With Nelson desperate to update his image and sound—to be thought of as more than just a former teen heartthrob with a velvety voice and pretty-boy face—Boylan stepped in and produced Nelson's comeback hit single in 1969, a country-rock Top Forty cover of Bob Dylan's "She Belongs to Me."

From there, now with a measure of music biz street cred in his back pocket after having also formed Nelson's critically acclaimed Stone Canyon Band (featuring a young, pre-Eagles Randy Meisner on bass), Boylan moved to Los Angeles, produced several more acts, including the Association and the Dillards, and then, through a friend, met Ronstadt in the Troubadour's front bar one evening. Founded by impresario Doug Weston in 1957, by the late sixties and early seventies the rustic-looking, five-hundred-seat club was *the* place for up-and-coming L.A. musicians to congregate, commiserate, contemplate, get drunk, and—occasionally, if they were good enough—perform.

With Ronstadt soon asking her new friend (and, for a time, boyfriend) Boylan to manage her after a last-minute deal with James Taylor's producer/manager Peter Asher fell through, Boylan hesitatingly agreed. But he knew that if Linda was going to be a success, to finally make it big, she was going to need a band of her own. Capitol, Ronstadt's record label, wasn't going to be patient forever—they wanted to see sales.

Shortly thereafter, in early 1971, as John Boylan sat in his usual position at the Troubadour's bar, nursing a beer and chatting with some friends, he noticed a man in his early twenties heading his way.

"You're John Boylan, right?"

"Yeah."

"I'm Don Henley, from the band Shiloh."

It immediately dawned on Boylan who Henley was. As the drummer for a little-known Texas-transplant country-rock group being groomed by the singer Kenny Rogers, Henley had recently sent Boylan a copy of Shiloh's debut album. Of course, lots of people sent recordings to Boylan—that was nothing unusual for a manager in a town full of aspiring musicians. But what stood out to him regarding Henley's efforts was twofold: first, Henley, atypically, wasn't looking to get a manager for himself or his band but had simply circled a song title on the back of the LP that he hoped Linda Ronstadt might want to record, and second, Boylan, after playing it, actually thought Shiloh had some promise.

"Yeah, you're the guy that sent me the album," Boylan acknowledged, extending his hand. In a business filled with plenty of phony "what can you do for me now?" types, John Boylan had a reputation for being friendly and straight up with one and all, no matter their status.

"You probably never listened to it," a smiling Henley lobbed back, clearly hoping for the opposite to be true.

"I did play your record. I liked it. It's good," Boylan confirmed, who then went on to explain that although the song Henley had written and submitted, "Same Old Story," wasn't quite right for Ronstadt, he and Henley should stay in touch anyway.

"You never know what might come up."

WITHIN A FEW WEEKS AFTER JOHN BOYLAN AND DON HENLEY met at the Troubadour Linda Ronstadt happened to run across Henley at the club too. With Shiloh on stage one Monday evening during the weekly, all-comers Hoot Night (short for hootenanny), their set included, among other things, Ronstadt's exact arrangement of "Silver Threads and Golden Needles," a song she had released a couple of years earlier on her *Hand Sown . . . Home Grown* album. Appreciative of their musicianship and style, Ronstadt especially enjoyed watching Henley play. *Now, there's a guy who knows how to lay down country-rock rhythm the right way*, she thought. Ronstadt also thought Henley would make a fine addition to her own band, presuming he would even be interested. With a new album to record, along with an upcoming tour, Ronstadt needed players.

After mentioning her discovery to Boylan, he then checked with Henley, who told him that he would indeed be interested. Ronstadt had her drummer. She then asked her live-in boyfriend, the songwriter J. D. Souther, to see if his best friend, a charismatic fledgling singer-songwriter from Detroit named Glenn Frey, might want to step aboard as her guitarist. With the financially strapped Frey jumping at the offer (his duo with Souther, Longbranch Pennywhistle, was on the same trajectory to nowhere as Shiloh), Boylan promised Henley and Frey $250 a week each, providing Linda Ronstadt with the crucial foundation of her new band. Of even greater eventual import, one-half of the Eagles were now in place, even if no one knew it yet.

But first things first for Ronstadt: she desperately needed a hit record in order to stay viable within an increasingly crowded marketplace of successful singer-songwriters such as James Taylor, Carly Simon, Carole King, Jackson Browne, and Joni Mitchell. Though Ronstadt didn't write her own material as they did, these artists were, by the early seventies, not only her Laurel Canyon–based friends and peers but also her primary competition. They represented a changing musical paradigm among a wide swath of prominent solo acts that had begun incorporating a more sophisticated pop-meets-folk (and, in

Mitchell's case, jazz) sensibility. The country-leaning Ronstadt, with her love for bluegrass and the songs of Nashville legends like Hank Williams and Johnny Cash, was in danger of falling out of step with the times, at least on mainstream Top Forty radio.

Yet true to her own vision, Ronstadt, by 1974 (after having released a couple of more poorly charting LPs), continued her quest to make the music she loved, regardless of whether it rocked enough. Her upcoming album, *Heart Like a Wheel*, though as usual slated to contain mostly country ballads, also, for a change, was to include a couple of notable exceptions. And it would be one of those two up-tempo, noncountry tunes—a remake of an old R&B number fueled by the unlikely contributions of a Beatles-obsessed high school kid Ronstadt had randomly met—that would soon transform her from a struggling club act into nothing less than a worldwide superstar.

ON JULY 5, 1974, INSIDE THE SOUND FACTORY AT THE CORNER of Selma and Cahuenga in the heart of Hollywood, Linda Ronstadt, along with her new producer, Peter Asher, and the studio's ace sound engineer, Val Garay, were preparing to cut a song called "You're No Good" that was to be included on Ronstadt's upcoming album, *Heart Like a Wheel*. It was a favorite of Ronstadt's from her live shows as a crowd-pleasing, up-tempo closer, and the soul songstress Betty Everett had recorded the best-known previous version back in 1963. With a dark, minor-key melody line and clever lyrics about a spurned woman's less-than-charitable feelings toward her ex and, in a neat twist, ultimately toward herself, the song offered universal appeal along with lots of room for a singer to emote.

As Asher had the latest members of Linda's band lay down a basic rhythm track of guitar (Ed Black), bass (Kenny Edwards), and drums

(Andrew Gold), he also asked them to leave a sixteen-bar instrument-free break in the middle. Asher then decided to have Gold step back in and play two tracks of Wurlitzer electric piano to complete the rhythm portion of the song. A musical wunderkind from practically birth, Gold was the son of famed film composer Ernest Gold (*The Defiant Ones, Exodus, It's a Mad, Mad, Mad, Mad World*) and his equally accomplished wife, Hollywood's premier "ghost" singer, Marni Nixon, who had dubbed in the singing parts for Natalie Wood in *West Side Story* and Audrey Hepburn in *My Fair Lady*, among many other musicals.

Gold, never short on initiative or ideas, originally met Ronstadt and her Stone Poneys bandmates when they played a concert at his private North Hollywood high school in the mid-sixties. Striking up a conversation with them following the show, Gold made an impression on Ronstadt with both his effervescence and overflowing musicality. Staying in touch afterward, the two became friends and, eventually, collaborators.

A gifted multi-instrumentalist, the red-haired, freckle-faced Gold mastered virtually anything he touched, from the guitar to the electric bass to the ukulele, along with possessing the ability to channel an amazingly accurate Ringo Starr style on the drums. Which came as no accident either. Having met the Beatles in 1964 at the age of thirteen following their performance at the Hollywood Bowl, the Fab Four–obsessed Gold from that moment forward took to inserting his love of the their sound into recording projects whenever he could. And "You're No Good" would prove to be no exception. With Asher and Garay scratching their heads over what kind of an arrangement and corresponding instrumentation might work best in overdubbing onto the open sixteen-bar section of tape, Andrew Gold finally raised his hand.

"How about if I give it a try?" he asked.

So Asher let him.

Hopping behind a candy-cane-striped, five-piece drum kit borrowed from a friend, Gold immediately got to work. He first laid down the slinkiest Ringo-like tom-tom-heavy pattern he could come up with, then pulled out Linda's black 1962 Fender Stratocaster (that John Boylan had found for her in a pawn shop) and stacked a bunch of lead and rhythm parts that sounded like George Harrison himself had just walked in the room. As a bit of sonic icing on the cake, what finally put the sound of Gold's playing over the top came when engineer Garay craftily ran the guitar (and other) tracks through a warped, British-made EMT digital delay unit, giving everything a uniquely jangly wobble. After tossing in a McCartney-esque bass line for good measure, Gold's attempt at filling up the sixteen-bar bridge section was complete, wowing both Asher and Garay.

But not so much Ronstadt.

After Peter Asher and Val Garay stayed up all night in the Sound Factory's Studio A control room painstakingly mixing the song to what they felt was close to perfection, the two were stunned the next afternoon when Linda Ronstadt, along with her boyfriend, the comedian Albert Brooks, stopped by for a listen. The singer clearly did not like what she heard.

"It sounds like the fucking Beatles," an exasperated Ronstadt exclaimed. "This isn't going on *my* record."

To make matters worse, Ronstadt then called Kenny Edwards on the phone and asked him to immediately come down to the studio. She wanted him to add some guitar riffs to help "fix" Gold's offending handiwork. Though with Edwards's mostly blues-style licks missing the mark and pleasing no one, the decision was ultimately made to let the song sit for a few days. Maybe a new idea would pop up.

But in the meantime the Andrew Gold version of "You're No Good" actually began to grow on Ronstadt. It may be Beatles-like, she concluded, but it's also good—very good. So she gave her approval, much to the relief of Asher and Garay. And because of her decision, a few months later Linda Ronstadt ended up with her first number-one hit. However, that was to be only the beginning. Not only for what would become a string of Top Forty chart successes for Ronstadt but also for her musical involvement with another red-haired guitar virtuoso, Waddy Wachtel.

WHEN IT CAME TIME TO BEGIN RECORDING FLEETWOOD MAC'S next album, Richard Dashut wasn't just afraid—he was downright terrified. Not wanting to appear "sniveling" to his friend and employer Mick Fleetwood, Dashut had dutifully accepted the position of coproducer, figuring he would just have to somehow fake it until he could make it.

In order to get away from Los Angeles and all the distractions it offered a now number-one band, Fleetwood decided to book recording time at the Record Plant in Sausalito, just across the Golden Gate Bridge to the north of San Francisco. The sister studio to both the New York and Los Angeles Record Plant locations, the Northern California version offered a private, bucolic setting along with state-of-the-art facilities. Which made it seem like the perfect choice for a road-weary band looking for a hideaway in which to relax and create what they hoped to be their best work yet. And it was, except for one thing: nobody got along.

With three couples—John and Christine McVie; Mick Fleetwood and his wife, Jenny (the sister of George Harrison's wife, Patti); and finally, once and for all, Lindsey Buckingham and Stevie Nicks—all in the process of breaking up, it left Richard Dashut, along with his coproducer and engineering whiz, Ken Caillat, caught in the middle.

Yet instead of taking time away to clear their heads and hearts or to perhaps even contemplate the formation of new bands, Buckingham, Nicks, and Christine McVie were determined to stick it out—and, in the case of Buckingham and Nicks, stick it to each other. The two began writing songs to and about their now not-so-significant other that hit home with every ounce of the intended vitriol. If the saying is to write about what you know, then three-fifths of Fleetwood Mac definitely wrote about what *they* knew—each other. Worse, each of the five members had to sing and/or play on the very songs every day in the studio that were quite obviously about themselves.

With Buckingham writing "Go Your Own Way" to Nicks ("Tell me why / Everything turned around / Packing up, shacking up / Is all you want to do"), Nicks returned the emotional artillery fire, penning the eventual number-one hit "Dreams" ("But listen carefully to the sound / Of your loneliness / Like a heartbeat drives you mad / In the stillness of remembering / What you had / And what you lost").

In a spate of lyrical jousting driven by broken hearts and raw emotions, the songs on *Rumours* by Buckingham and Nicks went round and round, explicitly addressing the fallout from their failed romantic relationship. Buckingham wrote "Second Hand News" and "Never Going Back Again" in further expression of his anger. Nicks countered with "I Don't Want to Know" and "Gold Dust Woman." Only Christine McVie's trademark musical paeans to love and hopefulness kept the record's otherwise angst-heavy, soap-opera-like content from weighing the whole thing down. Though even McVie's three delightfully optimistic compositional contributions—"Don't Stop (Thinking About Tomorrow)," "Songbird," and "You Make Loving Fun"—were little more than thinly disguised commentaries about *her* personal life regarding her now ex-husband, John McVie, and her new boyfriend, the band's lighting director, Curry Grant.

Then there were the drugs. Everyone in Fleetwood Mac (along with most of the other rock acts in Los Angeles at the time) smoked marijuana and hash, especially Buckingham and Dashut. If the two weren't already smoking a joint, they were likely about to roll one. But no one gave it a thought—getting high came with the territory; that's what musicians did and had done for generations. The esteemed big band drummer Gene Krupa had even been arrested for possession of cannabis as far back as 1943. Further, smoking pot seemed a whole lot less problematic than getting drunk. Nobody ever flew into a marijuana-fueled rage, for one thing, and it didn't cause agonizing hangovers either. In terms of firing up a fat doobie, laughing, making music, and getting the munchies was about as far as it all went.

In the mid-seventies, however, a much harder substance—cocaine—also began to make its presence felt throughout the L.A. recording studio scene. At first utilized mainly as a "harmless" stimulant to help musicians, producers, and others stay up all night while allegedly maintaining and even enhancing their creativity while the tape was running, cocaine was seen, at least at first, as merely a means to an end. "Better music through chemistry," as Lindsey Buckingham liked to say.

But unfortunately the means soon became the end for some. The amount of cocaine the members of Fleetwood Mac ingested got so out of control while recording *Rumours* that an increasingly paranoid—and willing coparticipator—Richard Dashut went to the extreme of spending one night curled up in the fetal position while hiding underneath the recording console in order to avoid everyone's madness. Nicks, as per her customary honesty, hit the subject head on when writing "Gold Dust Woman," the closing track on the LP, which dealt with, in part, how cocaine seemed to help a person cope, especially following a doomed romance like hers.

In another example of the importance of the drug to the band, a black velvet bag filled with extremely high-quality coke sat in a place of honor underneath the mixing console in the studio's control room during the recording of *Rumours*. Periodically, whenever the "need" arose, one of the band members would signal either Ken Caillat or Richard Dashut through the glass to bring the precious pouch to him or her.

During one recording session, however, Caillat finally decided to have a little fun with his bosses. Secretly substituting a replica bag full of harmless talcum powder for the real thing, he told no one but Richard Dashut of his planned subterfuge, then patiently waited. When next asked to ferry the coveted stash into the tracking room, Caillat, acting both oafish and oblivious, "accidentally" turned the fake bag upside down, letting its white powdery contents flutter to the floor. With the five members of Fleetwood Mac screaming in unison at the horror unfolding before their eyes, John McVie and Mick Fleetwood looked especially intent upon strangling Caillat before Richard Dashut's hysterical laughter coming from the control room made everyone realize it was simply a joke. Yet the point had been made: yes, maybe the music was still number one. But cocaine was running an awfully close second.

Though in no way dissimilar to many of their well-known musical peers in terms of enjoying illegal substances, Fleetwood Mac's band members perhaps loved the ritual surrounding the drug a little more than most; the small bottle the coke was kept in, the diamond-studded spoons, the velvet bags—it was as much a part of the recording of *Rumours* as were the guitars, amps, drums, and keyboards.

However, drug use and its negative consequences, although of only mild concern within Fleetwood Mac, at least temporarily, would prove to be a far bigger problem for other Los Angeles–based bands by the late seventies. In particular, both the Eagles and Chicago—arguably

Fleetwood Mac's chief Los Angeles–based hit-making counterparts—were about to experience their own very personal and tragic problems with the substance. Meanwhile the members of Fleetwood Mac were on the cusp of realizing more success than they ever could have dreamed possible.

AT THE SAME TIME IN THE SPRING OF 1976 THAT FLEETWOOD Mac busied themselves with cutting the basic tracks for *Rumours* in Sausalito (then later reconvening during the summer to record the instrumental and vocal overdubs back in Los Angeles at studios such as L.A.'s Record Plant, Wally Heider Studios, the Village Recorder, and other locations including, briefly, Criteria Studios in Miami, home of Eric Clapton's comeback album, *461 Ocean Boulevard*, and most of the mid-seventies Bee Gees' hits), Linda Ronstadt was beginning the preparations for *her* next album, this time including Waddy Wachtel.

With 1974's *Heart Like a Wheel* and 1975's *Prisoner in Disguise* having both gone platinum while spinning off several hit singles, Ronstadt was now a rising star. And with her newfound status came the pressure from her record label to come through once again. Having left Capitol for Asylum in a lucrative deal engineered by her manager and producer, Peter Asher, Ronstadt needed to earn her substantial keep. But not being a songwriter by trade put Ronstadt in a tougher position than most—she had to continuously scramble to find suitable songs rather than just pulling out a pen and a legal pad and writing some of her own. Fortunately Linda Ronstadt had plenty of talented friends upon whom she could rely.

While gathering material for her album, Ronstadt got a tip from her pal Jackson Browne about an unknown singer-songwriter he was producing named Warren Zevon. With a number of well-crafted, lyrically sophisticated songs in the can—and in need of money, as usual—Zevon let it be known that he would happily let Ronstadt use one or more. After listening to Zevon's catalog of work, which she instantly fell for, Ronstadt claimed the song "Hasten Down the Wind," which then became the title of her new LP as well. But it still left Ronstadt needing a powerhouse cut, something that radio would jump all over. She also needed someone who could play kick-ass rock-and-roll guitar on the song, whatever it turned out to be. And that's where Peter Asher came in.

As the shrewd, exceptionally intelligent, red-haired half of Peter and Gordon, a one-time British pop duo that charted no less than ten Top Forty hits in the United States during a three-year period from 1964 to 1967, Peter Asher knew firsthand what it took to get airplay. With his sister, the British actress Jane Asher, who was Paul McCartney's girlfriend during the same period in the mid-sixties, Asher had the additional benefit of a rare, insider's view of just how the biggest band in the world—McCartney's Beatles—went about creating *their* unending parade of hits.

Asher was also acutely aware of Ronstadt's particular affinity for—and facility with—doing remakes of popular oldies. That formula was the cornerstone of her suddenly booming career. Through a combination of his and her ideas, Ronstadt had already scored big with her versions of the chestnuts "You're No Good," "When Will I Be Loved," "Heat Wave," and "The Tracks of My Tears." Asher, knowing Ronstadt's fondness for the music of Buddy Holly and with Peter and Gordon having had a hit with Holly's "True Love Ways" in 1965, at one point tossed out the suggestion that she record "That'll Be the Day," one of Holly's biggest hits. Ronstadt immediately went for the idea and began including the song in her band's rehearsal set. After a decade on the music scene she was finally game to go from being known as the queen of country-rock to a full-on rock-and-roller.

WHEN WADDY WACHTEL WALKED IN TO THE SOUND FACTORY one day in early 1976 to drop off something for a fellow musician, one of the first people he ran into was the recording engineer, Val Garay, who was busy setting up a session. Wachtel, as usual, spoke without a filter, even though he had never met Garay until that moment.

"You look like a fucking Gucci wallet," Wachtel blurted as he eyeballed the darkly handsome, always nattily dressed Garay.

With the comment coming from so far out of left field yet with a grain of sartorial truth in it, Garay couldn't help but burst out laughing. From that moment on, he and Wachtel became tight studio pals, each knowing that the other always brought the musical goods. Which came in especially handy on one of their first projects together: the recording of "That'll Be the Day" for Linda Ronstadt.

After Peter Asher saw Wachtel playing live with Carole King and her band at UCLA during her *Thoroughbred* tour, the producer made a mental note to check on Wachtel's upcoming availability. With nasty guitar licks and a rock-and-roll attitude, Asher felt that Wachtel might be just what he needed to punch up Ronstadt's sound.

On the day in the late spring of 1976 when Ronstadt and her band cut "That'll Be the Day" at the Sound Factory, it was Ronstadt herself who suggested they all give the song a try. It had been one of many they had been rehearsing in preparation for possible inclusion on both the new album and the upcoming tour. But Ronstadt decided to take things a step further: she wanted the song cut completely live, vocals and all.

"That's the way Buddy Holly & the Crickets did it," she reminded everyone.

And so that's the way Ronstadt and her band did it too.

In the multitrack seventies, when almost everything was a bunch of overdubs, few artists ever bothered to record everyone playing together all at once. That was a quaint, sixties approach, something Phil Spector would have done back when there were hardly any open tracks upon which to record and just as Norman Petty, Buddy Holly's producer, would have been forced to do in his tiny studio in Clovis, New Mexico. But with forty-eight, sixty-four, and even ninety-six-track recording consoles the norm in L.A. studios by the mid- to late seventies, the necessity to record a bunch of sources live together onto just one or two available tracks was long gone. Every musician—for that matter, every sound—could have a separate track, allowing for isolating and recording each part of the song a little at a time, a method much easier to manage from an engineering perspective. Fewer people out on the studio floor led to fewer errors, not to mention more creative control. The downside was a loss of spontaneity and the ability of a group of musicians to play off each other. Call it the vibe, the mojo, or the chemistry—there was plenty to be said for everyone doing their thing at once.

As an unexpected bonus, Ronstadt's insistence on authenticity for "That'll Be the Day" proved to make all the difference. On the first take, after her drummer, Mike Botts (formerly of the soft-rock group Bread), counted off one-two-three-four, Ronstadt let loose with an impassioned, a cappella, one-word "Well . . . " followed by the rest of her backing singers, Kenny Edwards and Andrew Gold, locking in with her from the second note on. At the end of four bars the rest of the band kicked in with full-on instrumentation as Peter Asher and Val Garay simultaneously employed just the right sonic choices from the control room (including the liberal use of retro-sounding slapback echo, the same thing found on Holly's original). Linda Ronstadt's version of "That'll Be the Day" quickly gained a life of its own. With the performance's astonishing energy palpable to one and all, it took Gold and Waddy Wachtel in order to finally put it over the top into the realm of a modern-day classic.

When it came time for the tune's middle-eight guitar solo, Gold and Wachtel—being big-time Buddy Holly fans as well—simply turned on their musical jets, choosing to alternate two blistering yet complementary runs, with Wachtel playing the first four bars and Gold laying down the second four. The novel approach of trading licks within the same solo brought the song to even greater heights, in the process lifting Ronstadt's live vocal performance to arguably her best yet. After Gold and Wachtel then played the short guitar outro together to end the recording, the musicians all erupted in cheers. Everybody in the place knew it was a hit. And they were right.

"That'll Be the Day" became the powerhouse rock-and-roll smash Ronstadt and Asher were looking for to launch *Hasten Down the Wind*, with the single hitting number eleven and the album number three on the Billboard charts. More important, in terms of career direction, Ronstadt had finally broken away from her country-rock druthers for good while at the same time becoming the first female in popular music history to release three straight million-selling albums.

Hasten Down the Wind also transformed Waddy Wachtel in ways he never expected. Within the space of one LP Wachtel went from being one of the town's best-kept guitar-slinger secrets into a flat-out, in-demand, first-call musician—a status he would soon parlay into also becoming the coproducer of one of the most important and critically acclaimed albums of the seventies.

eight

ANGRY EYES

I'm going to feed my very best friend, Mr. Jerry Garcia.

—BUDDY MILES

I N THE FALL OF 1976, WHEN KEITH OLSEN'S PHONE RANG, HE had no idea his producing career was about to take a 180-degree turn.

After picking himself up and dusting off following the stunningly public end to his professional association with Buckingham, Nicks, and Fleetwood Mac, Olsen wasn't even sure if his phone *would* ring again. The band had gone so far as to let it be known to the major music trade publications that they viewed Olsen's legal claim as merely a "nuisance," implying that the producer had played but a minor role in their newfound recording success and was therefore simply trying to squeeze more money out of them. A charge with which Olsen vigorously begged to differ—he had a signed contract in hand entitling him to a specific percentage of the new album's sales, which had yet to be paid.

Nor was it Olsen's style to step into the mud and start flinging back. There would be no war of words, no rebuttal, no response of any kind on his part. Fleetwood Mac could say whatever they wished, however hurtful it might be. With the lawsuit recently settled in Olsen's favor (and with the specific terms to forever remain confidential), he just wanted to move on. But the public, like potential production clients, only knew what they read. And his name had been dragged around.

Which is why the identity of the person on the other end of the phone line proved to be such a surprise. It was Clive Davis, the chief potentate of Arista Records.

"Keith, I just signed a new band. I'd like you to produce them."

Olsen could barely believe his ears. Label heads—let alone legends—had better things to do than to call producers out of nowhere unless there was something important about to happen.

"Who is it?" Olsen asked, trying not to sound overeager.

"The Grateful Dead," Davis answered proudly.

IN MID-1971, FOLLOWING KENNY LOGGINS'S IMPROVISED MUSIcal showcase in Jim Messina's living room and after considerable thought, Messina decided to produce Loggins's first solo album after all. Loggins had something special to offer, Messina was sure of it. Few if any singers who Messina had run across did all that Loggins could do behind a mic. Plus, Loggins had the kind of charisma, presence, and boyish enthusiasm that naturally drew people in. Though after assembling and then rehearsing at length with a crackerjack, hand-picked band consisting of Larry Sims (bass), Merel Bregante (drums), Al Garth (sax/violin), Jon Clarke (sax/flute), Milt Holland (percussion), and Michael Omartian (keyboards), Messina began to realize something else: his involvement on the project was moving from strictly behind the scenes to back at the mic as well.

As Messina worked closely with Loggins on crafting the intricate rhythm arrangements and vocal harmonies for songs that one or the other had written, such as "Nobody But You" (Messina), "Vahevala" (Loggins), "Peace of Mind" (Messina), and "Danny's Song" (Loggins), it quickly became clear that the voices of the two musicians blended startlingly well—better than anyone had a right to expect. Which caused Messina to ponder whether he should perhaps assume a greater role in terms of visibility. If he did so, it might help in two ways. First, Messina had residual name value from his Buffalo Springfield and Poco days that at least some among the record-buying public and FM DJ world would recognize. It might give the unknown Loggins a sales boost in a very competitive marketplace if Messina's name could be attached in the right way. Second, employing both names would send a clearer message about what was now basically a vocal duo.

Maybe the album could be pitched as Jim Messina jamming with his good buddy, Kenny Loggins, or something casual like that, Messina figured. It certainly had been done before. CBS had enjoyed gold-record success utilizing a similar concept only a few years prior with the release of the *Super Session* LP. In that instance Al Kooper, the little-known multi-instrumentalist and founder of Blood, Sweat & Tears (and the walk-on organist on Bob Dylan's landmark "Like a Rolling Stone") had invited the acclaimed guitarists Mike Bloomfield and Stephen Stills—Messina's old bandmate, no less—to jam with him on *his* first solo album, with all three sharing equal billing.

After taking Loggins and the band into Studio A at CBS Records in Hollywood to cut Loggins's album—which took all of one week to complete, came in exactly on budget at twenty-five grand, and was recorded 100 percent live (except for some overdubbed backing voices)—

Messina felt it was time to have another chat with Clive Davis. But this time around Davis was the one resisting. He had signed Loggins as a solo act and wanted to keep him that way. Davis also thought Messina preferred to simply be a producer, not a performer.

"That's what you told me last time," Davis reminded him.

But Jim Messina, in his typically methodical, convincing manner, managed to change Davis's mind, at least to the necessary degree. They agreed that Loggins's album would officially be titled *Kenny Loggins (with Jim Messina Sittin' In)*. That way it could technically still be considered Loggins's "solo" debut, but with the reputation of Messina's name right alongside.

Which left Messina wanting to make one more important point to Davis.

"Just to be clear, I only want to be Kenny's temporary partner. I'll hang in there long enough to help him get his career off the ground. But after that he's on his own."

BY THE MID-SEVENTIES THE GRATEFUL DEAD, PARTICULARLY their lead guitarist and creative visionary, Jerry Garcia, were looking for a musical change. Having just ended a four-album run on their own label, Grateful Dead Records (distributed by United Artists), preceded by a seven-year relationship with Warner Bros. Records, the Dead had been doing things their way for the better part of a decade.

With the thought of perhaps being more cooperative and accepting of outside production ideas this time around—and maybe actually having a hit record for once (the Dead had yet to see even one of their songs crack the Billboard Top Forty)—Garcia and his six bandmates, Bob Weir, Phil Lesh, Bill Kreutzmann, Mickey Hart, Keith Godchaux, and Donna Godchaux, opted to sign a deal with the brand-new Arista

Records. After interviewing several producer candidates, however, the band still hadn't found the right fit. That's when Clive Davis suggested they consider Keith Olsen, someone Davis had known since the late sixties at CBS Records when Olsen and Curt Boettcher worked for him by producing specific electronic portions of various songs and albums (including "At the Zoo" by Simon & Garfunkel and *Sweetheart of the Rodeo* by the Byrds).

Back before Davis was thrown out, that is.

In 1973 CBS Records shocked many in the music business by abruptly firing Davis as its chief executive for allegedly using corporate funds to pay for his son's bar mitzvah, among other infractions. Though Davis remained adamant about his innocence, the CBS brass turned a deaf ear to whatever evidence he attempted to present and instead brought back the label's previous president, Goddard Lieberson (who would soon be replaced by yet another in-house exec, Walter Yetnikoff).

Barely a year following his dismissal, a determined, resilient Davis returned to the music business in 1974 virtually as prominent as ever, this time as the 20 percent owner of his own brand-new major record label, Arista. Davis created Arista after the movie and TV colossus Columbia Pictures hired him to step in and consolidate their three existing record labels (Colpix, Colgems, and Bell), and changes began to happen almost immediately. Davis got rid of a bunch of underperforming acts such as Brownsville Station, Terry Jacks, and others. Those Davis kept, including million-sellers Barry Manilow, the Bay City Rollers, and Melissa Manchester, fell decidedly at the saccharine end of the popular music spectrum, something Davis felt he could balance out with more rock and roll on the label's roster—the edgier the better. In particular, he wanted artists who offered a more lyrically sophisticated, guitar-oriented, provocative style. After signing alternative rockers Patti Smith and Graham Parker, Clive Davis then chose to go after the most counterculture, antipop band of them all: the Grateful Dead.

After Davis and Keith Olsen struck a tentative deal for Olsen to produce the Dead's next, as-yet-unnamed album, it was time for Keith to meet Jerry. Though the rest of the band certainly mattered and were all solid musicians, it was Garcia whom Olsen would need to impress the most. He was the Dead's musical center, and an opinionated one at that. Garcia, much like the notoriously acerbic John Lennon and Keith Richards, was not known to suffer fools gladly.

Likewise, Olsen wanted to make sure that Garcia and the others were going to be to *his* liking. Olsen knew the Dead's rep, as did everyone in the music business: they supposedly took massive amounts of drugs and could be prickly to work with. Among their peers, the Grateful Dead were considered to be a terrific live jam band who never could quite find their authentic groove inside the walls of a recording studio.

After Olsen flew up to meet with the band at their Northern California rehearsal space in San Rafael he found himself pleasantly surprised. Not only did he immediately hit it off with the clever, gifted Garcia, but after several sessions Olsen also found Kreutzmann and Lesh to be an especially potent rhythm battery. In fact, everyone proved to be friendly and could play well, drugs or not. And it wasn't like Olsen refused to partake when he felt like it—he was known to do his share of substances with clients. But he always made sure it came *after* the work was done. The music came first.

After returning to Los Angeles suitably impressed with the Grateful Dead, Keith Olsen finalized his deal with Clive Davis and then made a few more quick trips north to work with the band in order to get them ready for recording the new album. Except by the time they all reconvened at Sound City to actually begin laying down some songs, Olsen could get nothing usable out of them. No basic rhythm tracks. And it all came down to the drums.

With the Dead famously being among the first rock-and-roll bands to use two drummers at the same time, it had subsequently become a trademark part of their sound. Which worked well enough during their live shows because laying down a perfectly synchronized, in-the-pocket groove was never a priority; endless "space jams" with the Dead's many fans twirling and dancing and doing the "willow" were more what they were about. But it also left Keith Olsen in a bind. He never knew where the beat was. Mostly because the Dead didn't know either.

With Bill Kreutzmann laying back and playing slightly behind the beat while the naturally more aggressive Mickey Hart played on top of the beat, the combination of the two drummers' obviously different styles led to an indistinct, mushy blob in the studio.

"Can't you play *with* him?" a frustrated Olsen asked Hart at one point over the talkback mic.

Hart glaringly assured Olsen that he not only could but also had been doing so quite successfully for many years. With that Olsen then hit "record" and tried not to grind his teeth as the same thing happened again.

Finally Olsen stopped the session altogether. It was time to apply a dose of creative diplomacy to the proceedings.

"Do you guys know how they used to record Dennis Wilson of the Beach Boys playing the drums?" Olsen asked.

With no one offering up an answer, Olsen continued.

"Wilson played what's known as melodic drums. The engineer would cut a track of him playing straight time with the kick and snare only. Then they would come back afterward and have him do all the tom fills and cymbal crashes."

Olsen was referring to the latter-day, late sixties and early seventies incarnation of the Beach Boys when the band no longer used the Wrecking Crew's Hal Blaine as their primary drummer in the studio. With Dennis Wilson being an energetic though limited player, some of his recorded parts were done in separate pieces or takes.

"You have two drummers, so let's play it this way, okay? Billy, you lay back, just play the time. And Mickey, you do all the tom fills and cymbal crashes."

Which sounded like possibly a workable plan to everybody but Mickey Hart. To him it was nothing short of a demotion.

"So I'm just adding the fills?"

"It's more than that, Mickey. It's the other part," Olsen tried to explain. But Hart wasn't willing to buy in.

"No fucking way. Do it without me then."

And as good as his word, Hart walked out.

Yet true to his professionalism, he was back the next day, ready to play with no further questions, no apologies, and certainly not happy. But the Dead had an album to do, and Hart was a team player.

With the new division of drum labor, however, what had taken five weeks of going nowhere now turned into three days of rock-solid tempo and getting every last one of the basic tracks successfully in the can. The old melodic drum trick had worked. But the even bigger challenge remained for Olsen: What to do with all the snippets of musical ideas that Garcia had come up with?

When they had first met during rehearsals Olsen had asked Garcia to play him what he had. Which turned out to mostly be an interesting set of chord changes and a melody line that had popped into Garcia's head while driving. Combining them with typically poetic, elaborately embroidered lyrics by longtime Dead collaborator Robert Hunter, Garcia had what amounted to parts of three different songs ("Lady with a Fan," "Terrapin Station," and "Terrapin"). But that was it. Working with what he was given, Olsen then presented yet another idea to Jerry and the band.

"Why don't we put all these musical passages together like a symphonette? You know, like a small symphony. It could be a whole side of the album."

Not sure what to expect in response, Olsen steeled himself. Messing with anybody's musical vision could be a minefield, especially when it came to someone as talented and willful as Garcia. Except in this case the guitarist merely shrugged.

"Cool," Garcia said.

But it wouldn't turn out quite as sanguine as Garcia made it all sound. When it came time to get the Grateful Dead to stay put in the studio, all bets were off. With the members of the band and their crew often leaving the room to get high, meet with dealers, or play games of pinball out in the lounge, it was sometimes all Olsen could do to keep the sessions moving in a productive direction.

With the superior quality of the drugs they took—such as the 100 percent pure, pharmaceutical-grade cocaine in the little glass vials they somehow obtained directly from the corporate manufacturer, not to mention the LSD, mescaline, and different varieties of cannabis, hash, and sensimilla generally floating around—Garcia and most of the rest could (and would) get blitzed within a matter of minutes and then be of no practical musical value for hours to come. With a stake in the Dead's profits (as with all Grateful Dead employees), the Dead's tour manager, a burly, six-foot-four ex-con named Steve Parish, finally took it upon himself to nail a couple of eight-inch spikes into the door frame of Studio A, thereby keeping the members of his band safely, albeit unhappily, locked inside. Though with no restroom available, the Dead could also only stay sealed up for limited amounts of time. But at least the spikes got the job done. Some of the time anyway.

One night, around 10:30, while Olsen and Garcia were working together on a guitar part for the "Terrapin Station Part 1" symphonette, Garcia realized he had run out of cocaine. Asking Parish to remove the spikes, Garcia then sent one of the band's roadies out to score with a dealer. As Olsen and Garcia went back to work they suddenly heard a commotion coming from the hallway outside. And they knew just who it was.

"I'm going to feed my very best friend, Mr. Jerry Garcia," a wobbly, wasted Buddy Miles bellowed to one and all.

Miles, an almost four-hundred-pound African American drummer with a colossal, carefully combed afro and an appetite for anything and everything to match, had worked closely with a number of guitar legends over the years, from Jimi Hendrix to Mike Bloomfield to Carlos Santana. Possessed of a powerful R&B-meets-funk style behind the kit, Miles was also an accomplished singer and bandleader in his own right, having charted the FM favorite "Them Changes" on Billboard's Hot 100 back in 1970. Now at Sound City working on a new solo project in Studio B, Miles and his fellow musicians had become notorious around the facility for their wild behavior and overindulgences, particularly with PCP, a powerful disassociative drug that caused hallucinations and was sometimes used as an animal tranquilizer.

As the loaded Miles staggered down the hallway looking for Garcia, he had also managed to pick up a giant dripping hunk of meatloaf along the way. Having come across the Dead's nutritionist in the lounge where she was laying out their evening meal, Miles had decided to grab a fist full of the greasy, catsup-covered goodness for himself—and for his "friend," Jerry Garcia.

Garcia, however, wanted no part of Miles. Although Garcia was anything but moderate when it came to taking drugs, even he found Buddy Miles to be too much to deal with. To Garcia, Miles, who was at best a very minor acquaintance, was also totally obnoxious, especially when, like now, he was jacked up on angel dust (PCP's more poetic street name).

"Keith, cover me," Garcia said as he put down his guitar and slid out of the control room and back into the adjacent tracking room. "Keep Buddy away, okay? I'm going to pretend to use this phone out here. Tell him anything you want."

Just as Garcia picked up the receiver on the wall to begin his imaginary conversation, Miles walked into the control room, nonchalantly gnawing on his meatloaf.

"Where's Jerry?" he asked, wiping his mouth with his sleeve.

"Buddy, Jerry's talking to Jane Fonda on the phone right now," a pointing Olsen said, his face a mask of seriousness. "She wants him to direct her next film."

A chewing Miles nodded thoughtfully while watching Garcia through the glass.

"Okay, well, Keith, I gotta tell you, I really want to thank you for doing so much good work on my best friend Jerry Garcia's album."

With that, Miles clapped Olsen on the back with a catsup-smeared hand and left.

When Garcia eventually came back in the control room along with Steve Parish and Olsen's second engineer, Dave DeVore, they started to laugh at the sight of the giant red handprint on the back of Olsen's white T-shirt. When an oblivious Olsen asked no one in particular, "Why do I keep smelling meatloaf?" it sent the three over the edge into paroxysms of laughter.

But as funny as it was, there was nothing humorous about Keith Olsen's next adventure with the Grateful Dead on *Terrapin Station*.

GOODNIGHT, L.A.

BY THE FALL OF 1973 KENNY LOGGINS'S CAREER HAD INDEED taken off, just like Jim Messina had hoped. Only instead of Loggins being a solo act, Messina was still right there beside him.

It wasn't that Messina had wanted to continue as part of a duo; he had faithfully gone back to Clive Davis after the eventual gold-record sales success of *Sittin' In* to suggest that he now bow out as Loggins's "partner." Kenny was ready to go it alone, he felt. But Davis, with an eye toward the bottom line, would accept nothing of the kind.

"These kind of opportunities come very rarely, Jimmy," he said. "The two of you make a great combo."

And popularity-wise, Davis was right. Loggins and Messina, now officially a duo, would go gold with their first three albums. They had also placed three singles in the Top Forty, including what would be their biggest, 1972's "Your Mama Don't Dance." A silly throw-away tune the pair had worked up one afternoon in the studio while waiting for the rest of the band to arrive, to both Loggins and Messina "Your Mama Don't Dance" was about as far away as possible from who they really were as musicians. Written on a lark as a lighthearted poke at the stereotypically uptight mores of middle America during the fifties and sixties ("Outta the car, longhair!" their drummer, Merel Bregante, delightedly got to shout out midsong), the up-tempo rocker instead came to define them among most of the public, much to the duo's consternation. They felt that their other songs far better exemplified the depth of their craft, such as "Same Old Wine," "Till the Ends Meet," "Be Free," and perhaps especially, "Angry Eyes."

Carefully crafted from the ground up, "Angry Eyes," although not an AM radio Top Forty hit (but an FM staple at over seven minutes in length), nevertheless showcased the breadth of the entire band's premier musicianship, allowing room for everyone to shine. Though mostly improvised, the signature, all-hands-on-deck, groove-heavy, four-minute-fourteen-second instrumental jam smack in the middle contained important cueing elements that were in fact carefully sketched out by Messina ahead of time so the band would know when, where, and how to make their transitions. With powerful, no-nonsense words and music cowritten by Loggins and Messina, the song in many ways represented the pinnacle of their musical partnership. "Angry Eyes" was L&M, as the pair sometimes referred to themselves, at the top of their game. It was also an apt description of where the duo was headed next.

WHEN THE GRATEFUL DEAD TOOK OFF IN THE SPRING OF 1977 on a twenty-six-date East Coast arena tour, Keith Olsen took off for England. With him were the master tapes for *Terrapin Station*, upon which he planned to add a mass amount of orchestration to what would be side two's "Terrapin Station Part 1" symphonette. Having discussed the idea first with Jerry and the band to make sure they were all on board, Olsen mostly received a series of skeptical looks and an "Uh, okay, sure . . . " or two. Not only did the band members seem incapable of imagining the extent of what Olsen had in mind; they also seemed to not really care.

So Olsen, assuming he had everyone's blessing and also being the producer of the project, promptly flew to London, took a taxi to EMI's famed Abbey Road Studios, and set up shop with the esteemed composer, conductor, and arranger Paul Buckmaster. A graduate of the Royal Academy of Music, the thirty-year-old Buckmaster had built a major career on applying orchestration to rock and roll. His work on gold records for artists such as David Bowie ("Space Oddity"), Elton John ("Your Song"), Harry Nilsson ("Without You"), and Carly Simon ("You're So Vain") had made Buckmaster *the* go-to string man in the business by the mid-seventies.

After many days of working inside the hallowed halls and walls of the Beatles' former recording studio home, Olsen finally felt like he and Buckmaster had layered in just the right amount of violins, cellos, bassoons, violas, English horns, clarinets, trumpets, trombones, pianos, harps, piccolos, timpani, and standup basses to qualify the "Terrapin Station Part 1" suite as the Grateful Dead's own hippie-lite version of *Tommy*, the Who's legendary rock opera. The Dead, along with Clive Davis, had, after all, entrusted Olsen with the keys to the sonic kingdom. *Terrapin Station* was to be his baby all the way. They wanted something different, something that would also sell well.

Upon landing at John F. Kennedy Airport in New York City on his way back to Los Angeles with the newly orchestrated *Terrapin Station* master tapes in hand, Olsen, like everyone, had to pass through customs. In 1977, with no TSA in place and a comparatively cursory system of security procedures, returning Americans generally had little to do other than to show their passport and declare any goods they may have purchased outside the country. With nothing extra in his suitcase or on his person, Olsen assumed he would be quickly waved through. And he would have been, except for one thing: the tape boxes had the name "Grateful Dead" clearly printed on them.

Even in the pre-Internet, pre–cable TV era of the late seventies, a certain percentage of the general public had at least heard of the Grateful Dead. And that passing familiarity with the band usually also included the word "drugs." So it was with an eagle-eyed customs agent at JFK.

"Mr. Olsen, could you step this way, please?"

Before Olsen knew what was happening, he was taken to a private room and grilled extensively about his trip. What had been his business in London? Did he work for the Grateful Dead? Was he bringing in any illegal substances? With the answer to the last question being

Future producer extraordinaire Keith Olsen (second from left) posing with his Music Machine band mates in 1966. Olsen played the bass on the group's one and only Top Forty hit, early 1967's "Talk Talk," a raw, proto-punk rocker that still stands up today. Notice the single black glove on Olsen's left hand, part of the Music Machine's unique stage attire. *Photo courtesy of Keith Olsen*

Jackson Browne (left) with guitarist Waddy Wachtel (center) and drummer John Cowsill (right), who is now a member of the Beach Boys. This photo was taken circa 2011 during the filming of the excellent documentary about the Cowsills called *Family Band*. After a crazy fight in 1973 between members of the Cowsills in the control room of Studio A at Sound City, not only did Keith Olsen throw them out, but Jackson Browne and Warren Zevon wrote a song about the infamous incident called "Billy Ate the Tape." *Photo courtesy of Louise Palanker*

Sound City's exterior on Cabrito Road in Van Nuys, looking the same in 2013 as it did back in its glory days of the seventies and eighties. However, the recording studio inside the complex is now a private facility operating under a different name and ownership. *Photo courtesy of the author*

A profile shot of future solo star Kenny Loggins taken in the early fall of 1975 at his music partner Jim Messina's Ojai, California, ranch and recording studio. Behind fan favorites such as "House at Pooh Corner," "Danny's Song," "Angry Eyes," and "Be Free," the duo of Loggins and Messina (and their crackerjack band) packed venues during the early-to-mid-seventies. *Photo courtesy of Michel Rubini*

Jim Messina, looking pensive, at his Ojai ranch in 1975. He and Kenny Loggins were in the middle of recording what would turn out to be their sixth and final studio album together, *Native Sons*. A former member of both Buffalo Springfield and Poco, the gifted Messina was also Loggins and Messina's producer. *Photo courtesy of Michel Rubini*

Close pals Stevie Nicks and Richard Dashut mug for the camera during the late 'seventies. The sensitive, easygoing Dashut, with no previous record producing experience, found himself chosen by Mick Fleetwood in 1976 to co-produce what would become Fleetwood Mac's monster hit album, *Rumours*. *Photo courtesy of Bob West and Richard Dashut*

Merel Bregante, a drummer's drummer and member of the Loggins and Messina band, hits the skins here during the cutting of *Native Sons*. Known for his passionate playing and extroverted personality, Bregante gleefully got to shout, "Outta the car, longhair!" in the middle of Loggins and Messina's biggest hit, "Your Mama Don't Dance." *Photo courtesy of Merel Bregante*

Lindsey Buckingham and Richard Dashut sitting behind Studio D's mixing console inside the Village Recorder in West Los Angeles during Fleetwood Mac's *Tusk* sessions in 1979. Note L.A. Dodger great Ron Cey behind them. *Photo courtesy of Richard Dashut*

Another shot of the famous Studio D inside the Village Recorder. Based on the runaway sales success of *Rumours*, Warner Bros. Records had agreed to Mick Fleetwood's request to retrofit Studio D at the Village to the band's liking for recording their follow-up album, *Tusk*. More than a million dollars later, Fleetwood Mac had their very own custom-made, English-themed lair. *Photo courtesy of the author*

Keith Olsen (left) and his friend, songwriter, guitarist, and producer Jay Graydon, stand at the mixing console inside Davlen Sound Studios in North Hollywood in early1980. This is the same location where later in the year Olsen would produce the smash single "Hit Me with Your Best Shot" for Pat Benatar, breaking her career wide open. *Photo courtesy of Andy Zuckerman*

James Pankow, the band Chicago's trombonist, ace horn arranger, and hit songwriter, in performance during 2015. Still with Chicago today after fifty years, Pankow wrote the smash hits "Make Me Smile," "Colour My World," and "Just You 'n' Me," among many others. *Photo courtesy of the author*

Robert Lamm, Chicago's other brilliant in-house songwriter, plays his keyboard here during a concert in Portland, Oregon, in 2015. The smooth-singing Lamm, also an original member and the band's social and political heart since the beginning, penned the Chicago classics "25 or 6 to 4," "Saturday in the Park," and "Does Anybody Really Know What Time It Is?" *Photo courtesy of the author*

From left: Bob Cowsill, Paul Cowsill, Susan Cowsill, Waddy Wachtel, and John Cowsill during the filming of the *Family Band* documentary, circa 2011. Under the "guidance" of the Cowsills' violent and tyrannical father/manager Bud, Wachtel moved from the East Coast to Los Angeles in 1968 along with the family, hoping to make it big in music. After firing Bud, he did. *Photo courtesy of Louise Palanker*

Talented producer Bill Drescher (left) with pop/rock star Rick Springfield sometime during the early eighties. After Keith Olsen produced the #1, million-selling "Jessie's Girl" and the Top 10 "I've Done Everything for You" for Springfield in 1980 at Sound City, Drescher took the reins from the busy Olsen to complete the rest of what would become *Working Class Dog*, Springfield's first smash album. After Olsen returned in 1981 to produce Springfield's platinum follow-up LP *Success Hasn't Spoiled Me Yet*, Drescher stepped aboard once more to help Springfield generate another fistful of Top Forty hits through the mid-eighties. *Photo courtesy of Bill Drescher*

The band Boston's founder and mastermind, Tom Scholz, sitting in his tiny basement recording studio in Watertown, Massachusetts, during 1977. This is where the genius Scholz secretly played all the instruments (except drums) on every song but one that appeared on Boston's massive-selling 1976 debut album. The project's co-producer, John Boylan, ran interference for a grateful Scholz by making a big show of simultaneously installing the rest of the band in a "real" studio in Los Angeles, a ruse that fooled Boston's label, Epic Records, completely. *Photo courtesy of Ron Pownall/Michael Ochs Archives/Getty Images*

Glenn Frey (left) and Don Felder of the Eagles jamming onstage in 1977. Though Felder was and is a virtuoso (the band nicknamed him "Fingers"), the late Frey was an underrated player in his own right. Check out his beautiful lead guitar work on *The Long Run* gem "I Can't Tell You Why." *Photo courtesy of Gijsbert Hanekroot/Redferns/Getty Images*

From left: producer Bill Szymczyk along with Joe Walsh, Joe Vitale, and Kenny Passarelli of the early seventies Walsh-led, Szymczyk-produced group Barnstorm. Walsh, of course, later joined the Eagles (in 1976) where Szymczyk's jovial demeanor, golden ear, and steady hand in the studio played a vital role in helping turn that act into the biggest-selling American rock band of all time. *Photo courtesy of Bill Szymczyk*

Just off Santa Monica Boulevard in Hollywood sits the Record Plant, still one of the premier studios in the world. Its prior location on nearby West Third Street was often the recording destination of choice for L.A.-based superstars of every stripe during the seventies and early eighties, from the Eagles (parts of *Hotel California*) to Fleetwood Mac (parts of *Rumours*) and Chicago (*Chicago 17*, their biggest-selling album). The late, great Brad Delp also laid down his lead vocals (on top of Tom Scholz's prerecorded instrumentation) at the Record Plant for the band Boston's self-titled debut album. *Photo courtesy of the author*

The front entrance to Sunset Sound is seen here in 2015, just a few steps off Sunset Boulevard in Hollywood, looking virtually the same as ever. Don't be fooled by the simple exterior of this onetime auto repair garage, however. Since the sixties, dozens upon dozens of platinum records have been cut inside its state-of-the-art studios, including the Doors' first album (*The Doors*), much of *Led Zeppelin II*, and perhaps most famously, the singer Merry Clayton's passionate, chilling vocals on the Rolling Stones' "Gimme Shelter." *Photo courtesy of the author*

Singing superstar Rod Stewart (left) gets an earful from legendary, three-time Grammy-winning album cover designer John Kosh during an aborted photo shoot in Hollywood for Stewart's 1977 album *Foot Loose & Fancy Free*. The affable, charismatic, London-born Kosh, whose other work includes creating the classic covers for *Abbey Road*, *Who's Next*, and *Hotel California*, has always been known for his excellent rapport with clients, despite having to lay down the law on occasion. *Photo courtesy of Jim Shea and John Kosh*

The unchanged-by-time Studio A inside Ocean Way Recording Studios in Hollywood in 2012. Formerly known as United Recorders during the sixties and seventies and just up the street from Sunset Sound, Ocean Way was the hip place to record during the eighties, with stars such as Bonnie Raitt, Kenny Loggins, and the Rolling Stones regularly laying down tracks there. *Photo courtesy of the author*

A shot of EastWest's Studio 1 in Hollywood as it looked in 2012, also a world-famous "room." Originally known as Western Recorders (and during the eighties as a part of Ocean Way), EastWest's three internal recording studios have a pedigree and sound equal to any in town. Stevie Nicks, along with her musical director and lead guitarist Waddy Wachtel, recorded some of her *Rock a Little* album in the small-but-mighty Studio 3 in 1985, the same place where the Beach Boys cut many of their classic hits twenty years before. *Photo courtesy of the author*

The Red Rocker himself, Sammy Hagar (right), poses with his producer and friend Keith Olsen during the first day of rehearsals for Hagar's *Standing Hampton* album in the spring of 1981. Recorded at Goodnight LA, Olsen's personal "dream" studio built immediately next door to Sound City, this would be Hagar's first album to go gold and then platinum. *Photo courtesy of Keith Olsen*

Keith Olsen and Ozzy Osbourne sitting at the mixing console inside Olsen's Goodnight LA recording studio in Van Nuys during the recording of Osbourne's *No Rest for the Wicked* album in 1988. By this time, the always forward-looking Olsen was moving heavily into producing metal. *Photo courtesy of Keith Olsen*

Esteemed engineer and producer Val Garay sits next to Martha Davis, the lead singer of the Motels, circa 1982 inside Record One, Garay's state-of-the-art recording studio on Ventura Boulevard in Van Nuys. Designed by Garay to the last detail as an internal replica of the Sound Factory where he used to work, Record One proved to be an instant go-to choice for the likes of Linda Ronstadt (*Mad Love*), Jackson Browne (*Hold Out*), and Don Henley (*Building the Perfect Beast*). *Photo courtesy of Val Garay*

Val Garay and Kim Carnes hug at the 1982 Grammy Awards ceremony after the Garay-produced, Carnes-sung "Bette Davis Eyes" (recorded at Garay's Record One) won for both song of the year and record of the year. *Photo courtesy of Val Garay*

Waddy Wachtel playing his white Les Paul circa 2011. *Photo courtesy of Louise Palanker*

Keith Olsen sits in his increasingly quiet office at Goodnight LA in 1993. By this time, album (classic) rock had finally run its course in Los Angeles and elsewhere after Nirvana's groundbreaking grunge album *Nevermind* had come out in the fall of 1991. The irony? That seminal LP was recorded right next door to Goodnight LA at Olsen's original studio home, Sound City. *Photo courtesy of Keith Olsen*

an honest "no," it still didn't seem to satisfy the agent in charge, with Olsen being asked to remove his clothes. Doing as he was told, Olsen then experienced the greatest indignity of his professional music career, something even more unpleasant than witnessing the Cowsills' bloody in-studio melee or having Buddy Miles smear meatloaf on his shirt. It was a full-body search, including every orifice.

When the rubber-gloved intrusion finally ended and with the agent finding nothing, an angry Olsen dressed, gathered his belongings—along with the *Terrapin Station* master tapes—and headed for his connecting flight to L.A. After the harrowing ordeal at least Olsen felt he could find consolation in the fact that he had created a stunning piece of work, taking the "Terrapin Station Part 1" suite to new heights—just like the Dead said they wanted.

But when Olsen proudly played his masterpiece for the band back at Sound City, after having labored over it eighteen hours a day for a solid week alongside Buckmaster, the band said nothing while mostly looking stunned. Finally Mickey Hart broke the uncomfortable silence, echoing the others' thoughts.

"Well, that's an interesting choice of notes."

Not "we like it" or "we hate it." Those sentiments Olsen could deal with. The latter could maybe even be fixed to some degree in the mix. But "an interesting choice of notes" was their only comment? That was fucking disrespectful.

A crestfallen Olsen felt sandbagged. He thought he had made it perfectly clear before he left what he planned to do in adding all the strings and horns. Yes, it was ambitious. Probably a bit daring too. Perhaps even somewhat "out there"—but certainly no more so than the Dead themselves. Plus, that's why they had hired Olsen to begin with—to take their music to new places, which he did. The band *knew*. Now they were backpedaling. A rock opera the Dead wanted and a rock opera the Dead got.

Fortunately for Olsen, in the end the man who mattered most, Jerry Garcia, came around on the subject. After meeting up with Garcia at Kendun Recorders in North Hollywood a week or so later to do the final mixing and mastering of the full *Terrapin Station* LP, which needed to be delivered to Arista later that day, Garcia, in his inimitable way, finally gave the finished version of the project his blessing. Sort of.

"Well, Keith, there's some semblance of a human being singing some semblance of the English language. I like it."

And that was it from Captain Trips.

What about the Dead's fans—the ones who would have the final say at the cash register as to the album's ultimate worthiness? Many Deadheads found *Terrapin Station* to be a real head-scratcher. Other than some of the songs on side one, it didn't really even sound much like the Dead. Or at least what the Dead had sounded like up until then. But then an interesting phenomenon took hold: *Terrapin Station* started growing on people. At first selling only in mild numbers and even then only because of a big marketing push from Clive Davis and his staff, *Terrapin Station* actually began to gain steam both at retail and among critics. By the early eighties, a good four years out, the album began to enjoy a full-on rebirth, gaining sales each year and eventually earning the distinction as one of the Dead's best pieces of work.

For Keith Olsen there was little time to reflect on anything to do with *Terrapin Station*, however. With word getting out in the biz that he was a producer whose specialty was the ability to transform an artist's music and thereby their career, both the band Foreigner and the singer Pat Benatar were just about to knock on his door.

WHEN WRITING HIS SONGS, KENNY LOGGINS HAD A SECRET FOR-
mula: he would take a moment in time, focus on one specific emotion inside that moment, and make the feeling of that moment—and
therefore the song—as universally relatable as possible. And he was
good at it. But being one-half of a musical partnership with an equally
talented individual who was also the duo's producer—giving Messina
the final say on everything the pair did—left Loggins, by 1975, feeling
like a caged animal. A quick listen to the lyrics of his song "Brighter
Days" off the *Mother Lode* album from the year before—"But here I
am / Like a sea blown wind / Under my thunder and rain / I'll ride
the waves / 'Til the sunny day"—left little to anyone's imagination as
to how Loggins really saw his situation.

To Loggins, his relationship with Messina had become a stag-
nant mishmash of teacher-student, father-son, and big brother–little
brother—all of which he gradually came to resent. Loggins had a lot
to prove to himself and, in some ways, to Messina too. What had
started as a neophyte singer-songwriter in need of the steady, experienced hand of a seasoned producer had become a bourgeoning star in
desperate need of his unfettered freedom.

Never the types to get in major screaming matches, at least in
front of others, most of the time Loggins and Messina preferred a
more passive-aggressive approach in dealing with their faltering relationship. By the late stages of the 1975 tour the two were no longer
speaking. But that silence didn't necessarily extend to Loggins and
the rest of the band, whom he felt were no longer bringing the necessary energy. The band members, however, felt like Loggins considered them to be nothing but replaceable sidemen.

On November 14, 1975, at Utah State University in Logan, the
tensions finally boiled over. With the band having played a couple of
passages that Messina didn't like during the previous two shows, they
were asked not to do it again. They grudgingly agreed. Messina was

the man in charge, after all, and they respected him. But before the show that evening Loggins came to the band and told them, "I talked to Jimmy, and everything's cool." With the meaning apparently being that it was okay to play the musical passages after all. Which they did.

Following the show, however, it suddenly became a different story. In the dressing room backstage a livid Messina tore into the musicians.

"I thought I told you guys to leave those things out from now on."

Merel Bregante, the band's supremely talented, high-energy drummer and perhaps most outspoken member, stepped in to correct his boss.

"Jimmy, no, we were told by Kenny it was cool," a perplexed Bregante replied.

Loggins, standing nearby, then tossed in his version of the events. "He's a lying motherfucker."

Which was all it took to set Bregante off. The voluble, sometimes volatile, and always party-loving drummer may have been many things, but one of them was definitely not a liar. That's where he drew the line. He took pride in his honesty. Maybe Loggins had merely gotten confused over what had been discussed with Messina—or not. But calling Bregante a liar went above and beyond in the eyes of the drummer.

An irate Bregante dove at Loggins with every intention of beating the living shit out of him then and there. The angular, athletic Loggins, however, managed to slither out of Bregante's grasp and took off on a dead run.

With Bregante in hot pursuit, the fleet-footed Loggins eventually accelerated into the darkness of the venue's labyrinth of service tunnels, ending the would-be beat-down. Bregante and the rest of the band then regrouped to tell Messina their version of what had transpired. Messina, ever levelheaded, said he would take it from there. But there really was no "there" there anymore. The backstage confrontation had merely been a symptom of what was now an incurable disease.

Loggins and Messina, after a gold-record-filled five-year run, were on personal and professional life support.

In early 1976 the duo finally held a summit meeting at their manager's house in Los Angeles where Messina offered, "Things are fucked here, and we need to patch up our relationship."

"Why?" Loggins asked, clearly no longer interested in continuing.

"Because it's a bad way to begin solo careers, and it's a bad way to leave a friend," Messina said.

In characteristically logical, unemotional fashion, the duo then agreed to set a fixed date of September 25, 1976, for the partnership to cease. In the meantime they would put out one last studio album (*Native Sons*), followed by a final tour, just so they could depart—in the public's view anyway—the "best" of friends.

Kenny Loggins would finally have his coveted freedom. Which he would put to good use by becoming nothing less than one of the biggest music stars in the world by the turn of the decade.

nine

BABY, WHAT A BIG SURPRISE

Look, it has to be done here, this way.

—Tom Scholz

F ROM THE MOMENT JOHN BOYLAN HEARD THE FIRST SONG ON the demo burst forth from the speakers, he knew he wanted in.

Sitting in the offices of Paul Ahern, a savvy independent promotions man who had his ear constantly to the ground for new signees (Ahern, with his A&R friend, Charlie McKenzie, doubled as a wannabe artist managers), Boylan had been asked to render his opinion on some music McKenzie had recently discovered. Ahern also wanted to know whether Boylan—who was coming off not only his work with Linda Ronstadt but producing albums for Brewer and Shipley, Commander Cody, and Pure Prairie League as well—might be interested in stepping in production-wise to help get the project into a major label's hands and, from there, out to the public.

As he grooved along to the rest of the six songs on the spinning reel-to-reel tape, Boylan's mind began to whirl right along with it:

Why didn't the group responsible for such superb music already have a record deal? It simply made no sense. Featuring layer upon layer of crunchy, uniquely crafted Les Paul guitar riffs, catchy melodies, a swirling maze of Hammond B3 organ parts, relatable lyrics, and a passionate, emotive lead singer with a powerful tenor voice (and soaring falsetto) as good as any rocker out there, it was the tightest, most fully realized demo he had ever come across. Some of it could probably even be released to radio just like it was, which was saying something.

"So what's the name of this band?" an intrigued Boylan asked.

"That's the crazy thing about it," Ahern replied, shaking his head. "There isn't one. It's just a guy that put the whole thing together by himself in his basement."

BY THE EARLY SUMMER OF 1976 CHICAGO WAS ARGUABLY THE biggest band in America. Having just released *Chicago X*—their fifth-straight number-one LP—they were also routinely filling arenas around the world, sometimes several nights in a row in the same city, and had already starred in two of their own prime-time network TV specials.

Following the group's initial chart success with James Pankow's "Make Me Smile" and "Colour My World," along with Robert Lamm's "Does Anybody Really Know What Time It Is?" and "25 or 6 to 4," Chicago had wasted no time in racking up another *fourteen* Top Forty hits in the space of less than five years, including smashes such as "Saturday in the Park," "Just You 'n' Me," and "Old Days." In terms of concert revenue, record sales, and airplay, the band was a bona fide juggernaut. With a string of hit records that no other rock band could touch over the same period, just about the only achievement Chicago hadn't experienced during their first seven years of existence on the charts had been a number-one single. Top Ten? Plenty—but never the summit.

That is, until "If You Leave Me Now" came along.

Written and sung by Chicago's bassist, Peter Cetera, "If You Leave Me Now" not only became the band's first chart-topper but also, ever so quietly, ushered in a new, ultimately divisive direction for them. With a minimal amount of horns being used on the song—Chicago's signature element—"If You Leave Me Now" additionally became the band's first number-one adult contemporary hit, the chart where "soft rock" hits were ranked. Much to everyone but Cetera's horror, for the first time this put Chicago in the same musical conversation with such popular lightweight AC acts as Paul Anka, Helen Reddy, and Abba. It also served to subtly shift the intraband balance of power.

With Chicago's highly skilled producer Jim Guercio playing the exquisite acoustic guitar part in place of Kath on "If You Leave Me Now," everyone assumed Kath would likely come in and replace it later. Yet he never did, perhaps because it was so good. But also maybe, some theorized, because Kath essentially wanted nothing to do with that style of music.

To the purists among the band's fans along with most of the band members themselves, the first seven albums were the benchmark by which all others would be measured. *Chicago VIII*, their eighth LP, although maybe not quite as solid song for song as its predecessors, nevertheless spun off two Top Forty hits ("Harry Truman" and "Old Days") and another that just missed ("Brand New Love Affair"), along with several strong album cuts. But by the time of the recording of *Chicago X* in the spring of 1976 (*Chicago IX* had been a greatest-hits package), the rigors of constant touring had caused a creative drain, leaving the usual songwriting trio of Kath, Lamm, and Pankow short on viable material. And into this breach, ever so unobtrusively, stepped Peter Cetera.

Having written the Top Twenty love song "Wishing You Were Here" on *Chicago VII* (and cowritten the smash "Feelin' Stronger Every Day" from the year before with Pankow), the bass-playing, high-tenor-singing Cetera's development as a dependable tunesmith had been growing almost by the album. With a natural inclination toward ballads and well known among his bandmates for hating the heavy amount of horns found on most of Chicago's songs, "If You Leave Me Now" underscored where Cetera was headed as a musician. It also represented exactly where the rest of Chicago was not.

After "If You Leave Me Now" picked up two Grammys at the February 1977 ceremonies in Los Angeles (with the legendary love-song crooner Andy Williams appropriately being the host)—the first Grammy Awards in Chicago's history—it only served to solidify Cetera's power not just in terms of his creative impulses and output on a per-album basis but also in direct relation to the record label itself. To Columbia the only thing better than a Grammy-winning, number-one single was another song that sounded just like it and would hopefully perform just like it. Which the ambitious Cetera was only too happy to supply.

With "Baby, What a Big Surprise" on Chicago's next album, *Chicago XI*, released in the fall of 1977, Cetera almost revisited the same magic. Though the "If You Leave Me Now"–like ballad just barely missed hitting the summit with its similar set of softly sung sentiments, "Baby, What a Big Surprise" nevertheless rolled easily to number three on the charts, turning Cetera, once and for all, into the new voice of Chicago among the public. Notably, the song also served to reduce the role of the band's three-piece horn section even further into becoming more of an accent piece. By Pankow's design their potent sax, trumpet, and trombone combination had been arranged in the past on hit after hit and album after album to sound like an additional vocal line—something that had been part of Chicago's trademark style from the beginning. But, suddenly, no more.

Without quite realizing what was happening, the members of Chicago found themselves being pigeonholed as balladeers. Other than to Cetera, the appellation was a slap in the face to their unique, time-tested, kick-ass blend of jazz, rock, and blues. Though the new emphasis on ballads did help the band achieve success among a demographic of soft-rock-loving listeners, chiefly young women, Chicago's rejiggered, Cetera-centric sound and direction did little to satisfy their millions of existing fans. Nor did it excite the group's other six musicians, especially their guitarist, Terry Kath.

IN COLONIAL TIMES WATERTOWN, MASSACHUSETTS, ONCE RANKED right next to Boston in terms of its population size and land mass. Founded in 1630 as one of the original Massachusetts Bay settlements, segments of Watertown's geography were summarily lopped off and reassigned to other towns. Located only four miles west of Harvard Square, Watertown proper was down to a few square miles and just over thirty thousand souls. And although it had once been home to its share of accomplished citizens, including Helen Keller and Charles Pratt (an early oil tycoon and founder of NYC's Pratt Institute), by late 1975 the only current resident of the historic burg that mattered to West Coast–based John Boylan was a brilliant, introverted, music-obsessed, East Coast corporate engineer by the name of Tom Scholz.

From as early as he could remember, Scholz always liked to tinker. Taking things apart and putting them back together—maybe even better than they had been—gave him great satisfaction. Scholz also loved music. But not just any kind: he had specific tastes that mostly re-volved around power rock and roll. From his late high school years on through his time during the late sixties at the Massachusetts Institute of Technology, where he earned both bachelor's and master's degrees in mechanical engineering, the strikingly thin, six-foot-six Scholz took a particular liking to fired-up songs by the Kinks, the Yardbirds, and Iron Butterfly, with "All Day and All of the Night," "Shapes of Things," and "In-A-Gadda-Da-Vida" being personal favorites.

After slowly piecing together a hand-built recording studio in the basement of the apartment building where he and his wife lived, Scholz's fascination with guitar sounds began to take over. A key-boardist by experience (he had taken classical piano lessons as a kid), Scholz bought a 1968 Les Paul Goldtop reissue and worked as hard on learning how to play his new guitar as he did on everything else in his life. Alongside close friend and drummer Jim Masdea, Scholz then spent countless evenings and weekends holed up in his sub-terranean lair putting together songs—sometimes even calling in sick to his job at Polaroid, where he helped design various camera-related products.

Occasionally, too, Scholz would ask others to lay down a part here and there; local pros such as Fran Sheehan (bass) and Barry Goudreau (guitar) were among those used. But what really put Scholz's musical efforts over the top came when he met (through Goudreau) a local singer and guitarist by the name of Brad Delp. A Beatles nut from the second he saw their US debut on *The Ed Sullivan Show*, the sensitive, well-liked, curly-haired Delp played and sang in various rock bands around the greater Boston area while working a blue-collar day job making heating coils for Mr. Coffee machines.

Scholz, a frustrated nonsinger, knew that if and when he met a vocal talent that could make his lyrics sound the way he envisioned, he would need to stick to that person as closely as possible. All the marvelous melodies and wonderful words in the world would mean nothing without a lead singer who could bring it all home. With Scholz having auditioned many possible candidates over time, he eventually realized that finding a truly transcendent vocalist who got what he was trying to do was the hardest task of all. Good guitar players, bassists, drummers—those you could usually find without too much trouble. And lots of people could carry a tune. Fewer still could take a musical passage to new heights and make it their own. And then there was Delp.

With the uncanny ability to overdub layers upon layers of inventive, intricate harmonies to his own acrobatic lead vocal lines, Brad Delp was a one-man rock-and-roll chorus. His range also extended over several octaves, giving him plenty of headroom within which to apply his gifts.

Perhaps most important, Delp *felt* the music. Deeply. He poured his soul into every syllable of every word, expertly plumbing and probing for maximum emotional impact and resonance. The shy, self-effacing Delp whom his coworkers knew from the daily grind at the coffee machine factory became a completely different person in the evenings once he stepped behind a microphone in a darkened studio.

When Delp opened his mouth to sing, it was as if his vocalizations and Scholz's painstakingly crafted set of music and lyrics had been born *in situ*. It was a perfect match, making the sum of their efforts exponentially greater than the parts. The remarkable blend even made the usually skeptical Scholz start wondering about the possibility of actually attracting a record label. Not a million-dollar deal or anything—that would be crazy. Just a company big enough and connected enough so that if he was really lucky, he might get to hear one of his songs someday on local Boston radio, maybe even on the legendary WRKO. To Tom Scholz—who still thought of music as his hobby—that would be the thrill of a lifetime.

By the fall of 1977 Terry Kath was miserable.

Having toiled away for the better part of a decade in virtual anonymity as part of a faceless, albeit wildly successful, rock band, Chicago's lead guitarist—and, for that matter, their only guitarist—felt frustrated with what he regarded as a lack of personal recognition. When Jimi Hendrix had asked Chicago to open for him on his summer tour back in 1969 it was in large part because of his admiration for Kath's playing. The two subsequently spent hours backstage just jamming, talking shop, and grooving on each other's company. But while other guitarists of similar caliber, such as Jeff Beck, Eric Clapton, and Carlos Santana became household names, Kath remained largely unknown outside of his group and peers.

A self-taught virtuoso, Kath also loved to stretch his guitar work into every conceivable genre. When Chicago needed him to play jazz, as on "Italian from New York" on *Chicago VII*, he stepped up and played jazz. When it was time to rock, as on "25 or 6 to 4" from *Chicago II*, Kath rocked. And if a certain song required a heavy dose of nasty R&B, as on "Rediscovery" from *Chicago VI*, he was more than ready to get down and dirty. But the one style that left Terry Kath feeling flat was playing on fluffy love ballads. That was decidedly not the Chicago he knew and loved.

Kath too had a husky, bluesy, world-weary singing voice that reminded some of Ray Charles, a quality his fellow band members felt never received enough notice among the press or the public. During trombonist and songwriter James Pankow's frequent in-studio "sing-offs," where the three lead singers Kath, Robert Lamm, and Peter Cetera would each take a turn at the mic on one of Pankow's latest compositional efforts, more often than not Kath would be declared the winner.

To compound Terry Kath's insecurities over his lack of recognition, he looked nothing like a traditional rock-and-roll front man either. Square-jawed and thickly built of Norwegian ancestry, Kath seemed more like a lumberjack or a hockey player, especially onstage when wearing his favorite Chicago Blackhawks jersey and standing next to the movie-star handsome Lamm; the manly, often shirtless, leather pants-wearing Pankow; and the blond-haired, blue-eyed Cetera.

As the leader of Chicago, Kath also wore his ample heart on his sleeve. He would do anything for anyone, especially a fellow bandmate. And his passions ran deep and wide in other areas too. As crazy about cars, motorcycles, and guns as he was about guitars, Kath had a large collection of them all. If he wasn't cleaning, polishing, or working on one or more, he was usually driving, shooting, or playing.

On the evening of January 22, 1978, after another of the arguments with his common-law wife that had become all too commonplace, Kath showed up at James Pankow's Malibu home looking tired and down. He had been awake for several days and was high on various substances.

"Terry, do yourself a favor and lie down. Get some sleep, man," a worried Pankow said to his close friend. But Kath wasn't in the mood to do himself any favors. He was antsy, wanting to go to a shooting range to let off some steam instead.

"I think I'm gonna go to Donny's after that," Kath said, referring to the band's keyboard tech, Don Johnson. Kath indicated that he planned to get some rest there, maybe even crash for several days to clear his head. Keeping a guitar and amp setup at Johnson's place, it was Kath's mini-sanctuary, a home away from home.

Later the next day an even more burned-out Kath made his way to Johnson's Woodland Hills apartment, where, like Pankow before him, Johnson tried to step in. But this time the stakes were even higher: Kath had begun cleaning one of his guns at the kitchen table.

"Hey, man, you're tired," Johnson said, his concern evident. "Why don't you just put those guns down and go to bed?"

But Kath could be stubborn. He liked to do things his way.

"Don't worry about it," he replied, showing Johnson the compact, .380-caliber semi-automatic pistol. "Look—the clip's not even in it."

Slapping the empty cartridge back in place, Kath waved the weapon around.

"What do you think I'm gonna do—blow my brains out?" he laughed.

But what Kath didn't know was that one bullet still remained in the chamber. As the handgun moved through the air, his index finger accidentally applied just enough pressure to depress the trigger, causing the chambered round to discharge directly into the side of his head.

Terry Kath, the heart and soul of Chicago as well as one of the finest guitarists in rock-and-roll history, died instantly.

With his bandmates devastated by his passing—especially his best friend, Robert Lamm, who had the unimaginably difficult task of having to break the news to Kath's elderly parents—Chicago came very close to breaking up. But the love for music and for playing with each other that had propelled them since 1967 through a mind-boggling eleven straight platinum albums and twenty Top Forty hits somehow remained intact.

But as Chicago moved forward with heavy hearts into the eighties in Los Angeles, a new sound and leader would emerge within the group, surprisingly providing them with even greater popular success while at the same time threatening to tear them apart at the seams.

WITH JOHN BOYLAN FIRMLY ONBOARD REGARDING THE NEW music project he had heard in Ahern's office, the two soon thereafter took a trip down to San Diego to a CBS Records convention where they hoped to talk somebody into signing their new, as-yet-unnamed act. Which was always the key—and a crapshoot. No matter how much a manager and/or a producer might like a piece of music, someone at a label obviously had to like it too. And label guys—usually in A&R—were besieged with demos from anybody and everybody, most of the time unsolicited. As the gatekeepers, they hardly had time to listen to even the good submissions, let alone all the junk. Not to mention that they were also expected to go out and discover new acts on their own.

In the best of all worlds, in order to get personalized attention and therefore at least a fighting chance at radio and retail, there needed to be an in-house champion at a label, a person willing to enthusiastically take "ownership" of a single or album and shepherd it all the way up through the corporate ranks. Having each of a record label's departments come together and take a unified, rooting interest in a project was the gold standard. Which is where Lennie Petze, the VP of East Coast A&R for Epic Records, stepped into the picture after meeting with Ahern and Boylan.

"This is incredible," Petze enthused after listening to their tape. "It's a hit."

But Petze was also skeptical. He had actually passed on an earlier, less fully realized incarnation of the demo that had been mass-mailed to him and a couple of dozen other execs at various labels by Scholz and his wife. But Petze wasn't the only one to pass during the first round. An uninterested Clive Davis at Arista had also turned it down, as had Al Coury at Capitol, the same guy who took on the disastrous Paul Cowsill recording contract in order to keep Helen Reddy onboard ("I'd love the trip to Boston," Coury said about the Scholz demo, "but I don't think I can sell this.")

Because of that first demo, Petze already knew that Scholz, other than drums and vocals, was essentially a one-man band. Scholz played all the guitar, bass, and keyboard parts himself. And that just wasn't going to fly. Without a group of seasoned pros to send out on the road to play the music live, there would be no way to create any buzz. Concerts, airplay, personal appearances, interviews—it was all inter-connected and required real people. There needed to be a group. The image of some nerdy musical genius cooking up all the tunes alone in his basement was not going to help sell records.

Petze's immediate superior, an accomplished producer and head of Epic's A&R department named Tom Werman, also instantly fell for the unbridled power and utter originality of the music. Halfway through the song "Hitch a Ride," Werman thought he was being set up by *Candid Camera*—it was that good.

"Stop the tape," Werman practically shouted. "I guarantee you a record deal if this band is anything like this live."

Which then raised the question: What band?

Soon after, in order to appease Epic and lock in a deal, Scholz assembled a fixed lineup consisting of his longtime vocal ace Brad Delp along with Barry Goudreau, Fran Sheehan, and Sib Hashian (a drummer friend of Goudreau's) to join him in becoming a real band. In November of 1975 Boylan, Petze, and Werman then flew in to watch the five play a live set inside Aerosmith's nearby Waltham, Massachusetts, warehouse rehearsal space of what es-sentially would be the whole album. Coming away impressed with the group's unexpectedly tight onstage show, the Epic men shortly thereafter offered Scholz and Delp a record deal for the newly named "Boston," with the other three musicians to be salaried employees, at least to start.

But rather than give the untested Scholz free reign, there were two caveats. First, Epic, agreeing with Ahern and McKenzie, wanted John Boylan, not Tom Scholz, to produce the full album, citing the need for an experienced professional who had an ear for cutting commercially viable popular music. Second, the label wanted Scholz and his bandmates to rerecord the six-song demo, plus several other songs Scholz had been working on, this time in a state-of-the-art studio in Los Angeles. That way the label could be assured of the highest possible sonic quality while also keeping an eye on things. A homegrown basement tape was fine for demonstration purposes, but if Epic was going to throw their considerable corporate muscle behind the project, the recording process needed to be done among the big boys with the big toys.

But when John Boylan flew back to Boston to meet with Scholz inside his tiny apartment-house studio about getting the project under way, he immediately realized that his new client had other ideas.

"Come back to L.A. We'll do this the right way," Boylan offered, noting that Scholz would have his pick of the best audio equipment in the world.

To an unimpressed Scholz, however, doing it the "right" way meant something entirely different.

"Look, it has to be done here, this way, if I'm going to get those sounds again," he said, gesturing around his studio.

Yes, Scholz liked to be in control. And he could be unbending. But Scholz also knew himself and his music better than anyone. He was at his creative best when doing his own thing in his own space. Scholz would be out of his element anyplace else. His unconventional, pieced-together basement studio was a big part of why the original demo sounded so incredible. Being a trained mechanical engineer and tireless thinker, Scholz had designed and built much of his recording equipment himself; in that capacity he knew its nuances inside and out. Further, his in-studio gear was an extension of Scholz as a musician, the mastermind of the unique Boston sound. Take away any part of his personal production arsenal, whether it be his self-built guitar-amp power soak (created from a massive theater lighting unit) or his rare Scully twelve-track tape machine or his well-worn Hammond B3 organ, and it just wouldn't be the same.

Which left Boylan the odd man out. What was he going to do as the producer, he wondered—just sit in Scholz's apartment and do crossword puzzles while Scholz did everything himself downstairs? Truth be told, Scholz didn't really need his help anyway, certainly not for the basic tracking. Plus, there was the mandate from Epic about the album being recorded in Los Angeles. The label was adamant about that.

"Well, if it has to be done here, then I'm going to have to walk," Boylan said as got up to leave. No need to belabor a moot point. But as he opened the door and took one step outside, Boylan suddenly stopped. Maybe there was another way.

"Tell you what," he said, turning around. "You make the record here in your basement without me. We'll mix it and add the vocals out in L.A., and I'll keep Epic off your back in the meantime. Sound fair?"

Scholz was elated. It was everything he could have hoped for. Boylan trusted him and believed in him. That was his kind of guy. Now the album could indeed be done the "right" way.

But before Scholz could even utter "great" or "thank you," Boylan continued, adding one last sweetener that made the offer simply irresistible.

"And we'll split the 3 percent producer's royalty too, okay?"

Baby, What a Big Surprise

AFTER MAKING HIS GENEROUS OFFER TO TOM SCHOLZ ABOUT running interference while Scholz finished working on the Boston album in his little hideaway studio, Boylan had to then figure out how to pull the whole thing off. With Epic part of the CBS Records family of labels (as was the band Chicago's label, Columbia), Boylan was required to adhere to an existing agreement between CBS and the IBEW union that represented the company's electricians and broadcast engineers.

In the pact, which contained its fair share of stereotypical, union-style featherbedding, CBS had agreed that any recording done outside of a CBS-owned studio in New York City, Los Angeles, or Nashville but within a 250-mile radius of one of those studios required that a paid union engineer be present. With Scholz's apartment in Watertown being less than 250 miles from the main CBS recording studio in Manhattan on East 52nd Street, Boylan was therefore technically required to have an engineer present with Scholz at all times when recording. The thought of which made Boylan laugh as he imagined some timecard-punching union lifer sitting next to Scholz in the basement.

In an effort to create as much of a diversion as possible to avoid the union situation and to give Scholz his space, Boylan flew the rest of the band to California and made a big show of working with them in Capitol's Studio C, laying down the tracks for the one non-Scholz-penned song to make the album, "Let Me Take You Home Tonight," plus one other that proved to be a nonkeeper. At the same time Boylan even went so far as to pay out of his own pocket for the extra recording equipment Scholz needed back in Watertown, lest Epic's accountants begin to notice a non-L.A. paper trail.

While keeping Scholz's activities a secret from everyone at the label, especially from Petze and Werman, Boylan did confide in one person, Gregg Geller, who was Epic's West Coast head of A&R.

"Just don't tell anyone else," a surprisingly supportive Geller warned. "We'll present it when you're done."

After a number of weeks, once Scholz finished all of his guitar, bass, and keyboard re-creations based almost exactly on the original six-song demo (Hashian had come in and put down new, faithfully reproduced drum parts on all but one song), Boylan secretly flew to Boston for a listen. Loving what he heard, he and Scholz then made the return trip to L.A., where they settled in with Delp for the vocal sessions and, ultimately, the mix-down.

Although Delp's vocals were a breeze to capture, the mixing proved to occasionally be a battle of the fingers on the manual mixing console. Boylan preferred to push the faders up on some of the drum tracks in order to give the music more low-end punch. Scholz, at the same time, liked to nudge up the volume on the guitars, which sometimes caused a frequency cross-cancellation with the voice tracks, making Delp's lead work sound buried. But with Boylan patiently explaining his reasoning behind the way he wanted the record mixed—the average listener needed to be able to clearly hear the lead vocals over the top of the music on even the crappiest of car speakers—Scholz managed to come around.

When they finished the mix Boylan then got on a plane for New York to play it for Geller and the other Epic execs at the weekly CBS Records singles meeting, the place where the most promising radio-friendly songs were chosen for release. Playing side one of the album off a copy of the master tape, Boylan watched as the occupants of the room went berserk. So powerful was the impact that the president of Epic, Ron Alexenburg, took Boylan aside afterward and said, "Geller wants to hire you. I think it's a good idea." Suddenly John Boylan, a mildly successful independent producer with no particular grand career plan, was an A&R man for Epic Records, a prestigious position.

But that was far from the biggest news. Once the self-titled *Boston* LP hit retail shelves in August of 1976, barely a month after *Chicago X*, it took little time and almost no promotion for it to become a nationwide phenomenon. Fueled by word of mouth and the endlessly played Top Ten hit "More Than a Feeling," the album went gold in only three weeks and platinum within just three months.

With the public's appetite for the band's melodic, heavy-metal sound remaining unabated, *Boston* would go on to sell well over 5 million more copies throughout the rest of the seventies, in the process making it the biggest-selling debut by any American band in history up to that time. The album's success also not only cemented John Boylan's reputation as a rising star (he would go on to produce huge-selling albums for acts such as Little River Band, Quarterflash, and Charlie Daniels) but also led to a predictable me-too response from competitors. Within months of *Boston's* release other labels were lining up in an attempt to emulate Scholz's slick, powerful handiwork—a style of music that quickly came to be known, aptly or not, as "corporate rock."

And into this emerging genre would soon come Keith Olsen, once again presented with a band and production offer he couldn't refuse, something that would also lead to a stunning string of all-time classic albums.

ten

FOOTLOOSE AND FANCY-FREE

I just want a picture of me face.

—ROD STEWART

I N LATE NOVEMBER OF 1976, AS WADDY WACHTEL BUSIED HIM-
self with unpacking his suitcase and sorting through a pile of mail,
he heard his phone ring. Having just returned that day from a tour
of England with Linda Ronstadt in support of her recently released
Hasten Down the Wind album, Wachtel not only had a case of jet lag
but also a million things on his mind as he picked up the receiver.

"Hello?"

"Waddy?"

"Yeah?"

"Hey, it's Jackson Browne."

On the heels of such FM favorites as "Doctor My Eyes," "Rock
Me on the Water," and "Fountain of Sorrow" during the early to mid-
seventies, the folk-rock singing-and-playing Browne was a rising star
in the music world. With his latest album, *The Pretender*, having just

hit stores, Browne was about to go on tour in support of both it and its soon-to-be-released lead single, "Here Come Those Tears Again."

But first things first. Browne wanted to help out a mutual friend, an unknown (outside of the music business) singer-songwriter by the name of Warren Zevon, and Browne figured Wachtel might be just the guy to assist him.

"Hey, man, what's up?" a surprised Wachtel said, taking a seat. "I literally just walked in the door a few minutes ago from being on tour with Linda in Europe."

"I know," Browne replied. "That's why I'm calling."

Though Wachtel and Browne were acquainted, with Wachtel having played guitar on *The Pretender* and also on an earlier Browne-produced Warren Zevon album that went nowhere, they were hardly close friends.

"I read your interview," Browne continued. "You know, the one where you said I had my hands full and didn't really know what I was doing as the producer on Warren's last record."

Wachtel swallowed.

Oh, that interview, he thought—the one he had recently done with some British magazine where, as usual, he had spoken without a filter.

"Sorry about that, man," Wachtel said, half-chuckling in embarrassment.

Browne stopped him in midapology.

"No—you were absolutely right," he said. "That's why you're going to coproduce Warren's next album with me."

Wachtel wasn't sure he had heard correctly.

"What? Wait a minute—you don't even know me," he blurted in his typically blunt Brooklyn-ese.

"Not only do I know you," Browne countered, "but I know exactly where I stand with you."

Browne then added the clincher.

"More important, I need you," he said, sounding concerned. "Warren won't listen to me anymore. But he'll listen to you."

AT THE SAME TIME WADDY WACHTEL AND JACKSON BROWNE were reacquainting themselves with one another in the fall of 1976, in a nearby part of Los Angeles a different set of musicians (and Browne's good friends), the Eagles, were busy with the final stages of preparing the release of what would be their fifth studio album.

Having been graciously allowed by Linda Ronstadt to leave her touring band back in late 1971 to start one of their own, Don Henley and Glenn Frey quickly made it a foursome by recruiting Bernie Leadon (guitar, banjo) from the Flying Burrito Brothers and Randy Meisner (bass) from Poco. Vocalists all, the ability of the four to harmonize and even take turns doing leads fulfilled Frey's vision of putting together a unique ensemble where each member could sing and play with more or less equal facility.

After signing a deal with the fledgling, David Geffen–owned Asylum Records through their connection with Jackson Browne (Frey and Browne had met early on at the Troubadour, ultimately becoming close friends), the Eagles immediately scored a platinum record in mid-1972 with their debut album, the Glyn Johns–produced *Eagles*. Containing three Top Forty singles, "Take It Easy," "Witchy Woman," and "Peaceful Easy Feeling," it seemed to put the band on the fast track to stardom.

But after lackluster sales and up-and-down reviews of their second LP, 1973's cowboys-and-outlaws-themed *Desperado*, Henley and, particularly, Frey were adamant about making some changes for album number three. Tired of the exclusively country-rock direction forced upon them by Johns, the pair jettisoned him partway through the recording of what would become *On the Border* and brought in a new producer named Bill Szymczyk. A genial, gregarious, giant of a man at six-foot-four (at least compared to the substantially sub-six-foot Eagles), the former Navy sonar operator and all-around electronics whiz brought with him instant rock and blues credibility. Producing career-defining singles for B. B. King ("The Thrill Is Gone"), the James Gang ("Walk Away"), and the Edgar Winter Group ("Frankenstein"), it was especially Szymczyk's production work for Joe Walsh (whose manager, Irving Azoff, had just stepped in to also manage the Eagles) on "Rocky Mountain Way" that sealed the deal; the song rocked its ass off, just like Glenn Frey wanted his own band to do.

At the beginning of 1974, following a meeting between the Eagles and Bill Szymczyk at Chuck's Steakhouse on Third Street in West L.A. near Hollywood, the band and their hoped-for producer agreed in principle to work together. But it came only after Szymczyk made it clear over dinner that he had no interest in doing a country-rock record, a stance that especially pleased Frey.

After agreeing to recut *On the Border* (only "Best of My Love" and "You Never Cry Like a Lover" were kept from the original Johns-produced London sessions), Szymczyk gathered again with the band a week later and a mere two doors down from Chuck's at the red-hot Record Plant West. Opened in 1969 as the Southern California–based sister studio to its already-established New York City sibling, Record Plant East (and the soon-to-be-opened Record Plant Sausalito in the Bay Area), the Los Angeles location also became one of the first facilities on the West Coast to offer twenty-four-track recording capabilities, something that quickly made it a main competitor with Sound City, Sunset Sound, the Village Recorder, United/Western, American Recording, the Sound Factory, Crystal, and others. It was also no accident that the Record Plant West was Szymczyk's favorite studio in town—he had already produced successful albums there for the James Gang (*James Gang Rides Again*), the J. Geils Band (*The Morning After*), and B. B. King (*Indianola Mississippi Seeds*).

Though Bill Szymczyk's keen ear, strong studio skills, and rock-and-roll bent helped turn the rerecorded *On the Border* material into a less countrified presentation, Frey still wanted even more grit. In particular, he yearned for a third guitarist who could help give the Eagles a tougher sound. At the suggestion of Leadon, a call went out to an easygoing guitar virtuoso by the name of Don Felder. Having played in a mid-sixties high school band in Gainesville, Florida, with Leadon and also having informally jammed with the other Eagles (through Leadon) here and there backstage before their shows for over a year, the likable Felder was no stranger and an obvious choice.

After laying down some slide on "Good Day in Hell" and then adding a few lead and solo parts on "Already Gone," Don Felder, with the rest of the band suitably impressed, officially became the fifth Eagle. Because of his uncanny abilities on any kind of stringed instrument placed in his hands, whether acoustic, electric, six-string or twelve, Szymczyk and Frey soon began referring to him as "Fingers."

With *On the Border* successfully picking up where the first Eagles album left off in terms of chart position (seventeen) and more Top Forty singles ("Already Gone" and "Best of My Love"), the Eagles were back in business. But it was their next album, *One of These Nights*, that would turn them into superstars.

With three Top Five hits in 1975—"One of These Nights," "Lyin' Eyes," and "Take It to the Limit"—*One of These Nights* was a runaway success from the day of its release. The Eagles first number-one album, it was also Don Felder's debut as a contributing singer and songwriter, something he had very much hoped to do since the moment he joined.

"If you want to write for this band, create some instrumental beds [tracks] that are in a song structure," Leadon told Felder, who had been asking about how to get in on the action. "Then make demos of the songs and give them to Don and Glenn."

What Leadon meant was for Felder to take his guitar and lay down a melodic, compelling song that words could then be written for by Henley and Frey, who were the band's principle lyricists. The tune would also need to be in the common pop-music songwriting format of intro/verse one/verse two/chorus/verse three/bridge/chorus/outro.

Taking Leadon's advice to heart, Felder promptly fired up his home-based Teac four-track reel-to-reel tape recorder and got to work. Sometime after, with two of his compositions making the final cut for inclusion on the *One of These Nights* LP, including one, "Visions," that he actually sang the lead vocal on, Felder thought it would always be just that easy. As long as he wrote the music—even if someone else wrote the lyrics—then Felder would likely have a good shot at singing the song on the record too. In his experience that's the way bands worked—they were a democracy.

Further, from discussions with his bandmates it was Felder's understanding that he would always get to sing lead on at least one song per album. That was very important to him and among the reasons he left his position as a sideman for David Crosby and Graham Nash to join the Eagles. Felder thought he would now get to be an equal partner, including on vocals.

But much to Felder's chagrin, Don Henley and Glenn Frey would soon come to have a very different view regarding his level of participation in the band.

Footloose and Fancy-Free

DURING THE LATE SUMMER OF 1977, AS THE WELL-KNOWN album-cover designer John Kosh stood with his arms folded, absently watching a man's expensive black dress shoe float by in the pool of ankle-deep water, he knew something was wrong. He could feel it.

Having gone to great lengths and expense to craft a faithfully rendered replica of a standard-issue, Holiday Inn–style guest room inside of a giant waterproof tub—complete with suitably drab motel furniture, cheesy wall art, and a garish, custom-made flashing neon sign placed just outside a fake window—everything about the design and setup for the album cover photo shoot at hand had come off just as planned. No detail had been too small. No artful touch had been overlooked. Everything was perfectly in place for what Kosh felt just might end up being his grandest creative endeavor yet. Everything, that is, except for one crucial, all-too-obvious omission: the star attraction was nowhere in sight.

By the late seventies Rod Stewart had become one of the most popular rock-and-roll singers in the world. On the heels of hit singles such as "Maggie Mae," "You Wear It Well," and "Tonight's the Night (Gonna Be Alright)," the spiky-haired crooner with the sandpapery voice had become both a sex symbol and a huge moneymaker. Women threw themselves (and their underwear) at him during shows. His albums routinely sold in the millions. He played only the largest arenas. As superstars went, Stewart was among the biggest—with a sizeable ego to match.

Born barely six months apart during the last full year of World War II, Stewart, like Kosh, grew up in North London. And once upon a time, in the early to mid-sixties, they also each held a particular fondness for the Mod lifestyle, a fashion-obsessed existence then popular among certain segments of British youth. Dandies both, Stewart and Kosh would have recoiled in horror at the mere notion of venturing out among the public in anything that might have been considered naff—local jargon for "in poor taste." But all tailor-made, narrow-lapel Carnaby Street suits and pointed-toe, leather winkelpicker shoes aside, that is where the similarities between the two ended.

Stewart's childhood in Highgate featured all the trappings of the upwardly mobile, with his middle-class parents spoiling him silly, and where he especially excelled in playing English football (soccer). Kosh, however, grew up a confirmed nonathlete in Friern Barnet, a rough-and-tumble, mostly working-class area better known for its endless rows of lookalike council housing and prominent Cockney accents. In lieu of organized sports, one of Kosh's favorite early activities included playing with friends in old V-1 bomb craters left from the German air raids during the war while at the same time doing his precocious best to look up girls' dresses.

By the mid-seventies, with Stewart's well-known reputation preceding him in terms of doing whatever he wanted whenever he wanted, the ever-professional Kosh nonetheless decided to take on the task of helming the design for Stewart's first album release on Warner Bros. Records. Titled *Atlantic Crossing*, the partially Los Angeles–recorded LP's cover featured a colorful, stylized rendering of a glam-rock-like, jumpsuit-wearing Stewart taking a giant stride across the Atlantic Ocean from London to New York. The image slyly referenced both his recent defection from his old label, Europe-based PolyGram (the same company that put out *Buckingham Nicks*), to the Burbank-based Warner Bros., along with the fact that Stewart had also just moved to America, more specifically to Hollywood, just as Kosh had done the year before.

With *Atlantic Crossing* going platinum after making the Top Ten on the US album charts in 1975, Stewart wanted to use Kosh's services again on his follow-up release in 1976, to be called *A Night on the Town* and to be cut at Cherokee Recording Studios in Hollywood. Once more

Kosh designed an eye-catching cover, this time humorously inserting a sketched likeness of a jaunty-looking Stewart into a crowd scene in the middle of a famous Renoir painting (*Le Moulin de la Galette*). And just like the last time, Stewart scored a platinum record.

So it was little surprise to Kosh when "Rod the Mod," as the fanzines dubbed him, turned to him for yet another album cover. As a couple of expat Brits in the middle of creating new lives for themselves far from their homeland, Stewart and Kosh by this time had become occasional lunch partners too. Of course, watching Stewart zoom up in his black Porsche 911 Turbo in front of Ye Olde King's Head pub in Santa Monica (their favorite watering hole) usually meant that Stewart's wallet would somehow mysteriously fail to materialize when it came time to pay the tab. Yet the two got on well, if perhaps occasionally fueled by more than their fair share of Bass Ale and Guinness Extra Stout.

Despite the commercial success and relatively pleasant working relationship that resulted from their first two vinyl collaborations, however, the third time was definitely not the charm for Rod Stewart and Kosh. On *Atlantic Crossing* and *A Night on the Town*, Stewart's presence had not been required to create the cover art (both were drawings). For *Foot Loose & Fancy Free*, it was.

Stewart had agreed to be photographed in a (for him) stereotypically debauched, semicomatose pose while sprawled across an unmade motel room bed as an overflowing bathtub flooded the premises. The singer loved the concept when Kosh initially pitched it to him. Stewart got the humor of it all, plus it would give him a chance to poke a little fun at his well-publicized partying persona.

But by the end of the first day of the shoot there was no sign of the enigmatic singer inside of Kosh's Hollywood production studio. Just plenty of water, a hell of a set, and at least one ownerless shoe.

As day number two rolled around, with Kosh bringing back all the well-paid hair, makeup, and lighting crews, still no Stewart. By day three Kosh was through. It wasn't that he had never been forced to deal with the absences of a recording artist before—he *had* worked with the Stones and the notoriously tardy Keith Richards on several occasions. But at least good ol' Keef always turned up soon enough, certainly never missing days at a stretch without bothering to report in. In the current situation the meter was running on the Stewart project, and Warner Bros. had already made it clear to Kosh that they were not happy about the hefty bill being run up.

Finally getting through to Stewart's manager Billy Gaff on the phone, Kosh laid it on the line as straight as he could.

"Look, Warner is getting really upset about this," he said, hoping to light some kind of fire. "They're in so far for about sixty grand."

Mere afterthoughts until *Sgt. Pepper's Lonely Hearts Club Band* by the Beatles came along in 1967, the cardboard jackets surrounding vinyl albums suddenly began to matter. By the mid- to late seventies elaborate, expensive-to-produce LP covers and their associated inserts such as posters, stickers, and booklets had become commonplace. With recent releases by all sorts of front-line music acts—from Earth, Wind & Fire to Yes to Led Zeppelin—selling millions of copies with extraordinarily rendered artwork and sleeves, the better a record's packaging looked, the thinking went, the better the chances were to increase sales.

Yet even by 1977's fanciful, free-spending standards by the major record labels, the cost of creating Rod Stewart's album art on his latest project was becoming a problem. By comparison, Kosh's design work for the Eagles on the acclaimed *Hotel California* album package from the year before, which included an extravagant gatefold and poster, cost only $42,000 for the finished product.

"I'll see what I can do," came Gaff's reply.

Just to be on the safe side, however, Kosh also placed a strategic call to Mo Ostin, the president of Warner Bros. Records, to keep him up to date on Stewart's wayward tendencies. No need in having the boys at the record label pissed off for some reason at the man with the sketchpad—better to stay on their good side. Kosh knew that he undoubtedly would have further business with them down the road on other albums by other artists.

"You know, you've got a really difficult client here," Kosh began, stating the painfully obvious.

Ostin let out a sigh. He needed no reminding.

"Why do you think we call him Rod the Sod?" he wryly responded. Sod, with its roots in the word "sodomite," was British slang for a brat, among less flattering things.

"Well, are you going to cover my ass, then?" Kosh asked while laughing, the double entendre of his question hard to miss.

"Yes, son," Ostin replied.

By day four, however, the powers-that-be had apparently done their jobs. Rod Stewart, however grudgingly, dutifully appeared at the photographic studio on Vine Street (directly across from Capitol Records and next door to the legendary Hollywood Canteen) where Kosh, crew, and a waterlogged set had been sitting idly by for the better part of a workweek. It was the defining moment everyone had been waiting for, the big payoff. Excitement filled the air. Validation for a job well done seemed imminent.

Yet after taking one look at all that had been so carefully, so painstakingly crafted on his behalf and at his behest, Stewart suddenly had other ideas.

"Nah, I don't want to do this anymore," he said with a wave of his hand. "I just want a picture of me face."

Kosh couldn't believe what he was hearing. Did the guy have any idea what went into creating something like this? Let alone that it would make a brilliant album cover?

But after an uncomfortable exchange, with a pouting Stewart ultimately turning away from Kosh like a little kid who knew he had done wrong but didn't care, the short discussion between the two onetime North Londoners abruptly ended. The hugely expensive motel room set would be no more. Rod the Sod would indeed have his way. Several days later Kosh and photographer friend Jim Shea found themselves at the top of the Hollywood Hills on Mulholland Drive taking a picture of Stewart's face, just as ordered—something that originally could have been done for a fraction of the cost. But for Kosh, the client—even one as stubborn and self-absorbed as Rod Stewart—was always right.

Most of the time anyway.

WHILE JOHN KOSH BUSIED HIMSELF WITH ROD STEWART'S album-cover antics, Waddy Wachtel had problems of his own to deal with just a few blocks down the street from Kosh's Sunset Boulevard office.

Having agreed to coproduce Warren Zevon's next album with Jackson Browne at the Sound Factory, the project had gone relatively smoothly most of the way. The hard-drinking, fast-living, often-abrasive Zevon, who was usually too much for most people to handle, actually listened to Wachtel, just as Browne had predicted. Zevon liked and respected Wachtel not only for his premier musicianship but also because of his no-nonsense attitude. The guitarist would readily call bullshit whenever he saw or heard it, no matter how famous or cantankerous his employer might be. He had serious guts in a music business where fear usually governed the tongue. There was nothing artificial or contrived about Waddy Wachtel—what you saw is what you got. He was loyal too. And funny, often inadvertently. All of which had endeared him to the mercurial, temperamental Zevon ever since their days playing together for the Everly Brothers.

But the current issue for Wachtel as coproducer had nothing to do with Zevon; instead, it had everything to do with one of the tracks on Zevon's new album, *Excitable Boy*. After many different combinations of session drummers and bass players had given it a shot—including local L.A. stalwarts such as Russ Kunkel, Jeff Porcaro, Michael Botts, and Gary Mallaber on drums, along with Bob Glaub and Lee Sklar on bass—Wachtel and Zevon had thrown up their hands. Though not planned as anything other than an album cut, the rhythm portion of "Werewolves of London" still needed to be right.

Written a couple of years prior with nonsensical lyrics by Wachtel and Zevon about a swarm of suave-yet-lethal werewolves out on the town in London dining at places such as a Chinese restaurant and Trader Vic's—even walking with the Queen—the song was purely a romp. There were no hidden meanings or agendas or ironic characterizations. But it also had an undeniably catchy riff that Wachtel's friend Leroy Marinell had come up with. The tune materialized one day when Wachtel stopped by Zevon's house for a few minutes while out running errands. When Zevon happened to mention to Wachtel that Phil Everly had encouraged him to write a song with the odd title of "Werewolves of London," Wachtel asked quizzically, "You mean like, *ahh-ooo*?"

"Yeah, yeah," Zevon replied, laughing at Wachtel's attempt at howling.

"That's easy, man," Wachtel said, a bolt of creativity zapping through him. "Roy, play that guitar figure you've been fooling around with for the past year."

As Marinell did so, picking out a simple-yet-mesmerizing eight-note pattern over and over on his acoustic guitar—dut-duh dut-duh dut-dut-dut-duh—Wachtel began making up words.

"I saw a werewolf with a Chinese menu in his hand," Wachtel sang off the top of his head, "walking through the streets of Soho in the rain."

Before anyone knew what was happening, Wachtel suddenly had the entire first verse of the song done.

"He was lookin' for a place called Lee Ho Fooks. Gonna get a big dish of beef chow mein."

As they all jumped in on singing a big round of *ahh-ooo*'s and then the words "werewolves of London," the three collapsed in hysterics. Zevon, for one, loved it.

"That's great," he exclaimed.

"Really?" a surprised Wachtel said, who thought it was all just a big goof. "Okay, well, there's your first verse. I gotta go to town."

And with that, Wachtel was gone, forgetting the song within minutes.

But after Wachtel's visit, Zevon continued to work on the rest of the lyrics, finally completing them sometime later. But rather than putting it on the first solo album that Zevon had done with Browne as his producer, Browne wanted to save "Werewolves of London" for another time, perhaps on Zevon's next album.

"We need room right now for your more important stuff like 'Hasten Down the Wind,' 'Carmelita,' and 'Mohammed's Radio,'" he explained.

Unfortunately for all concerned, the album, titled simply *Warren Zevon*, promptly vanished at retail in 1976. But it did lead directly to Zevon's reputation as a tunesmith to contend with among those in the know in the music business, leaving Linda Ronstadt and others clamoring to record his work.

In the fall of 1977, when it came time to cut Zevon's next LP, *Excitable Boy*, there was "Werewolves of London," still waiting for its turn on vinyl. But, as before, it needed the right bass and drum feel. Though Zevon, Browne, and Wachtel had gotten plenty of decent versions of the song out of the various session musician combos they kept bringing in, to Wachtel at least, the song continued to come up short. It needed to be played straight up.

"I think it's really good like it is," Browne offered.

"No, man, it's too cute. It's got to be heavy," Wachtel said.

After the studio cleared out one afternoon following another failed attempt, Wachtel sat in a back office by himself looking depressed. As he wracked his brain about whom he could find to come in and do "Werewolves" the right way, Wachtel heard a voice coming from behind him. It was Jorge Calderón, his old pal from the early days with Keith Olsen over at Sound City. Calderón—perhaps Zevon's best friend ever since he had helped a drunk, keyless Zevon get back inside his apartment by jokingly saying, "Don't worry, I'm Puerto Rican. I can get into anybody's house"—had stopped by to check on the album's progress and to cheer Zevon on.

"Hey, Waddy, how're you doing?" Calderón said brightly, extending his hand.

"Oh, man, Jorge," Wachtel replied, shaking his head, "you know, we've gone through six or seven different rhythm sections on "Werewolves of London," and we can't get a fucking track. A song so simple, and they all play too much."

Calderón nodded. A quiet, astute, musician's musician, perhaps his best attribute was being a good listener, whether it be to a friend in need or to the nuances of the music itself. Having played many a song with many a band, he knew exactly what Wachtel meant. Simple songs are sometimes the hardest for rhythm sections to play because they instinctively want to spice things up. The trick is to find a drummer and bassist combo who is into laying it all down old-school style, with a hard beat, a big groove, and little or no extraneous fills or runs. To Calderón it obviously needed to be a pair who had played together for a long time and had a natural, almost organic approach.

And then it dawned on him.

"How about Mick and John?" Calderón suggested, referring to the rock-solid, joined-at-the-hip pairing of Mick Fleetwood and John McVie. Through Lindsey Buckingham and Stevie Nicks during the *Buckingham Nicks* era and beyond, Wachtel already knew both Fleetwood and McVie, as did Jorge Calderón.

For their part, Fleetwood and McVie were as unadorned and groove-heavy as any rock-and-roll rhythm battery in the business, which had especially pleased Keith Olsen when recording the *Fleetwood Mac* LP at Sound City several years earlier. Just like on that record's first hit, "Over My Head," Fleetwood and McVie knew precisely how to provide a song with a simple-yet-powerful foundation that allowed the instrumentation and voices to stand out. That ability was the duo's trademark. Of course, given that by the fall of 1977 they were also now in one of the biggest bands in the world because of the success of *Rumours*, their interest in playing on a cartoonish album cut for Warren Zevon—hardly a household name—could well be nada.

"That's a great idea," Wachtel said, his eyes opening wide. "But would they even be available?"

Having just returned from hanging out with Mick and the rest of Fleetwood Mac in Miami at one of the band's huge outdoor concerts, Calderón was now one of Fleetwood's best friends too. So Calderón called Fleetwood and passed along the info about Zevon and Wachtel's song predicament. With Fleetwood surprisingly expressing interest and, more so, actually knowing all about Zevon, Wachtel then gave the drummer a call to nail down the details of the session.

"You want us to come there and play with you guys? Oh, Waddy, that's a real honor," Fleetwood said gushingly. "John and I would love to."

With Mick Fleetwood being one of the most famous drummers on the planet by this point, to Wachtel the over-the-top compliment didn't quite make sense.

"What? Uh, yeah, well just get down here, would ya?" he replied with his characteristic bluntness.

Once Fleetwood and McVie set up their instruments and started playing around seven o'clock at night along with Wachtel (lead guitar), Zevon (piano), and Wachtel and Browne's friend Danny Kortchmar on rhythm guitar (whom Wachtel had fought for on the Carole King tour), they all knew within seconds that it was the right combination. Finally. The corny monster tune now had a hook and a groove that just wouldn't quit.

But, then, neither would Mick Fleetwood.

At the end of the second take Wachtel walked over to the control room and mentioned to coproducer Jackson Browne that he thought maybe they had what they needed. But Browne felt they should do a few more takes, just to have some solid choices to pick from. Except that a few takes then turned into dozens, and the next thing everyone knew, it was five o'clock in the morning.

An exhausted Wachtel approached Fleetwood, who was sitting behind his drum kit, looking game for even more.

"I think we're done," Wachtel said, hoping Fleetwood and everyone else would go home so he could record his guitar solo for the song.

"We're *never* done, Waddy," a wild-eyed, sweat-soaked Fleetwood said in his growling British accent.

By seven o'clock that morning, however, they really were done. Wachtel and Browne could take no more and agreed that, after a monstrous twelve-hour recording session and out of almost sixty takes, take number two really was the best of the bunch. And after Wachtel laid down his nasty Les Paul guitar solo, that was that—until the suits at Warner Bros. Records got ahold of the song.

With stellar compositions such as "Roland the Headless Thompson Gunner," "Accidentally Like a Martyr," "Nighttime in the Switching Yard," and "Lawyers, Guns and Money," the *Excitable Boy* album was filled with examples of Zevon's unique and exquisitely sophisticated songwriting talent. No one could come up with an offbeat musical idea or phrase like he could and make it both funny and poignant at the same time. But none of that mattered to the execs; instead, the one and only cut they thought could be a hit was "Werewolves of London," something that enraged both Wachtel and Zevon. It was just a joke song, not even close to Zevon's best work—didn't anyone understand that?

Yet "Werewolves of London" did indeed become Zevon's first Top Forty hit, blasting out of radios everywhere during the spring of 1978. It was also his only song to ever make the Top Forty, leaving most of the general public forever unaware of Zevon's true brilliance.

eleven

MEXICAN REGGAE

Only do an inch, man. This shit'll kill ya.

—GLENN FREY

W HEN DON FELDER FIRST CAME ACROSS THE CHORD PROGRES-
sion for "Hotel California" on his Martin acoustic guitar, he
knew he was tapping into something special. Sitting inside his beach-
front rental house in Malibu with the doors wide open and overlook-
ing the sparkling blue of the Pacific Ocean, Felder had been absently
picking and strumming his way through what suddenly became a
basis for a song. A very good song, Felder thought. Dashing into his
little studio in a spare bedroom before he forgot anything, Felder got
the basic chord structure down on tape.

From there, over the next several days Felder continued to play
around with the song, layering in various almost Jamaican-like rhythm
and harmony parts on acoustic and electric guitars, plus some electric
bass, and even a slinky Samba beat courtesy of his trusty old Rhythm
Ace analog drum machine. When he was done the eclectic mixture

seemed to Felder like a possible standout. It was certainly different from anything he had ever written, let alone emerging so fully realized. But the only way to gauge its true potential as a fit for the Eagles was to send it off on cassette to Henley and Frey for their opinions. That was the protocol.

After Don Henley gave the tape a listen, which contained more than a dozen song ideas of varying quality and length, something caught his ear. Sure enough, it was the musical piece with the Caribbean sound and the Latin beat.

"I really love the one that sounds like a matador, like you're in Mexico," he told Felder. "What's it called?"

With Felder having never bothered to name his composition, Henley gave the song the working title of "Mexican Reggae" and then got busy conjuring up a story. With legal pad in hand and with a conceptual contribution from Frey, Henley ended up penning a surreal tale about a lone driver who ends up stranded for the night—and perhaps for life—inside a freakish inn. A metaphor in some ways for Henley's view of Southern California—and, for that matter, America itself—as the increasingly tarnished land of opportunity, the song, soon renamed "Hotel California," became the basic thematic foundation (and title) for the entire album. With the narrative arc slowly yet inexorably shifting from innocence and optimism to that of experience and pessimism over the course of the nine tracks, critics and fans alike rapidly anointed the LP as the Eagles' crowning achievement.

Going platinum within a week of release and hitting number one within four, *Hotel California* additionally generated two number-one singles ("New Kid in Town" and "Hotel California") and delivered two more Grammy Awards (the band had previously won for "Lyin' Eyes").

It also was the beginning of the end for the Eagles.

DURING THE EARLY PART OF THE TWENTIETH CENTURY IN SOUTH-
ern California few architectural styles possessed greater allure than
that of Spanish Colonial Revival. With its use of smooth stucco fin-
ishes, low-pitched clay-tile roofs, and terracotta accents, it borrowed
elements from a wide variety of earlier movements, particularly those
of Spanish Baroque, Moorish Revival, and Mexican Churrigueresque,
with a dash of Pueblo thrown in for good measure. And no architect evidenced a greater skill in its creation than George Washington
Smith of Santa Barbara.

Renowned for his imaginative use of polychrome Spanish and Tu-
nisian tiles, hand-forged, wrought-iron window grilles, and heavy,
wood-beamed ceilings, Smith's inimitable designs put him in great
demand among the wealthy and powerful. Though most of his one
hundred–plus homes were to be found in posh coastal communities,
one of his masterpieces—and the only example of his work in L.A.
proper—was the Henry Kern estate on Carolwood Drive in fashion-
able Holmby Hills, just off Sunset Boulevard near the UCLA campus.

Situated on a lush, two-acre rise with breathtaking views, the
home's long private driveway wound its way up a gentle, immacu-
lately manicured slope, where it passed under a Saracen arch at the
top, finally spilling out onto a huge white and beige flagstone-paved
motor court, complete with splashing fountain in the middle. The
house itself featured a mammoth two-story marble entry hall filled
with Art Nouveau accents; massive living and dining areas containing dozens of pieces of Gallé glass, Erté paintings, and Ruhlmann
cobra torchères (candle stands); a winding grand staircase; and too
many bedrooms and bathrooms to even bother counting. In short, the
cavernous, impossibly ornate dwelling was fit for a king.

Or, by 1978 standards, one Roderick David Stewart.

Having moved into his palatial digs a couple of years earlier along with his girlfriend Brit Ekland, the beautiful Swedish actress and one-time Bond girl, Rod Stewart, riding high on the success of three consecutive, multiplatinum-selling, Kosh-designed albums, had already begun recording a fourth. And he knew exactly what he wanted to call it too: *Blondes Have More Fun.* All Stewart needed now was to get Kosh on board to make the visual magic happen one more time.

Despite some bruised feelings that understandably had come with the *Foot Loose & Fancy Free* album cover debacle from the year before, Kosh held no grudges. That wasn't his style. This *was* the record biz, after all, and he had been around long enough to realize that rock-and-rollers were nothing if not tempestuous—they sometimes did crazy, impetuous, illogical things. But they also just as often created incredible music. They were artists, like him. Besides, Mo Ostin had been true to his word: Warner Bros. Records found it within themselves to pay Kosh in full for all his flooded motel room efforts, which went a long way toward helping him want to do business with them again. And as for Stewart, well, he was forever just Rod. Take him or leave him.

Kosh therefore took it in stride when he received a phone call at his office one day in the early fall of 1978 from Stewart, who wanted to hire his services once more. The occasional disagreement aside, their exceptional track record together spoke for itself. After Stewart explained his idea about stocking his swimming pool with a bevy of beautiful blondes (with himself in the middle) as the basis for his new album's cover, Kosh said he would be willing to design it. He would also set up all the details, including putting the flamboyant, roguish singer in touch with the Playboy Modeling Agency so Stewart could handpick his own buxom aqua mates. Following that, it would just be a matter of Kosh taking a little trip down the road to Holmby Hills to get it all down on film.

Home at various times to luminaries like Walt Disney, Humphrey Bogart, and even Hugh Hefner (the Playboy Mansion opened there in 1971), Holmby Hills boasted the distinction of having one of the highest per capita income levels of any neighborhood in the United States. Along with Beverly Hills and Bel Air, it formed what the locals referred to as the "Platinum Triangle." Into this luxurious land of Lincolns, Bentleys, and the occasional Maserati motored Kosh, proudly piloting his beloved, gold-colored, long-out-of-production 1950 Hudson Commodore.

A streamlined postwar behemoth (it had the lowest center of gravity of any US-built passenger vehicle), with a straight-eight engine, a 128-inch wheelbase (compared to the 1950 Cadillac Coupe De Ville's 126-inch), and plenty of horsepower, Kosh's colossal car satisfied both his undying love for over-the-top American automobiles and his well-cultivated taste for the offbeat. Not to mention his sense of humor. Gas crisis or no, the grander the gas-guzzler the better, thank you very much.

As Kosh pulled up in his beloved antique sedan in front of Stewart's magnificent manse, he couldn't help but marvel. In his four years in Hollywood he had been invited to many a rock star's elegant abode. Sometimes to work, more often to party. Nothing new there. Living large was all part of the gig. But Stewart's place took first prize for out-and-out ostentatiousness. To Kosh, it looked like the second coming of the Palace of Versailles, with lawns going down to lawns going down to lawns, all neatly bisected by a stunningly designed stepped waterfall of scalloped seashells that emptied its cascading contents into an enormous rectangular swimming pool.

Shortly after Kosh rang the home's front bell, a buoyant Stewart, cocktail in hand, opened the door wide.

"Come on in, mate," he said warmly.

With Kosh preferring to remain sober when he worked, he politely declined to join his host in enjoying any libations. Though there had been a couple of exceptions, like the time Glenn Frey and one or two of the other Eagles stopped by his office to take a look at some of the planned artwork for *Hotel California* and, before Kosh knew what to say, Frey had poured a lengthy line of cocaine on the table, then provided a sincere warning.

"Only do an inch, man. This shit'll kill ya."

Kosh knew to do as he was told. In his experience the old rock-and-roll adage that the bigger the band, the better the drugs was something not to be trifled with. But in the main and unlike a good share of his clients, Kosh was a teetotaler during working hours. There was too much at stake otherwise. In his profession a reputation for mistake-free excellence meant everything. Besides, there was always plenty of time for imbibing, inhaling, or snorting when not on the clock.

Following a quick exchange of pleasantries, Kosh and Stewart then made their way through the house and out a sliding-glass door to Stewart's impossibly verdant back lawn (the Sod's sod, so to speak). There they joined Stewart's music producer, the legendary Tom Dowd (Aretha Franklin, Cream, Otis Redding), who had been quite contentedly occupying himself by watching a number of gorgeous Playboy models arrive in their bikinis by the pool area far below.

After Kosh said hello to Dowd and vice versa (they had met each other several times before), Stewart could wait no longer to spring his latest album cover ambition on the unsuspecting art director. And this time it was one for the ages.

"I've got this concept for you, Kosh—it's great," he enthused. "Remember, now, the album is called *Blondes Have More Fun*. So I've decided to dress up in full Nazi regalia, complete with a monocle, and I'm going to be kissing a nun."

Apparently the pool-full-of-girls idea had now gone the way of the floating-motel-room idea. Maybe Stewart somehow just hated water.

A dumbfounded Kosh could only stare, silently hoping—praying, even—that Stewart was only joking. But the inebriated, peroxide-blond vocalist seemed to be anything but.

However, unlike almost any other bizarre request made of Kosh by any other artist—and there had been many—Kosh simply said no. Not this time around. Not something this blatantly offensive.

"Can you imagine the Bible Belt's response?" he asked incredulously while simultaneously scanning Stewart's face for some sign of sanity. "No, I won't do it."

Kosh could easily imagine the irreparable damage it might do to his own career, much less that of Stewart's. It would be professional suicide for one and all. But Rod Stewart was used to having his way, and this was no exception. Who did Kosh think he was talking to anyway?

An enraged Stewart then turned belligerent as an equally intransigent Kosh gamely stood his ground. Pointing at the twenty or so blonde models now assembled below—models he had personally chosen—Stewart barked, "I wouldn't fuck any one of them!" As if Kosh somehow actually cared either way.

From there the conversation between the two—if it could even be called one—became nothing more than a foul-mouthed flurry of every expletive in the book, finally descending to the level of a couple of common guttersnipes, with Stewart absurdly shouting, "Don't call *me* a cunt, you cunt!"

By that point, seeing that he was getting nowhere, Rod Stewart simply came unglued, doing the unthinkable. The athletic, sinewy-strong, hot-tempered singer reared back to throw what seemed likely to be a roundhouse punch straight at Kosh's face. Something that Kosh could see unfolding before his eyes as if in slow motion. But somehow, within the last precious milliseconds, just before metacarpus met mandible, as Kosh resigned himself to spending some quality time at the nearest medical facility, a hand suddenly came out of nowhere and stopped Stewart's fast-moving arm cold. It was Tom Dowd.

Not known as any kind of physical specimen, the small, compactly built, unprepossessing producer, who was easily twenty years older than either Stewart or Kosh, somehow managed to restrain the livid, out-of-control Rod Stewart, in the process slightly calming him down. It then became a brief grumble-grumble, mutter-mutter standoff between Kosh and Stewart, with Kosh finally walking away in disgust. There would be no photo shoot of any kind—he was through with Stewart's bullshit. Let the barmy arsehole design his own effing album cover.

But what the entertainment gods taketh, they sometimes giveth in return. Not long after the craziness of the Stewart incident, Kosh had some good news come his way, something that provided a nice salve. Based on his work for his friend Linda Ronstadt when he created the jacket art for her latest best-selling album, 1977's *Simple Dreams* (which knocked Fleetwood Mac's *Rumours* from the top of the Billboard album chart after twenty-nine straight weeks), Kosh won his first Grammy for Best Recording Package. A triumphant moment, it put him on top of the art direction world within the music business. The impoverished Cockney kid who once played among the bomb craters had created a thunderous impact all his own.

Following the Grammys Kosh's phone rang almost nonstop for the next several weeks, with one congratulatory message after another flowing in. Then, in an only-in-Hollywood moment, out of nowhere came a call from the man who had caused Kosh more anguish and aggravation than all his other clients combined: Rod Stewart, the last person Kosh wanted to talk to.

But instead of apologizing for the appallingly nasty confrontation that had occurred at his home or at least offering a congratulations on the big Grammy win, Stewart, true to form, merely said, "Hey, Kosh, let's do another album together."

And so they did.

THOUGH DON FELDER HAD HOPED AGAINST HOPE THAT HE might get to sing "Hotel California," as he had written almost all the song's music, the vocal duties ultimately fell to the song's lyricist, Don Henley, who, by 1976, had become the Eagles' primary lead singer. With his raspy, world-weary voice and natural-born storyteller's gift for phrasing, there were few, if any, in popular music who could "sell" a song as well as Henley. Which no one disputed inside the Eagles, especially Felder. He knew the pecking order.

With the addition of Joe Walsh in place of the recently departed Bernie Leadon just prior to the start of the recording sessions for *Hotel California*, Felder readily acknowledged that he was the worst singer in the band. He was fifth out of five. But that in no way meant he was a bad singer either. In fact, Felder was pretty good, notably at harmonizing with the other four, which was an essential job requirement—at their core the Eagles were a vocal group, after all.

But getting to sing the actual lead on a song for the high-flying band, who had by the time of *Hotel California* flown past Chicago, the Doobie Brothers, and other superstar American acts to become *the* most popular group in the country, now required being a whole lot more than "pretty good." With Henley, Frey, Walsh, and Meisner all having enjoyed Top Forty success as lead vocalists, those four had a virtual lock on the number of available tracks.

Yet despite the realities of being in a world-class vocal group with four other singers more adept than he, Felder clung tight to the notion that he had been promised the chance to sing lead on at least one song per album. In particular, he wanted his turn at the mic for *Hotel California* to be on "Victim of Love," another unique chord progression he had written, recorded, and submitted via cassette to Henley and Frey. With Henley, Frey, and J. D. Souther subsequently writing the lyrics about a woman's desperate search for late-night Hollywood-style companionship, no matter the personal cost (something the three knew plenty about), and with Felder's raw, catchy guitar licks, "Victim of Love" quickly made the cut to become one of the nine tracks earmarked for inclusion on *Hotel California*. Which then still left open the question as to who was going to sing it.

Temporarily shifting their recording operations away from the Record Plant West to Miami's famed Criteria Studios (Bee Gees, Eric Clapton, Lynyrd Skynyrd) during the summer of 1976, the Eagles got down to putting "Victim of Love" on tape. But this time the band decided to do something out of the ordinary. They wanted to make a point of cutting the instrumental portion of the song entirely live, with only the vocals to be overdubbed later. Stung by accusations in the press that they were only capable of recording their songs piece by piece, then having their ace producer, Bill Szymczyk, bail them out by editing everything together after the fact, the Eagles decided to put their musical prowess on display.

With Felder on lead guitar, Walsh on slide, Henley on drums, Frey on rhythm guitar, and Meisner on bass, the basic tracking went even better than expected, yielding a powerful, driving, and funky instrumental bed. The Eagles proved to themselves and anyone who would care to listen or read (Szymczyk subsequently scratched "V.O.L. is a five piece live" on the vinyl LP's side-two run-out groove) that they were very much a standout live band in the studio when they wanted to be. Now all the song needed was a killer lead vocal to put it over the top.

But with Henley and Frey obligingly giving Felder a shot at singing lead on "Victim of Love," after a number of takes they decided that his pleasant-enough voice wasn't nearly giving the song the edge it needed.

"Okay, let's hold on that," Frey said over the talkback mic to Felder, who was standing alone out in the studio wearing a pair of headphones. "We'll pick it up later."

Except there was no later.

That evening, at the urging of Henley and Frey, the Eagles' devoted manager, Irving Azoff, slyly took Felder out to dinner in Miami to keep him away from the studio for several hours. In the meantime, back at Criteria Henley laid down *his* lead vocal interpretation of the "Victim of Love" lyrics (that he had written), creating what Henley, Frey, and Szymczyk instantly realized to be a vast improvement.

Once Felder found out the next day he had been duped, however, it caused a deep and permanent wound. Felder felt betrayed by those with whom he was presumably the closest. How could his very own bandmates trick him? With Henley and Frey wanting the best possible lead vocal on "Victim of Love" and also not wanting to get into some overheated shouting match with Felder about it, they simply chose to finish the song without him. In their minds the case was closed. In Felder's view, not so much.

Like the Beatles, the Rolling Stones, Creedence Clearwater Revival, and many, if not most of history's major rock-and-roll bands, a benevolent dictatorship—perhaps sometimes not even all that benevolent—has usually run the show. And so it was with the Eagles. Though there existed an equal legal partnership between the original four (then five) members, Henley and Frey were always clearly in charge of the band's artistic direction, like it or not. To them, when it came down to the option of being either a five-man democracy with equal input or of creating the best possible records, the decision had to come down on the side of the music every time. Doing what was "best" for the Eagles is the way the pair often explained the rationale behind their decision making. And by the summer of 1980, with four consecutive number-one albums (including the landmark *Hotel California*), sixteen Top Forty singles, and countless other tracks in regular rotation on the huge number of album-oriented rock (AOR) stations on FM radio around the country, few could argue against the fact that Henley and Frey, heavy-handed or not, did indeed know what was best for the Eagles. And then there was Don Felder.

As burned out as the rest in the band from too many years of grinding out album after album and tour after tour while at the same time partying as if Bolivia and Peru were in imminent danger of running out of coca leaves, for Felder—who never got over his lead-vocal snubs—something had to give. On July 31, 1980, the final night of the Eagles' sixty-four-date worldwide trek in support of their latest (and almost three-years-in-the-making) studio album, 1979's *The Long Run*, that "something" proved to have a name and a face: US Democratic Senator Alan Cranston.

Ever environmentally conscious and politically aware, the left-leaning Don Henley and Glenn Frey had agreed on behalf of the Eagles to stage a benefit concert in Long Beach, California, in support of the liberal Cranston's upcoming reelection campaign. Don Felder, however, avowedly apolitical, neither knew nor cared a whit about Cranston. Mostly, though, Felder had just grown tired of playing concerts free of charge whenever Henley and Frey unilaterally made the decision that the Eagles would be doing so.

Backstage before the show, during a meet-and-greet with Alan Cranston and around a hundred guests, the long-festering resentments between Don Felder and Glenn Frey finally reached the point of no return. As the senator and his wife made their way down a lineup of the five Eagles to shake hands and offer their thanks, the last one they came to was Don Felder. After Cranston passed along his appreciation to Felder, Cranston's wife, trailing slightly behind her husband, then politely added, "It was very nice to meet you."

"Nice to meet you too . . . *I guess*," Felder replied, adding the last two words mostly under his breath and with a notable level of sarcasm.

Loud enough, however, for Cranston's wife, Norma, to catch as she glanced back over her shoulder while walking away. The nearby Glenn Frey also overheard the words.

"Don, I need to speak to you in the dressing room right now," a stone-faced Frey said, approaching Felder.

As the two entered the backstage locker room used as a dressing area for both sports teams and music acts alike, all pretense of good will between the two longtime bandmates immediately dissolved as Frey smashed a longneck bottle of Budweiser against the wall.

"You fucking asshole," Frey bellowed as he got up in Felder's face. "Where do you get off insulting the senator and his wife like that?"

At first trying to explain his comment as having been an inadvertent slip of the tongue and that he was apologetic, Felder gave up even trying as Frey's four-letter-word tirade continued. Finally, fed up with the continued haranguing and with Frey in general, Felder tossed off a "fuck you" of his own and walked out.

But that hardly ended the matter.

Feeling both challenged and disrespected, a still-seething Frey let his enmity boil over later that evening onstage during the concert, something that rarely happened among bands in general and had never occurred within the Eagles.

As a horrified Timothy B. Schmit (Randy Meisner's replacement in the Eagles following *Hotel California*) and Joe Walsh looked on (Don Henley was behind his drum kit), Frey and Felder kept up their hate-filled dialogue throughout the show on open mics.

Fueled by various alcoholic beverages strategically stashed behind their guitar amps, Frey and Felder laced into each other with increasing vitriol.

"You're a real pro, Don, all the way," Frey sneered at Felder during one song.

"Yeah, you are too," Felder volleyed. "The way you handle people. Except for the people you pay. Nobody gives a shit."

"Fuck you. I've been paying you for seven years, you fuckhead," an increasingly unhinged Frey barked back.

Toward the end of the two-hour show a glaring Frey kept up the attack.

"Only three more songs, asshole. I'm gonna fuckin' kill you. I can't wait."

But for all the heavy-duty onstage huffing and puffing between Frey and Felder, no punches were ever thrown.

Instead, after the Eagles came back out to do their second encore before the roaring crowd, which consisted of playing "Already Gone" and a Joe Walsh solo tune called "All Night Long," the band simply said its thanks, took a bow, and then they were gone. Not only from the stage but from each other's lives. The five separate limousines waiting for them downstairs at the loading dock said it all. After a remarkable eight-year run of being the very personification of what it meant to be a successful rock band in L.A. during the seventies, the Eagles were no more.

twelve

DAMN THE TORPEDOES

I'll sell fucking peanuts before I give in to you.

—TOM PETTY

IN THE SUMMER OF 1961, WHILE AIMLESSLY PLAYING IN A PILE OF pine needles in the front yard of his run-down Gainesville, Florida, home, an eleven-year-old Tom Petty looked up to hear the words that would forever change the course of his life: "How would you like to meet Elvis Presley?"

They came from Petty's visiting Aunt Evelyn, whose husband, Earl Jernigan, had just told her he could set up a meeting with Elvis himself. Having been on a veritable cinematic tear after his much-publicized release from a two-year Army hitch, Presley was in Florida to film no less than his fifth postservice flick in a mere fifteen months, this one to be called *Follow That Dream*. For his part, Petty's uncle found a way to hire on to the local production crew and had somehow ingratiated himself with the legendary singer.

"Me and Elvis are buddies," Jernigan liked to brag.

On the day of the big event the small-for-his-age, towheaded Petty stood next to his aunt, uncle, and several cousins as they watched Cadillac after Cadillac pull up at the shooting location, dropping off one mohair suit–clad, pompadour-wearing member of Elvis's personal posse after another. Hundreds of frenzied girls behind a nearby chain-link fence screamed with every arrival.

"Is that him? Is that him?" Petty asked over and over, only to be disappointed.

Finally, after almost an hour of waiting, with everyone growing weary, one last Caddy motored into view. With a bevy of bodyguards scrambling to be the first to open the gleaming black limo's back door, out stepped a man with an aura so magnetic that Petty could feel it from fifty feet away.

"*That's* him!" he cried out, triumphantly.

But as Elvis made his way over to greet the Jernigan/Petty clan, the future front man and namesake of Tom Petty and the Heartbreakers suddenly froze. After all, who was he to speak to the most famous musician on the planet?

"These are my nieces and nephews, Elvis," Jernigan said, pointing, as Presley smiled and nodded. Though Petty burned to say hello, he instead stood wide-eyed and mute, as if he had just borne personal witness to the Second Coming.

"Nice to meet y'all," Elvis offered, then ambled off toward his trailer.

And that was all it took.

From the moment Petty returned home from the encounter, his mind reeling, all he could think about was Elvis. Or more precisely, all he could think about was how he—Thomas Earl Petty, a poor kid with no apparent musical aptitude—might someday, someway become the *next* King of Rock and Roll.

AT THE SAME TIME TOM PETTY FOUND HIMSELF FALLING UNDER Elvis Presley's spell, a thousand miles to the north another youngster began his would-be professional musical odyssey under an entirely different set of circumstances. Born to Martha and Milton Yakus just outside Boston during the late 1940s, Sheldon "Shelly" Yakus virtually grew up in a recording studio. With his parents owning a small-yet-thriving local facility called Ace Studios, the precocious Yakus spent most of his free time as a kid acting as an in-house assistant to his father. Young Shelly enthusiastically learned how to do such things as fix tape machines and cut acetates (lacquer-coated demonstration records) while his friends were busy outside playing Little League baseball and cowboys and Indians. To be near his beloved father was a joy; to be working in an actual recording studio, if only a small one, was an even bigger joy.

One day, at the age of seventeen, Yakus received what would become a life-altering after-school assignment.

"Shelly, I want you to take this reel of quarter-inch tape down to New York and have it mastered so we can get some 45s pressed," his dad said.

Thrilled to be making his first trip to see a big-time recording studio in action, Yakus was all eyes and ears from the moment he stepped inside Mira Sound on West 47th Street in Manhattan. And as his luck would have it, a recording session was just getting under way featuring a Queens-based, Top Forty–hit-making "girl group" called the Shangri-Las, who were being produced by industry veteran Brooks Arthur. Of further good fortune, the local musicians' union rep not only happened to be on hand that day but also took a shine to the teenage Shelly.

"Hey, Brooks, this kid here is from out of town, and he's crazy about record making. You mind if he watches your session for a little while?"

"Uh . . . sure," Arthur replied distractedly, his eyes never leaving the mixing console in front of him. "Just tell him not to make any noise."

From the moment the recording began on the future hit single "Give Us Your Blessings," Shelly was in awe. It was like nothing he had experienced back home in Boston. This music was *alive*. From the high-end Neumann microphones and the state-of-the-art Scully four-track tape machine to the way Arthur's fingers flew across the faders as he deftly mixed the sound while incorporating the unique acoustics of the studio, everything seemed to mesh so perfectly. Yakus was instantly hooked, realizing that audio engineering was what he wanted to do—what he *must* do—for the rest of his life.

IN FEBRUARY OF 1964 TOM PETTY FINALLY FIGURED OUT HIS entry point into the world of rock and roll. Having obsessed over Elvis and anything even remotely rockabilly-related for the better part of two years, the now-thirteen-year-old Petty had been spinning his small collection of 45s so incessantly that his parents began to worry, thinking he might need to see a psychologist. "Does the kid ever do anything but play records?" his father would ask in exasperation.

But the night the Beatles made their first appearance on the *Ed Sullivan Show* that all changed—in an instant. Petty took one look at John Lennon and George Harrison on the TV screen playing their gleaming Rickenbacker and Gretsch electric guitars and decided then and there he would become a guitarist just like them.

Though perpetually low on disposable income, Petty's doting mother (in contrast to his often drunk and violent father) somehow managed to scrape together enough money to buy her son a cheap, $35 Kay electric guitar and a tiny portable amp from Sears. And with the same level of dedication he showed in playing his cherished Elvis singles over and over, Petty now turned his attention toward mastering everything he could about his new axe.

After learning a few basic chords from some neighborhood pals and then teaching himself to play "Wooly Bully" by ear, Petty soon decided it was time to form a band of his own. He wanted his group to be just like the Fab Four, who met the only set of criteria that mattered to him: they wrote their own music, played their own instruments, looked like they were having a good time, and, perhaps most important to a kid with a turbulent home life, were self-contained—the Beatles were in *control*.

With an evolving set of names like the Sundowners and the Epics, Petty and an ever-changing cast of fellow underage musicians played any Moose club, birthday party, and fraternity function that would pay—and some that didn't. Petty instinctively knew that it was all valuable experience, something bound to come in handy down the line.

In 1969 the now-eighteen-year-old Petty received an Ampex reel-to-reel tape recorder from his mother for his birthday that changed his world. Finally he could get his musical ideas down on actual tape, putting him one step closer to his goal of becoming a real recording artist.

By the time Petty graduated from high school several months later the core of his band, unbeknownst to him, was now essentially set for the next forty-plus years. The Epics had metamorphosed into a new outfit called Mudcrutch via the defection of a couple of members and the addition of future Heartbreaker mainstays Mike Campbell (lead guitar) and Benmont Tench (keyboards). Through playing gigs virtually nonstop throughout Florida in the early seventies, Mudcrutch became tight and accomplished. Their southern-blues-meets-British-rock sound and repertoire consisted of a string of Petty-written originals, with the occasional Beatles rocker thrown in for good measure, such as "Day Tripper" or "Birthday." Petty's unique, nasally vocals led the way on stage as the band steadily gained a large and loyal regional following.

In the fall of 1974 Tom Petty decided it was time to make his big move. Dreaming of nothing more than having a nationwide hit to call his own, Petty and one of his band's roadies impulsively hopped into a beat-up Chevy van, Mudcrutch demo tape in hand, and drove three thousand miles to Southern California to knock on as many record-label doors as possible. With no connections and even less guile, Petty naïvely hoped he could find someone who might at least consider listening to his work. Instead, much to his astonishment, he received no less than three offers for his services on the *first* day, something virtually unheard of in the music business.

Having written his own songs for a number of years, Petty had a flair for coming up with catchy lyrics and melodies, which in turn had caught the ear of Denny Cordell at Shelter Records. Co-owned by Cordell and Leon Russell (the solo star and onetime Wrecking Crew studio musician), Shelter had a reputation for putting out authentic, southern-style rock, blues, and Americana by the likes of J. J. Cale, Dwight Twilley, and Freddie King—about which the record album–obsessed Petty was already fully aware. So despite offers from big-money labels MGM and London, Petty chose to go with the smaller Shelter, primarily because of Cordell.

Born in Argentina but growing up in England, the lanky, aristocratic, chain-smoking Denny Cordell had become a full-fledged music business phenom before even reaching his twenty-fifth birthday. In 1964, at the age of only twenty-one, he produced "Go Now" for the Moody Blues. Two years later he produced "A Whiter Shade of

Pale" for Procol Harum. Cordell then moved on to produce Joe Cocker's first several hits, including the classic "With a Little Help from My Friends." Based in the United States by the mid-seventies, the flamboyant-yet-pragmatic Cordell now saw his future musical fortunes in the form of Tom Petty and band. But first the boys from Florida would need a little education.

"We're not making an album right away, mates," Cordell declared. "We're going to take some time to expose you to lots of people, lots of records."

And expose them he did. Each evening at six o'clock for several weeks they would all gather in Cordell's office for an hours-long tutorial on just what great music was supposed to sound like.

"Have you ever heard of Lloyd Price? Or Larry Williams?" Cordell would ask, seldom waiting for a reply. He would then slap the respective platter on the turntable.

"You hear that? Now *that's* the shit!"

Petty soon realized how far he needed to go as a songwriter. What worked in Gainesville might not play in Peoria. As he and the band diligently fine-tuned their sound over many months (while being housed and supported by Shelter), Petty eventually found himself chucking every one of the original songs from the Mudcrutch demo tape in favor of a complete set of new compositions.

Finally, in early 1976, the debut LP by the rechristened Tom Petty and the Heartbreakers was ready for primetime. Except primetime wasn't quite ready for it or them. The album took a full year before it made so much as a dent on the Billboard charts. In the meantime Petty and his band scrambled to play whatever gigs they could get, mostly in England, where they had become cult favorites.

By mid-1977, however, with the benefit of some well-placed word of mouth from a few East Coast disc jockeys, the almost-punk-sounding album suddenly took off, especially among college students. The self-titled *Tom Petty and the Heartbreakers* then stayed on the charts for over a year, even after the band's second album, *You're Gonna Get It*, was released in early 1978. Petty's long-cherished dream of being a bona fide rock star was coming to fruition. With hits such as "American Girl," "Breakdown," and "I Need to Know," his distinctive voice was fast becoming an FM radio staple. People knew him by name. He was on the cover of magazines. After years of focus and hard work, it was all coming together. Yet in mere months, while beginning recording album number three, Petty would see his newfound success on the verge of being totally stripped away.

WHEN SHELLY YAKUS PULLED HIS RENTAL CAR INTO THE PARKing lot of Sound City for the first time in late 1978, he wondered what he had gotten himself into. Having never seen the studio before, to his eyes it didn't look like much. Housed in an industrial complex in a rundown neighborhood, Sound City's exterior evidenced nothing of what actually went on inside. Yakus figured it could just as well have been a factory, which it once was. After walking inside, Yakus's suspicions were further confirmed. The place had none of the gloss or high-end accoutrements he was accustomed to inside the big New York studios, things like gorgeous wood paneling, sumptuous lounge areas, and gourmet kitchen facilities; instead, Sound City proudly featured raggedy-looking orange shag carpet, a beat-up sofa, and a broken candy machine.

Through working his way up the recording studio ladder in New York during the heart of the seventies, first at Phil Ramone's vaunted A&R Recording, then at the world-famous Record Plant on West 44th Street, Yakus had established himself as one of the most important engineers in all of rock and roll. His contributions on helping shape the sound while sitting side-by-side with John Lennon on the ex-Beatle's smash LP *Walls and Bridges* was the stuff of legend. Not to mention Yakus's "other" work with the likes of Alice Cooper ("School's Out"), Van Morrison ("Moondance"), and Bruce Springsteen ("Born to Run").

So when Yakus received a phone call from a hot young NYC-based producer named Jimmy Iovine about going to California with him to cut the next Tom Petty record because Denny Cordell had become too busy running Shelter, Yakus understandably had his reservations. Working with Petty might be one thing—the guy had several hits and obvious momentum. But why record it at some no-name studio out in bumfuck Egypt or Van Nuys or wherever the hell the place was?

Once Yakus found himself inside Sound City's Studio A, however, his mind began to change. With the state-of-the-art Neve 8028 mixing console that Keith Olsen had installed several years earlier, along with a fantastic-sounding live room, especially for drums, Yakus could see the potential. Plus, it was the only place Petty liked to work.

For Iovine, recording what would become *Damn the Torpedoes* with Petty and Yakus was all about intuition and believing in the "power of three"—not just the three of them sitting behind the console making all the sonic decisions but also the fact that this was Petty's third album. And Iovine very much believed in third albums. He felt the third time out often proved to be an artist's best work. Springsteen's *Born to Run* and Patti Smith's *Easter* (which Iovine produced) were two among many examples he liked to cite.

When Iovine sat down with Petty in the studio at Sound City during preproduction for the new album, the ever-blunt producer got right to the point. He hoped there might at least be something useable within Petty's ever-present notebook of tunes.

"Play me what you got."

So Petty did. Grabbing his Gibson Hummingbird acoustic guitar, he proceeded to strum and sing "Refugee," followed by "Here Comes My Girl." Both of which left his new producer breathless.

"Holy crap. You don't *need* anymore songs," Iovine gulped, sitting back in his chair. "Those two are hits."

As the actual sessions got underway, however, two things quickly became apparent: Shelly Yakus didn't like the sound of Heartbreaker drummer Stan Lynch's drum kit. And Jimmy Iovine just plain didn't like Lynch.

During the first official day of recording, as Petty and the Heartbreakers ran through some of their material to help establish the best microphone placement out in the studio, Yakus felt compelled to have a little heart-to-heart chat with Lynch.

"Stan, can we talk for a minute?"

"Sure, Shelly, what's up?"

Yakus cleared his throat, and then continued.

"Well, uh, you know, I don't want this to sound insulting or anything, but your drums sound pink."

"*Pink*? What the heck does that mean?"

"It means they sound like a toy, like a little kid's drum set. We need to get you a better kit, something with more power. This record is gonna require that. C'mon, let me take you drum shopping."

Yakus and Lynch then spent the rest of the day down at the local percussion store painstakingly testing and then selecting just the right combination of snares, tom-toms, kicks, and cymbals. To Yakus, getting the right drum sound in the studio was the single-most critical element in successfully building a song from the ground up. He felt that without the correct percussive foundation, a recording had every chance of ending up lifeless, no matter how great the composition or performance.

But for Lynch, the matter of his "pink" drum kit would prove to be far less problematic than his relationship with Jimmy Iovine.

A later addition to the band as well as a few years younger than the rest, Stan Lynch oozed both power and finesse when playing. By most standards he was an excellent drummer—certainly no one could question his passion. But he also naturally tended to play on the back of the beat, which was not quite the same place rhythmically as Petty's singing. This, combined with the fact that Lynch had an over-the-top personality, forever rubbed the equally extroverted Iovine the wrong way.

One afternoon, during the recording of "Even the Losers," Iovine stopped the session cold from inside the recording booth. He had heard enough: the drumming—and the drummer—had finally gotten to him.

"What pattern do you want?" Petty asked, trying to be diplomatic as he and the producer stepped out into the studio.

"I just thought he should play straight," Iovine replied, clearly exasperated.

Overhearing the exchange, a less-than-pleased Lynch decided to toss in his thoughts from behind the drum kit.

"Dude, there's a glass window back there," a smirking Lynch said to Iovine, pointing toward the control booth. "You're supposed to be on *that* side of the wall."

With the diminutive producer knowing better than to take on the towering Lynch in any sort of physical confrontation, no matter how much he would like to, Iovine chose instead to end the encounter with a piece of barbed humor.

"That's it," he barked in mock dictatorial style to Lynch, Petty, and the rest of the Heartbreakers. "You're gonna sound like the Motels on this record!"

After the guffaws subsided, they all went back to work. But the damage had been done. Shortly thereafter Lynch was asked to leave the band midrecord. Ultimately, however, when no suitable replacement could be found after several weeks of auditions, Lynch returned, but he remained under strict orders to keep his mouth shut around Iovine.

Which isn't to say that Iovine was always easy to work with either. The producer's big personality and domineering ways could also take their toll, sometimes even on Petty. One day Keith Olsen, who was busy down the hall in Studio B, happened to poke his head in Studio A's control booth just as Mike Campbell suggested to Petty that "maybe they should get Jimmy's opinion." Petty had but a two-word response for his lead guitarist: "Fuck Jimmy." After which the three of them, along with Shelly Yakus, broke into gales of knowing laughter.

AS RECORD LABELS OFTEN DO, THE GIANT MCA BOUGHT TINY Shelter in 1979—on its face just another garden-variety Hollywood deal between a whale and a comparative minnow competitor. The history of the music business is replete with a long list of such mergers and acquisitions. Bigger players have made it their practice to swallow up the smaller ones for decades, ever since the Radio Corporation of America (RCA) took a flyer in 1929 and purchased the Victor Talking Machine Company, the world's largest manufacturer of phonographs and phonograph records. But in the case of the MCA/Shelter accord, the two labels made a grievous error in judgment. No one at either place bothered to say so much as "boo" to Tom Petty about the impending transaction—something both companies would soon come to regret.

Whether through incompetence or hubris, when MCA took over Shelter they failed to honor a clause in Petty's Shelter contract that required his approval before he and his band could be "sold" to a new label (known as an "artist's guarantee clause"). Petty's song publishing rights—which Shelter had obtained from Petty several years earlier without Petty even understanding what he was giving up—also went along as part of the MCA deal.

Prepared to accept it as perhaps an honest mistake, Petty and his attorney then scheduled a meeting with the brass at MCA. But when they sat down to talk over the illegalities involved, much less the ethical violations, they were stunned at the response they received from MCA's head record man.

"Too bad," the label head said with a shrug. "You're in no position to fight a big corporation. You're staying with us."

A combative sort by nature, particularly when he felt wronged, Petty came out swinging. His two managers, Tony Dimitriades and Elliot Roberts, along with his legal team devised a plan for Petty to file for Chapter 11 bankruptcy protection, thereby nullifying his contract with MCA. Of course, given that no popular musician had ever done such a thing, Petty quickly drew the attention and ire of virtually every label in town. They worried that if Petty could get away with this tactic, then what was to prevent a deluge of other unhappy musicians from doing the same thing? In essence Petty's precedent-setting maneuver put him more than merely in a battle with one record company; it put him in a war with them all.

MCA, of course, did not take kindly to Petty's gambit—anything but. They immediately sued him and also filed for an injunction to prevent Petty and his band from signing—or playing—anywhere else. And they made sure to freeze all of Petty's royalties too, thereby cutting off his cash flow. Fortunately for Petty and the Heartbreakers, however, Elliot Roberts then stepped in and personally bankrolled the hefty cost of recording *Damn the Torpedoes* at Sound City, a price tag north of fifty grand in 1979 dollars. Roberts, along with the Heartbreakers' chief roadie, Alan "Bugs" Weidel, also took the extraordinary measure of spiriting the master tapes home in their cars after each evening's session, lest MCA try to sneak in and get their mitts on them. Petty made it clear that he didn't want to know where the tapes were being kept either in case he was deposed at some point. "Don't tell me *anything*," Petty ordered Roberts and Weidel.

Yet despite the intense outside pressure of the looming lawsuit, the recording of *Torpedoes* inside Sound City (and occasionally at Cherokee in West Hollywood) hurtled along almost as if Petty and his Heartbreakers hadn't a care in the world. The songs were coming together practically by divine guidance, like it was all meant to be. In one instance, when they were all working on "Here Comes My Girl," the idea suddenly popped into Petty's head to just talk his way through the verses and then sing the chorus, something he had never tried. To Yakus it sounded like something right out of the Shangri-Las' Top Forty playbook from back in his New York City days. And it worked perfectly. Petty's impromptu narration helped the message of the song come across all the more powerfully.

On another occasion, with Mike Campbell wracking his brain to come up with a guitar solo on "Even the Losers," Petty said to him, "Well, what would Chuck Berry do?" Campbell knew just what the singer meant. Both Petty and Campbell were longtime, ardent admirers of Berry, known for his trademark style of picking two strings at a time. Within a matter of minutes Campbell had a blistering solo in the can.

Sometimes the ideas even came from interested bystanders. While on a break from recording an early take of "Refugee" one day Petty happened to run into the noted session drummer Jim Keltner in the hall just outside Studio A's door. In Keltner's hand was a Latin percussion shaker.

"This is what that track needs," Keltner said, rhythmically shaking the small, buckshot-filled metal canister. "Sometimes it's the little things."

With no one noticing, the drummer apparently had been listening in the back of the control booth during the session. And with an undeniable groove happening right before his ears, Petty was sold on the spot.

"Let's do it," he said.

After Keltner finished overdubbing his shaker part in one take, Petty, Iovine, and Yakus looked at each other dumbfounded as they listened to the playback. Keltner couldn't have been more right: one simple percussion effect, placed correctly in the mix, had utterly transformed the feel of "Refugee," giving it the hit-quality mojo it needed.

IN MANY WAYS TOM PETTY WAS THE EMBODIMENT OF THE AMERican dream: a hardworking, independent-minded, principled individual seeking his rightful place in the world. A rebel, even—someone known for taking exactly zero shit. The very image, of course, that record labels love to cultivate to make more money. Rule number one in the music business has always been that bad boys (and girls) sell more records.

Lou Reed, Jim Morrison, and Led Zeppelin are but three among countless examples. The public remains utterly fascinated with each of them decades after their last hits. Great artists all, but these acts had more than just chops; they were also unique and copped a 'tude. More so, they were outsiders who did things their way.

It was all about rebellion in every conceivable manifestation. A monotone-sounding talk-singer by trade, Reed made a career out of exhibiting a well-practiced disdain toward any kind of authority. Morrison allegedly exposed his genitalia on stage in Miami and subsequently drank and drugged himself to death. Zeppelin's much-publicized debauchery while on tour in the seventies (including the infamous "mud shark" incident with a groupie in Seattle, which by now has taken on many of the hallmarks of an urban legend) forever cemented that band's reputation as the very definition of sex, drugs, and rock and roll.

There have always been more skilled musicians on the scene, of course. Plenty of hired-hand session pros can play laps around the stars they work for in terms of sheer ability. It's been that way at least since back in the sixties, when the Wrecking Crew first played in the studio in place of bands such as the Beach Boys.

But that's not what matters most. Not if the goal is to make it to the top of the heap. To really break through, to become a true rock god or goddess, it requires much more. Swagger, mystery, and charisma are the qualities that sell out stadiums and earn platinum album awards, not mere dexterity on a fret board or the ability to carry a tune. And if the act is difficult, then so much the better. It's almost perversely axiomatic among popular rock-and-roll musicians, as long as the underlying talent exists: the bigger the asshole, the better the sales. To the labels, three chords and a sneer have always been worth a thousand jazz standards.

Which is where the irony came in when it came to MCA. They *wanted* Petty to be insolent. They *wanted* Petty to be uncompromising. They *wanted* Petty to be a rebel. Until, of course, it turned on them.

At one point during a set of pretrial depositions being taken from Petty and others, MCA's high-powered lead counsel got in the singer's face in an attempt to intimidate him into capitulating.

"Listen, kid, you're going to forget all this, and you're going to go make your records and shut up," the lawyer said, leaning in.

"I'll sell fucking peanuts before I give in to you," Petty fired back. And he meant it.

On the eve of the trial, however, MCA finally blinked. They floated an eleventh-hour offer that included allowing Petty to be on his own record label within MCA (to be called "Backstreet") as well as letting him retain full creative control over all musical decisions. As the parent company, MCA would merely oversee the manufacturing, distribution, and marketing. The singer-songwriter could have all of his publishing rights back too. Knowing vindication when he saw it, Petty accepted.

In a rare instance of clear-headedness within the music business, MCA had created a win-win for everyone. Tom Petty was back in charge of his artistic destiny, and MCA was rewarded with arguably the best album of Petty's career. From the moment of its release, *Damn the Torpedoes* was a runaway hit. Containing no fewer than four smash singles ("Here Comes My Girl," "Refugee," "Even the Losers," and "Don't Do Me Like That"), the album shot to number two on the Billboard charts, behind only Pink Floyd's *The Wall*. It also went platinum several times over, making the suits at MCA very happy.

Damn the Torpedoes additionally had the effect of making radio stations realize that rock and roll had some teeth left in it, that old-school rockers could still kick disco, punk, and new wave's collective asses when they had a mind to. Maybe even if they hadn't had a hit record in years. Which was exactly what a new Keith Olsen client by the name of Carlos Santana planned to do next.

thirteen

WINNING

Carlos may be a little difficult from time to time.

—Bill Graham

D URING THE LATE WINTER OF 1978, AS MICK JONES, THE LEAD guitarist and founder of the band Foreigner, sat in front of the mixing console inside Studio A at Atlantic Records' Columbus Circle recording facilities in New York City, he slowly began bending a pencil in his right fist. And the more Jones heard from one of the people in the room with him, the harder he squeezed.

Having recorded and released their first LP, *Foreigner*, the year before, Jones and his five fellow group members, including Foreigner's world-class, leather-lunged lead singer and front man, Lou Gramm, were attempting one of the hardest tasks in all of rock and roll: to follow up a multiplatinum debut with something hopefully even better.

Containing anthem-like FM favorites such as "Feels Like the First Time," "Cold as Ice," and "Long, Long Way from Home," Foreigner's first album had become one of the industry's biggest sellers in 1977, quickly going gold and then platinum within weeks of its release. And despite the chorus of critics who gleefully condemned the band and their highly produced, power-chord-driven sound as being yet another manifestation of the subgenre of rock and roll derisively referred to as "corporate rock" (alongside fellow practitioners Queen, Styx, Boston, and Journey), Foreigner nonetheless had become one of the most popular acts in the country within mere months of hitting the charts.

But Mick Jones wanted to take the next step. Having been a mainstay in his previous band, Spooky Tooth (with Gary Wright, later of "Dream Weaver" fame), as well as playing guitar on many high-profile sessions in his native England for musicians such as George Harrison and Peter Frampton, Jones had been around the industry long enough to know that he and his band were going to have to raise their game in order to prevent a sophomore slump. They needed to come up with an even tighter, tougher, more aggressive approach to stay competitive within a hard-rock music scene that featured such heavy hitters as Kansas ("Carry on Wayward Son"), Aerosmith ("Walk This Way"), and Blue Öyster Cult ("Don't Fear the Reaper"). That meant writing even better songs. It also meant hiring a new producer. That was part of Jones's secret formula. No matter that Foreigner had experienced remarkable success with John Sinclair and Gary Lyons in charge of the production on *Foreigner*, it was still time to move on. "One album isn't enough for a producer to inflict his style upon us," Jones liked to say.

During the same period, with Keith Olsen's reputation growing by the record following his work on *Fleetwood Mac* and *Terrapin Station*, it was but a matter of a few phone calls back and forth between Olsen's highly connected manager, Bob Buziak, and Foreigner's manager, Bud Prager, before Olsen found himself installed as Mick Jones's new man behind the glass. On Olsen's part, working with Foreigner would provide the chance for a musical challenge of a different sort:

instead of working to elevate the success of a well-known niche band who had been around for years without earning even one gold album as he had done with both Fleetwood Mac and the Grateful Dead, this time Olsen would get the opportunity to dive in midstream and help make a big-time hit-maker even bigger.

Forgoing his preferred recording environment at Sound City, Olsen agreed to Jones's request that the basic tracks for the new album, *Double Vision*, be cut in New York City at the in-house studio owned by Atlantic Records, the band's label. After flying to the Big Apple and taking a short-term lease on a Central Park South apartment, Olsen got right to work with the band. And he immediately liked the songs Jones and Gramm began laying down, two in particular.

Giving evidence that musical inspiration can come from the unlikeliest of sources, the album's title track, "Double Vision," developed while Jones and Gramm attended a New York Rangers hockey game. After an injured player left the ice at one point following a fight, the announcer described him as suffering from "double vision" and therefore was unable to return. With the British Jones being unfamiliar with that particular turn of phrase, it stuck in his mind, leading him, along with Gramm, to soon cowrite a driving rocker about the inability to be monogamous (though many listeners erroneously assumed "Double Vision" to be about drug use). And though the song would ultimately hit number two on the Billboard Hot 100 in the fall of 1978—yet another smash for the band—it was the lead single "Hot Blooded" off the new album that had Keith Olsen intrigued and Mick Jones perturbed.

Developed in the studio when Mick Jones and Foreigner's drummer, Dennis Elliot, locked in on a groove together that had everyone instantly tapping their feet, it was also the suggestive set of lyrics conjured by Gramm and Jones that made the song a particular standout. Spewing out innuendos like, "Come on baby, do you do more than dance?" and "Now it's up to you, we can make a secret rendezvous," there was no mistaking the lead singer Gramm's libidinous intentions. The baseness, the coarseness, the utter primitiveness of the words gave rise to the song's universal appeal, certainly among teenagers and young adults, especially of the male persuasion. It represented the age-old rock-and-roll go-to: when in doubt, sing about sex. Which thrilled Keith Olsen to no end. To him "Hot Blooded" was a relatable, brilliantly rendered little story song, just as Carole King had instructed him back in 1974. That's what people wanted to hear—that's where hits came from.

Yet however catchy "Hot Blooded" may have been, the simplicity of its sentiments did not exactly excite everyone in the studio during the playback session when Mick Jones held his death grip on the Dixon Ticonderoga no. 2 pencil. The person standing next to Olsen in the control room, John Kalodner, had a less than positive opinion of the song. Kalodner, who had both found and helped bring Foreigner to Atlantic Records, was one of the label's A&R men and a rising star. This band was his baby. Though still early in what would become a lengthy and legendary career through his work in revitalizing acts such as Aerosmith, Sammy Hagar, and Cher, the longhaired, bearded, almost Jesus-looking Kalodner was born with an uncanny instinct for what the public wanted to hear. And he was sure the words to "Hot Blooded" were not it.

"Keith, where did you get those lyrics? Those really suck."

Just as the caustic comment came flying out of John Kalodner's mouth, the pencil in Mick Jones's hand finally snapped from the tension. His anger evident, Jones began to rise from his chair with the intention, Olsen was sure, of knocking Kalodner's block off. But before Jones could do something he might regret, Olsen put a hand on the guitarist's shoulder and gently pushed him back down. It was time for the producer to do some flexing.

"John, you and me, out in the hall," Olsen said to Kalodner, pointing.

After a brief, heated exchange in which an angry Olsen made sure Kalodner understood that slamming an artist's songwriting in front of that very artist would under no circumstances be tolerated, a smarting Kalodner trudged off, leaving Olsen alone for the rest of the project. However, with Foreigner under a severe time constraint due to a string of intermittent tour dates, including an appearance before three hundred thousand fans at the prestigious California Jam II in March of 1978 at the Ontario Motor Speedway, it took every ounce of Olsen's patience to get the album in the can. Though once it was there and after returning to his home base at Sound City to do all the mixing alongside Mick Jones, Olsen knew it was a hit. At least he felt certain "Hot Blooded" would be a big deal. And it was.

Rocketing to number three on the Hot 100, "Hot Blooded" quickly and forever became Foreigner's signature song, propelling the *Double Vision* LP to platinum status, then double, then triple—eventually reaching 7 million units sold, surpassing Foreigner's first album by a cool mil. Keith Olsen had done his job. He had helped take the band to the next level, just like Jones wanted. Even John Kalodner finally came around following many months of disliking Olsen for giving him a studio hallway comeuppance. After "Hot Blooded" cracked the Top Five, Kalodner called Olsen at Sound City, clearly looking to make amends.

"Keith," he began in his usual slow and measured way, "you're a genius." Kalodner's nasally voice and Philly-born-and-bred accent were famous in the biz.

"John, it was a momentary lapse of judgment, that's all," an equally conciliatory Olsen responded, referring to Kalodner's in-studio comments in front of Mick Jones. "*You're* the genius and you know it."

"I know," Kalodner replied.

But Keith Olsen had little time to reflect on either Foreigner's latest success or his renewed friendship and business relationship with John Kalodner (who on the *Double Vision* back-cover credits Mick Jones and Lou Gramm had cleverly listed as "John Kalodner: John Kalodner"). Several more major recording artists would soon be stepping forward to grab most of Olsen's increasingly precious studio time—the first, a lightning-fast guitarist originally from the central coast of Mexico.

BY THE SUMMER OF 1979 RECORD BUYERS ACROSS AMERICA WERE fed up. At least those who loved straight-ahead rock and roll. With disco music and its relentlessly pulsating four-on-the-floor percussive style saturating the airwaves with the seemingly endless number of songs spun off from the multimillion-selling *Saturday Night Fever* soundtrack album, something had to give. The general public could only take so much of the Bee Gees and their friends. And the catalyst for that something would prove to be the antithesis of all things disco, something as traditional as it was tranquil: America's favorite pastime, baseball.

When an outspoken, rock-and-roll-loving local Chicago disc jockey by the name of Steve Dahl decided that enough was enough, the shock jock took it upon himself to arrange a "Disco Demolition Night" at Comiskey Park, home of the Chicago White Sox. Hyping it on his radio show for days beforehand, Dahl encouraged his many listeners to bring the vinyl disco albums of their choice to the upcoming doubleheader against the Detroit Tigers, where all the offending records would be dynamited into glorious oblivion.

Worrying that not many people would appear for the promotion, both Dahl and White Sox officials received the surprise of their lives when, instead, over fifty thousand fans showed up for the game on July 12, approximately thirty-five thousand more than the White Sox usually drew. Further, with the stadium ultimately selling out, almost another twenty thousand people who couldn't get in milled about outside.

As the first game progressed, a throng of unruly, beer-swilling fans began flinging their albums onto the field like so many sharp-edged would-be Frisbees, causing players on both teams to scurry out of the way. Some, such as Tigers outfielder Ron LeFlore, refused to take their batting helmets off. Between games, after the highly anticipated ten-second countdown and a mammoth explosion near second base of several giant crates filled with albums, the crowd simply went berserk, leaping over seats, railings, and fences to flood the field in a mindless frenzy of destruction. They tore up the turf, stole the bases, and fought with anyone who got in their way. With the melee spiraling out of control as a giant bonfire burned unchecked where the records had once been, the police were called in, a flurry of arrests were made, and game two was canceled before it ever began.

But the image of tens of thousands of people rioting over disco records was a lasting one. The national wire services were quick to pick up on the story, and video footage made the evening newscasts in city after city. Some argued that the melee was less about true opposition to the music and more about being racist and/or homophobic, given the diversity found among disco's performers and fans. But whatever the motivation behind each of the individuals and their participation, one thing was certain: a seemingly minor publicity stunt had unleashed a startling amount of pent-up vitriol across the country, enough to knock King Disco right off his platform shoes.

Far from realizing that its favorite source of easy revenue might actually dry up anytime soon (disco albums were often comparatively cheap and fast to make), the major record labels were ill prepared for the sudden downturn in airplay and corresponding sales across the country. Underscoring the precipitous decline, the single "Good Times" by Chic, one of the best-known disco songs of all time, first hit the Top Ten during the week of the demolition, one of an astonishing six to make it. A month later only three disco songs were in the national Top Ten. And thirty days after that it was down to zero.

At the same time the rallying cry of "Disco Sucks" began sweeping the nation, creating a fierce blowback inside a great number of record stores that were already packed to the rafters with way too many albums by the soon-to-be-forgotten, booty-shaking likes of Tavares, Heatwave, and Foxy. After retailers ultimately shipped back millions of unopened disco LPs to the record companies for credit (most labels offered a 100 percent return policy), the music industry, once considered recession-proof, in 1979 experienced its first year-over-year downturn since World War II, with revenue sliding a whopping 11 percent.

With sky-high oil prices also a contributing factor along with disco's untimely decline (petroleum was/is the central component in manufacturing vinyl), CBS Records, the parent company of the Columbia, Epic, and Portrait labels, in but one example of the fallout, fired 120 employees in August of 1979 on the heels of cutting 52 others just weeks before, for a total of 6 percent of its workforce. By November Warner Bros. Records, the last of the majors to make cuts, lopped off 55 of its employees (8 percent of its workforce) after waiting to gauge the market viability of Fleetwood Mac's *Tusk*, upon which they had based their fall quarter sales projections.

Furthering the dearth of desirable product in stores, disco's popularity during 1977 and 1978 had also caused the major labels to hold back on both developing new rock artists and also aggressively promoting many of the ones they already had on their rosters. When disco abruptly fell out of favor in mid- to late 1979, it left album-rock fans feeling victorious. But it wasn't only disco that put a dent in the dominance of album rock; it was also the growing desire among a good share of young listeners to experience other styles of music like punk and new wave. Bands like the Sex Pistols, the Clash, the Ramones, Blondie, and the Talking Heads were starting to set the agenda.

Though the Los Angeles–based album-rock artists who had flourished during most of the seventies tried their best to adapt to changing tastes, all too often their efforts came up short. Fleetwood Mac, after its colossal success with *Rumours* in 1977, abruptly shifted direction in 1979 with *Tusk*, an edgy, spare, double album of bold musical choices that alienated many of their fans. Rather than doing a *Rumours II*, as Warner Bros. had hoped, the Lindsey-Buckingham–driven, yearlong *Tusk* sessions at the Village Recorder in L.A.'s Westwood neighborhood (whose owner spent a then-record $1 million on building an entirely new studio within the studio just for the band) were all about visiting new horizons. But with sales coming in at a fraction of what *Rumours* had rung up, many considered *Tusk*, fairly or not, to be a major disappointment, despite selling a couple million units. "You went too far," a disappointed Mick Fleetwood said to Buckingham afterward.

Though perhaps the most high-profile example, Fleetwood Mac was far from the only well-known rock-and-roll outfit working in the Los Angeles studios who tried to find a way to remain relevant. The band Chicago, after the shocking death of their guitarist, Terry Kath, in late 1977, regrouped several months later in an effort to find its artistic footing in the face of the rapidly changing music environment. Putting out the albums *Hot Streets* in 1978, *13* in 1979, and *XIV* in 1980, Chicago desperately tried to reinvent themselves to fit the times. With well-intentioned stabs at disco and power pop mixed in with their traditional horn-driven blues-rock sound, the hodgepodge of styles found on *13* and *XIV* especially were less than satisfying to their many fans, with *13* barely going gold and the Tom Dowd–produced *XIV* not even coming close.

Not long after, following a virtually unparalleled twelve-year hit-making run together, Columbia Records finally dropped Chicago, signaling the end of an era. But it wasn't just Chicago who was no longer a major player; as the eighties arrived, the Eagles disbanded, as did Steely Dan, and the Doobie Brothers, who cut the bulk of their albums at Warner Bros. in Burbank and experienced an unexpected last hurrah with their Michael McDonald–infused *Minute by Minute* and *One Step Closer* albums, were about to do the same. Linda Ronstadt would soon abandon rock for good and turn her attention to nostalgic, heavily orchestrated ballads from the forties and fifties. The group Boston, after putting out their second album, *Don't Look Back*, in 1978 to lukewarm response, dissolved in 1980 amidst a flurry of lawsuits between its band members (Tom Scholz would reemerge with Brad Delp and an otherwise new Boston lineup to release *Third Stage* in 1986). As for the California Sound singer-songwriters such as Carole King, James Taylor, Joni Mitchell, Carly Simon, Warren Zevon, and others who had achieved so much success in the early to mid-seventies—well, they were running out of hits too.

It was the musical changing of the guard. Along with the influences of punk and new wave, a flurry of overwrought, overproduced power ballads were becoming rock and roll's newest darling. Those acts who wanted to stay in the game were going to have to reinvent themselves with all that in mind. Some would make it; many would not.

IN EARLY 1967, AS CARLOS SANTANA PEERED THROUGH THE grimy kitchen window of the Tic Tock drive-in located in San Francisco's Mission District, he instantly felt a wave of certainty wash over him: he knew on the spot that he was going to become a music star.

Pulling up outside the restaurant in their limousine to grab some hamburgers were the five members of the Grateful Dead, a local band who had recently released their first album on Warner Bros. Records. Santana, having been around the Dead on the local music scene since they were known as the Warlocks, was sure that if *they* could do it, he could do it. He had, after all, been playing guitar in clubs, both strip and otherwise, since he was twelve years old and living in Tijuana, Mexico, with his family. After they moved to the Bay Area during his early teen years, Santana, who was by then a virtuoso and had dropped out of school for good, picked up small-time gigs wherever he could while also working odd jobs.

After sitting in one night with the Paul Butterfield Blues Band at the Fillmore Auditorium, Santana received his first critical acclaim. He thereafter started gaining a local following, enough to attract the high-powered impresario (and owner of the Fillmore) Bill Graham as his manager. With the savvy, tough-as-nails Graham steering his career, Santana assembled a band, developed a unique Latin-rock sound, signed a record deal with Columbia, scored a Top Ten album (*Santana*), a Top Ten single ("Evil Ways"), and appeared onstage at Woodstock, all by the time he was barely twenty-two.

Following this breakout success in 1969, Santana kept up the pace. He and his band, also called Santana, racked up several more huge hits in the early seventies, including "Black Magic Woman," "Oye Como Va," and "No One to Depend On," along with an LP, *Abraxas*, that would go down as one of the finest in rock history. But as his commercial and material success grew, so did Santana's egotistical ways. Stunning many in the music business, he ended up splitting with his original band in 1971 after only three albums. More than anything he longed for a sense of centeredness and spirituality.

During the sixties, seventies, and even into the early eighties the quest for enlightenment and inner peace was an all-consuming pursuit for many famous musicians. George Harrison, after a trip to India in 1968 with his fellow Beatles (and others such as Mike Love of the Beach Boys) to sit at the feet of the Maharishi Mahesh Yogi, subsequently became an ardent practitioner of Yogi's Transcendental Meditation. Harrison's bandmate, John Lennon, later tried utilizing a variety of current self-help philosophies, including Primal Scream therapy, while his wife, Yoko Ono, favored EST (Erhard Seminars Training). For every rock-and-roller so inclined, there seemed to be a correspondingly personalized path to the hoped-for attainment of bliss, which also often included the time-honored options of booze and drugs. For Carlos Santana, who, after his breakout commercial success, had partied for a while just like the rest of his musical peers, the way toward fulfillment would eventually materialize in the form of a robe-wearing Bangladeshi expat mystic by the name of Sri Chinmoy.

WHEN KEITH OLSEN ANSWERED HIS PHONE TO FIND BILL GRAHAM on the other end of the line, he couldn't have been happier. By the fall of 1979 the San Francisco–based Graham was one of the most powerful men in the music business, with concert promotion and artist management companies that worked with only the biggest names. With Olsen's own work for Fleetwood Mac, the Grateful Dead, and, most recently, Foreigner putting him on the short list of the most sought-after producers around, Graham wanted to see whether Olsen had any interest in taking on Carlos Santana.

After a red-hot start to the seventies, then a long dry stretch, followed by a brief resurgence in late 1977 with the album *Moonflower*, the superstar Santana's record sales had, for the most part, slowed to the point where he was lucky to go gold with each new release. Perhaps, Graham hoped, Olsen could jumpstart his famous client's career, just as he had done for others.

"Now, Carlos may be a little difficult from time to time," Graham said, chuckling. "But you know that, right?"

A battle-tested Olsen shrugged it off.

"Yeah, I've worked with difficult artists before."

Olsen wanted the gig. Even with slowing album sales, Santana was still a hell of a big name. Plus, Olsen figured he had already seen pretty much all there was to see inside a recording studio. But that came before he knew that he would be answering to not one but *two* people on the new Santana project: Carlos Santana as well as his personal guru, Sri Chinmoy.

Instead of recording the basic tracks at Sound City, Santana wanted to work in his new favorite studio, a place in downtown San Francisco called the Automatt. Formerly owned by CBS Records and before that by Bill Putnam's Coast Recorders, the facility had become—along with the nearby Wally Heider Studios, Pacific Recording in San Mateo, Fantasy Studios in Berkeley, and the Record Plant in Sausalito—one of the main studios in the Bay Area. Though it wasn't Olsen's first choice—he much preferred his own equipment back at Sound City—the rock band Journey had started working at the Automatt. So had the famed jazz musicians Herbie Hancock and Chick Corea, who cut several albums there. There were worse places Olsen could have ended up. Mostly he just needed to figure out how and when he could get some songs down on tape.

With Carlos Santana usually busy on Wednesdays enjoying his life and then spending the next day meditating and also atoning with Sri Chinmoy via long distance, there were automatically two days of the week unavailable for recording. That left Mondays, Tuesdays, and

Fridays, plus here and there on the weekends to put together what would become the *Marathon* album.

However, even then, as each song was recorded, sometimes just parts of songs, Santana—who had officially changed his full name to Carlos Devadip Santana in honor of his spiritual beliefs—insisted that the musical passages and/or lyrics be played over the phone to Sri Chinmoy back in New York City so the guru could determine whether they were of sufficient "oneness." If they were, then Chinmoy would give his blessing for Santana, Olsen, Dave DeVore (Olsen's lead engineer), and all the gathered musicians in Santana's band to continue. If not, the song would have to be reworked. With Olsen knowing little about Eastern religious philosophies and exactly nothing about Sri Chinmoy, he had to cross his fingers and hope for the best each time the oneness call was placed.

But despite the oddness of the production process, Olsen genuinely liked Carlos Santana as a person and certainly respected his incredible guitar-playing skills. More so, Olsen wanted to produce a smash album for him. After all, that was the reason Bill Graham hired him in the first place. To do so, Olsen knew he would need to identify at least one standout track among the bunch they had been recording that could be released to FM album-rock radio. That's what still drove album sales in 1979: airplay. And more than anything, picking the right song was arguably Olsen's chief skill—he usually knew a hit when he heard one.

Realizing there were two single possibilities that had been put down on tape during the sessions—one, an up-tempo rocker called "Winning" penned by Russ Ballard and the other a midtempo power ballad called "You Know That I Love You"—Olsen very much wanted to go with the former. It would be a perfect lead track on the new album, and radio would probably jump all over it.

Bill Graham also loved it.

"Oh, my God, that's a hit," he said, practically dancing around the room after Olsen played a demo for him. "Finally, we're going to have another hit with Santana."

But there was no need to even call Sri Chinmoy for his opinion this time around. When Carlos Santana heard the "Winning" playback with his band's lead singer, Alex Ligertwood, passionately belting out the overdubbed lines, "I had a dream / But it turned to dust / What I thought was love / That must have been lust," Santana turned as white as the linen pants and gauze shirt he was wearing.

"Nooo!" he yelped. "That song can't be on my record!"

As Olsen would quickly learn, Sri Chinmoy had a thing about lust. Temptation, lust's nasty little partner in crime, led to impurity, which then led to preventing a person from becoming a fully God-realized follower. Oneness was apparently okay. But any sort of "twoness" was definitely out.

All of which left Olsen incredulous. "Winning" was easily the best song on the album as well as the most commercial. And now it had to be tossed, all over one word. When Olsen broke the news to Graham, after a brief four-letter word outburst, the tears simply rolled down Graham's cheeks as he imagined the money pouring out of his pockets. CBS Records was already excited enough by an advance copy of the track to begin negotiating a new lucrative record deal with Graham on behalf of Santana. Now *Marathon* would have to be released without "Winning." Graham's leverage was gone. A dejected Olsen returned to Sound City with the master tapes, dutifully did all the mixing there, then turned in the final product to the label, ready to move on.

But temptation and impurity would win out.

As the vicissitudes of mysticism would have it, not long after the release of *Marathon* in the fall of 1979, Santana abruptly parted company with Sri Chinmoy after years of tutelage, thereby opening the door for the song about lust to be released after all. CBS quickly tacked "Winning" onto Santana's next LP, *Zebop!*, which came out a mere seven months after *Marathon* in April of 1980. Sure enough, "Winning" won, zooming to number two on the Mainstream Rock Charts and making it to number seventeen on the traditional Billboard Hot 100, Santana's best showing in almost a decade. Carlos had his comeback hit, Graham secured a new contract for his client, and Keith Olsen had come through once again. Barely.

fourteen

VIDEO KILLED THE RADIO STAR

You want to record "Jessie's Girl"?

—RICK SPRINGFIELD

ONE DAY IN THE SPRING OF 1980 KEVIN BEAMISH, AN UP-AND-coming sound engineer and record producer, received a phone call from Kevin Cronin, the lead singer of REO Speedwagon. Beamish and REO were in the early stages of gathering tracks for possible inclusion on a new album. It would also be REO's tenth for Epic Records without ever having seen one of their single releases make the top half of the Billboard singles charts.

"Can you come over?" Cronin asked, sounding amped up.

"Yeah, man, what's up?" Beamish replied, wondering if he should be worried.

"Just come over. I've got something to show you."

Virtual rock gods throughout the Midwest during the seventies (they were originally from Illinois), the now Los Angeles–based REO

Speedwagon was still barely known on either coast outside of a smattering of hardcore fans. Able to sell out basketball arenas with ease in cities such as St. Louis and Des Moines, they were lucky to draw a thousand or two to their shows in places like Boston and Seattle.

Sales-wise, the best REO had ever done at the cash register had come with their 1978 album, *You Can Tune a Piano, But You Can't Tuna Fish*, recorded at Sound City and executive produced by John Boylan (who was by then the West Coast head of A&R at Epic after his mammoth success with the band Boston). *You Can Tune a Piano* had been REO's first LP to crack the Top Forty, peaking at number twenty-nine (and eventually going double platinum) while spinning off a couple of heavy-rotation FM AOR favorites too, with the rockers "Time for Me to Fly" and "Roll with the Changes." With the success the band seemed poised for a breakthrough.

But REO Speedwagon's next album, the highly anticipated *Nine Lives*, took an inexplicable step backward, barely going gold. Radio mostly reacted with a big fat yawn. And by then, in 1979, Epic had finally used up the last of its patience too. After eight years of support, the execs wanted hit singles for a change. REO had already been on the label longer than anyone except for the legendary British guitarist Jeff Beck. And he had outsold and outcharted them on his last two albums without even having any vocals.

It was time for REO Speedwagon—named after a brand of flatbed truck popular during the first half of the twentieth century—to earn their keep or find a new recording home. Cronin and the other four were put on notice: the new album would be their last chance. The reality of it made everyone in the band nervous, especially Kevin Cronin. He was the front man and the one most likely to come up with some radio-friendly hits. Which is why he had wanted to see Kevin Beamish, who was coproducing, right away.

After Beamish arrived at Cronin's suburban Los Angeles–area home in the upscale San Fernando Valley neighborhood of Encino, he found Cronin at the piano.

"Remember when you talked to me about all the songs you said we didn't have time to write because we're on the road all the time?" Cronin asked as he began to play.

"Sure, yeah," Beamish replied, remembering it well. That's why he had lobbied Epic to do the recently released "best of" compilation (*A Decade of Rock and Roll 1970 to 1980*)—it bought the band time. REO needed some easy current income to forgo their normally heavy touring schedule and instead focus strictly on writing. If the new album was to achieve any kind of meaningful success, it was going to need an infusion of some seriously strong material.

"You should have seen by the look in my eyes, baby," the high-tenor Cronin began to croon as his hands danced over the keys. "There was somethin' missin'."

It was the rough version of a song Cronin had been working on called "Keep on Loving You." Beamish sat transfixed, especially when Cronin hit the chorus.

"And I'm gonna keep on loving you, 'cause it's the only thing I want to do."

When the performance ended, all an overwhelmed Beamish could utter was "Phew." He knew then and there in Kevin Cronin's living room that he had just heard a smash. What's more, he couldn't wait to tell the rest of the band about it, especially Gary Richrath, the group's founder and longtime leader. After phoning Richrath to share his enthusiasm, he got even more good news: Richrath had a song *he* thought might be a hit too, something called "Take It on the Run," which Richrath then proceeded to play and sing over the line.

With two potential gems and various other promising possibilities in hand, Beamish then booked several weeks of rehearsal time for REO at S.I.R. (Studio Instrument Rentals) in North Hollywood on Tuesdays, Wednesdays, and Thursdays, and they all set about fashioning an album's worth of cohesive material. But when it came to "Keep on Loving You," Richrath—a country-born-and-raised man's man and a kick-ass, Les Paul–playing guitar hero by trade—would have none of it.

"I'm not playing this pussy-mother-fucking song anymore!" a red-hot Richrath bellowed as he unhooked his guitar and tossed it across the room one afternoon. "We're a boy's band, and it's a damned love song. I'm not playing it, and we're not putting it on this record."

Having played "Keep on Loving You" over and over to get the arrangement into workable form, Richrath could simply take no more. He had tried blasting his guitar through his Marshall amplifier stack as loud as he could to drown out Cronin's singing and playing, but the resolute Cronin refused to be minimized or intimidated—he knew he had a good song.

At the same time, however, an interesting phenomenon occurred during the in-studio showdown between the group's two principal songwriters: the combination of Cronin's vocal and piano work in conjunction with Richrath's raw, distorted guitar sounds provided, to Cronin's ears, an unexpectedly ideal counterbalance on "Keep on Loving You." Richrath's wrath managed to keep the tune grounded and relatable, providing a little bit of toughness to go with the sugar. Despite his hissy fit and all the petulant electric guitar pyrotechnics— or, more accurately, precisely *because* of them—Richrath had inadvertently helped create an arrangement that perfectly prevented the song from veering into the terminally vanilla land of Barry Manilow and Air Supply. That was something nobody in REO wanted, not even Cronin, the group's resident romantic with the folkie soul.

To mollify the burly, stubborn Richrath, however, Beamish subsequently pointed out to the guitarist that the weird, high-pitched sounds heard on a board tape from one of their recent weekend shows where REO had played an early version of "Keep on Loving You" were, in fact, a hoard of women screaming their lungs out at the end of the song. Not a bunch of birds, as Richrath had erroneously thought upon first listening. The reason to even bother playing Cronin's prized composition finally started to make sense to the self-appointed alpha male of the band: yes, REO was a boy's band. But boys brought their girls to the shows. And girls were crazy about "Keep on Loving You."

After feverishly cutting demos of the best of what they had during a two- to three-day period at Crystal Recording in Hollywood— coincidentally the first studio Beamish had worked in when getting in the business many years before, just like Fleetwood Mac's Richard Dashut had done before him—REO then reconvened at Kendun in North Hollywood shortly thereafter to record the real deal. But after Beamish sat down with Cronin to listen to the playback of the new album (Cronin had also been playing it for several days in his car), the two came to the same surprising conclusion: for the most par, the quick and dirty demos of the songs recorded at Crystal actually sounded *better* than the newly created masters that had cost a whole lot more money. The energy, enthusiasm, and quality of the originals could not be duplicated, let alone surpassed.

So Beamish, along with Cronin, Richrath, and REO's Alan Gratzer (drums)—the four coproducers—made the unusual decision to add overdubs to the nine demo songs where needed, cut a tenth song ("Out of Season"), mix it all down, master it, and then offer the finished stereo version of the album to Epic for approval. With the depth of songwriting and performances, they were sure it was their most commercially viable album yet.

But REO Speedwagon's record label had other ideas.

After Beamish shipped a copy of the master tape to Frank Rand, Epic's East Coast vice president of A&R—the guy who made the decisions for the New York–based company regarding which albums to release—Beamish waited. And waited.

When he finally called Rand more than a week later to see what was going on, Beamish was stunned at the executive's reply.

"I'm rejecting your record," Rand said flatly. "There aren't any hits on there."

After failing to talk Rand out of his decision, a shaken Beamish took the bad news back to Cronin and Richrath, who came unglued. They agreed that Rand didn't know what he was talking about: Had the guy even *listened* to the album? They decided it was either going to be put out just as it was or the label could go ahead and drop them. REO would then shop it elsewhere, potential lawsuits be damned.

Shortly thereafter Beamish called Rand one more time on behalf of Cronin, Richrath, and the rest of the group.

"You all do what you want," Beamish said to the Epic executive, "but I would suggest you go ahead and release it anyway. The band is standing by the record."

He then added one final tip.

"By the way, service Top Forty radio with 'Keep on Loving You.'"

"Oh no," Rand replied, recoiling like he had been shot through the heart with a poison dart. "That track is awful. It's way too sappy."

But after Beamish convinced him that the label had nothing to lose because they didn't believe in the album anyway, Rand did just that. He had his promotional team start working "Keep on Loving You" at stations around the country. Six weeks later Kevin Cronin's battered little love song leapt to number one on the Billboard Hot 100 and practically everywhere else in the universe. Furthermore, REO's new album, with a memorably lascivious cover designed by John Kosh and named *Hi Infidelity* as a nod to the marital struggles of some of the band members, also rocketed to number one, becoming nothing less than the single-biggest-selling album of 1981.

But aside from the huge personal success enjoyed by REO Speedwagon with the release of their tenth album, the music industry ramifications in the wake of *Hi Infidelity* ran much deeper and wider. The power ballad was here to stay. And rock music in general was getting lighter and poppier seemingly by the day. Those who wanted to survive in the changing marketplace were either going to have to rebrand themselves accordingly or face the prospect of reduced popularity.

No one, however, expected what was about to happen next.

AT 12:01 A.M. EASTERN DAYLIGHT TIME ON AUGUST 1, 1981, just after the images of a rocket blasting off and then an astronaut walking on the moon flickered across the TV screens in the small number of homes actually able to receive it, the following words were heard: "Ladies and gentleman, rock and roll."

And from that moment on, the music business would never be the same.

Spoken by John Lack, the chief operating officer of a new cable network called Music Television (MTV), the simple sentence served to launch a new broadcasting concept of providing twenty-four hours of nonstop pop and rock video programming. Starting slowly on just a handful of cable networks around the country, the New York City–based MTV wasn't even initially available to viewers on its home turf in Manhattan. Although a seemingly obvious concept in retrospect, airing music videos twenty-four hours a day across the nation had never been done.

Yet a plentiful number of one-off music videos had been around for years. Many were created as stand-alone promotional pieces and/or to be aired in conjunction with an appearance by a band or solo artist on a TV show either in the United States or overseas. One of the more famous examples occurred in 1974 when the Rolling Stones, rather than touring in support of their latest album, instead chose to appear in a video featuring them jamming on their instruments (while, oddly, wearing sailor suits) to their recent hit song, "It's Only Rock 'n' Roll (But I Like It)" as they hopped about inside a giant plastic tent as rising water and soap bubbles slowly submerged them.

Prior to its launch, MTV's creator and programming chief, Robert Pittman, made the brilliant move of hiring five engaging, telegenic VJs (for "video jockey") to become the resident talking heads. Within a year, as more cable systems around the country signed on, Nina Blackwood, Mark Goodman, Alan Hunter, J. J. Jackson, and Martha Quinn would become huge stars. But the most pressing concern for the first day on the air, at least, dealt with which videos the new channel would play. The world, such as it was, would be watching.

Electing to lead off with a relatively obscure (yet ultimately more prophetic than anyone knew) video of a song called "Video Killed the Radio Star" by the London-based Buggles, which only made it to number forty for one week on Billboard's Hot 100 in 1979, it was actually the *second* video MTV played that would provide an indication of where music was truly headed.

AFTER WRAPPING THINGS UP WITH CARLOS SANTANA, KEITH Olsen had begun looking for his next big-name project. He also had it in the back of his mind that he might want to own a studio of his own. Though he had briefly been a partner in Sound City in the early days, Olsen held no particular interest in the business aspect of it. Studios were dicey propositions in terms of revenue flow. Someone had to continually beat the drums, so to speak, to keep customers coming in the door. But what *did* interest Olsen was the idea of having a place for his use only.

With so many high-profile projects now coming his way, it was getting harder and harder to reserve adequate studio time at Sound City. Though Olsen was the star attraction there, he nevertheless was also far from being the only producer, band, or singer wanting to use the facilities. Studios only make money when they are occupied, so Joe Gottfried and his partner naturally took business from anyone who was willing to pay for it. Which occasionally left Olsen on the outside looking in, at least regarding Studio A, where his beloved Neve 8078 mixing console sat. But studios also cost a lot to build, and they had to be situated in the right building with the right acoustics in the right neighborhood. Olsen didn't have a lot of time to race all over town looking for the right location, nor did he want to spend a fortune out of his own pocket to create a sonic environment that would satisfy his exacting needs. Fortunately for him, a series of events would soon conspire to create the perfect answer to his dilemma.

BY 1980 PATRICIA MAE ANDRZEJEWSKI WAS LOOKING FOR A NEW record producer. Known to the public as Pat Benatar, the petite, Long Island–born singer with the knockout looks and operatic voice who could belt out a song like album rock's answer to Big Mama Thornton had scored a huge debut hit in late 1979 with "Heartbreaker." But after a platinum-selling album (*In the Heat of the Night*) that had been more or less produced by committee, Benatar wanted some consistency and more personalized attention for album number two. Given her breakout success, she felt she had earned it.

With Bob Buziak, Keith Olsen's manager, once again working his magic behind the scenes at the highest of levels, Buziak managed to secure his client the gig. The next thing Olsen knew, he was sitting in a meeting with the brass at Chrysalis Records, Benatar's label, brainstorming about song possibilities. Just as with Foreigner, Olsen's job was to make a big act even bigger. But it would take strong material to do it. And Olsen had just the song in mind.

At around the same time he signed on to produce Pat Benatar's next record, Olsen had received an inquiry from another record label that wanted him to produce a little-known Canadian singer-songwriter by the name of Eddie Schwartz. After Schwartz sent Olsen a demo of a bunch of his stuff, Olsen dutifully gave it all a listen. Although most of the tunes were decent but not really standouts, one of them practically leapt off the tape. It was a simple, relatable little story song (Olsen's favorite kind) about somebody in a relationship putting on a brave front when they are about to get dumped by the person they love.

Knowing a great composition when he heard one but not crazy about Schwartz's vocals, Olsen gave him a call.

"Really, you want to sing this, Eddie?"

Featuring the lines, "You're a real tough cookie with a long history / Breaking little hearts like the one in me," the delivery just didn't work for Olsen. In his view it was a song a girl should be singing, not a guy.

But Schwartz was insistent.

"Oh, yeah, yeah—that's me," he replied, unconvincingly.

"Well, you know, I'm working with this female singer, Pat Benatar, who's already had a big hit, and I think this song would be perfect for her," Olsen countered, the implication clear. If Schwartz gave Olsen the song, there might be some serious bread to be made—for everyone. Which turned out to be all Schwartz needed to hear.

"Okay," he quickly said.

With Olsen's prized song now in hand, it then took a little arm-twisting for Benatar to want to sing it. She and her bandleader (and boyfriend), Neil Giraldo, disagreed with Olsen's assessment. Not only did they not like "Hit Me with Your Best Shot" at first, they also didn't see it becoming a hit. Benatar's artistic inclination was to go for more lyrically sophisticated material in the same vein as Bruce Springsteen, one of her idols. But Olsen, in his friendly, charismatic, ever-persuasive manner, was as insistent about Benatar singing the song as Eddie Schwartz originally had been about keeping it for himself.

Subsequently booking time at Davlen Studios in North Hollywood (Sound City was temporarily full), Olsen, Benatar, Giraldo, her band, and Chris Minto, Olsen's talented engineer, began laying down the tracks for "Hit Me with Your Best Shot." With Benatar offering up a stinging, sneering, defiant vocal performance worthy of an Academy Award and with Giraldo supplying his customarily blistering guitar work, the song came out even better than Olsen had expected. He was sure it would be a smash.

With everyone then agreeing that they felt they could work well together, plans were made to reconvene at Sound City to cut the rest of what would be called *Crimes of Passion*. But while working on the album Olsen received another overture about working with yet another artist. This time the request came from Joe Gottfried, Sound City's beloved co-owner. The genial though far-from-shrewd Gottfried had somehow gotten a record deal with RCA for a young singer-songwriter–guitar player he was grooming, and he wondered if Olsen would be willing to handle the production for a couple of songs to release as advance singles. The label wanted them as soon as possible. Which is the moment Olsen realized just where his new state-of-the-art recording facility was going to come from.

"Joe, I'll tell you what. I'll cut those two songs on your artist for points and a studio next door."

Gottfried looked confused.

"You mean the old radiator shop that closed down?"

"Uh huh," Olsen said. "I'll put in the gear, and you do all the build-out."

"Okay, you've got a deal," Gottfried said as the two shook hands.

And while Olsen soon thereafter had his own gorgeous new recording studio called Goodnight LA (in partnership with investor and best friend, Gordon Perry), positioned immediately adjacent to Sound City no less, in the same horseshoe-shaped business complex, perhaps the bigger gain was snagging a percentage of the struggling musician Gottfried needed produced: Rick Springfield.

Born in Australia as Richard Springthorpe, the tall, dark, and exceedingly handsome (and by now thirty-year-old) Springfield dreamed of nothing more than being a successful musician. Having enjoyed a brief taste of the charts in 1972 when his song "Speak to the Sky" made it to number fourteen in the United States on the Billboard Top Forty, Springfield's career soon evaporated when rumors circulated that Capitol Records, his label, had secretly bought up a bunch of his albums in order to boost the sales ranking.

Following an extended fallow period that left Springfield essentially broke and out of the spotlight for the rest of the seventies, his luck finally changed when Gottfried stepped in as his manager and benefactor. Treating Springfield like a son, Gottfried gave him free studio time to work on his craft and also a stipend of a $150 a week to help pay the bills (which Springfield augmented with the income from occasional small acting jobs). But musically Springfield felt that being produced by the great and powerful Keith Olsen was an incredible gift and maybe his only hope.

With a bunch of demo songs on a cassette that Springfield had meticulously written and recorded over the past year or more, he was more than ready for the big meeting scheduled up at Olsen's house. Olsen wanted to listen to everything Springfield had so he could pick the two best of the bunch. As Olsen lent a critical ear to each song in turn, the one that really caught his attention was about a guy's unexpected love for his pal's girlfriend. Based loosely on an encounter with a woman Springfield noticed in a stained-glass-making class he took while waiting for the RCA deal to happen and originally titled "Randy's Girl," then "Gary's Girl," it was far from the best of what Springfield felt he had to offer.

"Really?" he asked, dumbfounded. "You want to record 'Jessie's Girl'?"

"It's the best one you've got. A great story song," Olsen replied.

Knowing Olsen's reputation for picking hits, Springfield decided to go with it. He was in no position to argue anyway.

After Olsen then strategically asked Pat Benatar's husband-to-be, Neil Giraldo, to play guitar and bass on the song (along with composing his own parts)—how could Pat get mad if time was taken away from her own album under those circumstances?—Olsen got "Jessie's Girl" and another tune, written by Sammy Hagar (a future Olsen client too), called "I've Done Everything for You" in the can over one weekend at Sound City, then mixed them both the following Saturday. Three days, all in. From there Olsen immediately returned to work finishing up the *Crimes of Passion* LP for Benatar plus getting the construction under way on Goodnight LA, all the while giving "Jessie's Girl" little further thought.

In the fall of 1980 "Hit Me with Your Best Shot" became a giant hit, as did *Crimes of Passion*. Pat Benatar was now an even bigger star. And Keith Olsen was rewarded with the opportunity to produce (along with Neil Giraldo this time around) her next album, *Precious Time*, which would also end up going multiplatinum in the summer of 1981. But it was neither the incessant radio airplay of "Hit Me with Your Best Shot" nor any of the other huge songs from either *Crimes of Passion* or *Precious Time* that would turn Benatar into a household name. That job fell to MTV.

On its first day on the air MTV had gone with "Video Killed the Radio Star" as its lead, which did little to revive the Buggles' fading career. But the second video MTV aired during the wee hours of that morning—"You Better Run," featuring a finger-snapping Pat Benatar in a black-and-white top suggestively telling a paramour to get lost if he knows what's good for him—blew the lid off her career. It instantly established the photogenic, take-no-shit Benatar as one of MTV's early darlings, her videos played over and over. The heretofore-untapped power of video as a promotional tool, compared to radio's traditional reach, was mind-boggling. Benatar's album sales shot up, as did those for most of the other acts MTV favored. Suddenly, making a video became the central component of any major artist's promo plans.

MTV quickly metamorphosed into the province of those, like Benatar, who were attractive, willing to spend the time and money, and able to act (or at least lip sync in a reasonably entertaining fashion). Within a startlingly short period of time from its launch in August of 1981 MTV had made it so that what a music artist *looked* like mattered as much—maybe more—as what the music itself sounded like. Looks had always mattered in rock and roll, of course, from the Beatles' celebrated mop-top haircuts in the early sixties to David Bowie's ever-changing personas in the seventies. But now appearances were everything.

Anathema to rock-and-roll purists, video really did kill the radio star by the early eighties. Or at least many of them. With album-rock radio already reeling from the body blows it had absorbed over the years from the pernicious incursions of disco and new wave, MTV provided the ultimate smack-down. Pretty boy (and girl) musicians suddenly ruled for often little other reason than their appearances. All of which served to help Rick Springfield just when he needed it most.

His album, the ten-track *Working Class Dog*, released in late February of 1981 (and produced by Bill Drescher at Sound City on the other eight, non-Olsen songs), at first received scant notice. Nobody knew about it. RCA, leery of pushing Springfield's brand of pop-rock at a time when power ballads, new wave, and the remnants of disco were still popular, sat on the LP without promoting it. Finally, after some nudging by Joe Gottfried and the by-now well-connected Keith Olsen, RCA hesitantly released "Jessie's Girl" as a single at the end of March. They then gave Springfield the princely sum of $900 to go make a rudimentary video of him singing the song that could be used on various TV shows instead of spending a bundle on indie radio promoters.

After an agonizingly slow build over nineteen weeks spent in the Hot 100, during the first week of August—at the precise moment MTV hit the air—"Jessie's Girl" became the number-one song in the country. With RCA then racing to hand over the cheaply made "Jessie's Girl" video to MTV's programmers, who were hungry for content, Springfield, like Benatar at the same time, became one of the new cable channel's biggest stars. Further, REO Speedwagon, fresh off the unbridled success of *Hi Infidelity*, appeared in the ninth, seventeenth, and forty-seventh videos played on MTV's first day, becoming another of the channel's regular acts.

As for Keith Olsen, without even trying, he had unwittingly become part of the so-called video generation. Which would prove to be both good and bad for him and for the rest of the rapidly changing L.A. music industry as the eighties rolled forward.

fifteen

FREE FALLIN'

I'll bet you a couple of grams this is a . . . smash hit.

—WADDY WACHTEL

WADDY WACHTEL ALWAYS HATED GOING HOME. BEING AN EX-
trovert by nature and loving the company of other musicians,
Wachtel would often swing by a recording studio just to have the
chance to hang out with some pals after leaving a session of his own
elsewhere. And if the place he was visiting also happened to have
some adult beverages available, then so much the better.

While cruising down Ventura Boulevard one afternoon in January
of 1981 in the San Fernando Valley neighborhood of Sherman Oaks,
Wachtel decided to stop in at Record One, a new, state-of-the-art recording studio co-owned, built, and operated by the producer Val Garay. Long wanting to have a place of his own after having spent many
years working mostly at the Sound Factory, Garay had partnered with
the billionaire shopping-mall builder Mel Simon to create a facility

that instantly became a favorite among many recording stars, including James Taylor, Linda Ronstadt, and Don Henley.

As Wachtel stepped inside through the back alleyway door, designed so Record One's high-profile clientele could come and go unnoticed, Garay came hustling over.

"I'm really glad you're here," he said. "Josh is sick. Would you mind filling in on Kim's session?"

Josh Leo, a brilliant guitarist who had been diagnosed with cancer, fell ill at the last moment, leaving him unable to make that day's scheduled recording date for the singer Kim Carnes. Coming off a Top Ten hit from the year before, "More Love," the attractive, blonde-haired, husky-voiced Carnes, who had been putting out albums since 1971 and writing songs even longer, was finally poised to become a headliner after years of working in the shadows. With Garay, her new producer on board, Carnes was in the middle of rehearsing for her new album, to be called *Mistaken Identity*.

While actively looking for quality songs for the new Carnes project, both Carnes and Garay were receptive when Donna Weiss, a well-known backup singer and songwriter, called one day to ask if she could swing by the studio.

"I've got a song that would be *perfect* for Kim," Weiss enthused.

"Sure, come on over," Garay replied. He loved finding unexpected gems.

But as Weiss sang the much-anticipated tune for Carnes and Garay while Weiss's friend provided accompaniment on Garay's office piano, it quickly became clear that it just wasn't the right fit, at least not for Carnes.

"Nah, I don't think so," Garay said politely as he glanced at Carnes, who was equally ambivalent.

"Well, you know, I have another song that I gave to George Tobin and nothing ever came of it," Weiss offered.

Tobin, a well-known pop music producer, had worked with Carnes on her last album, *Romance Dance*. It was her decision to discontinue work with him after that project, which had led to Garay stepping in as her new producer. And Carnes had liked the song too when Weiss first presented it the year before. But Tobin somehow didn't want to cut it.

"Well, give *me* the demo," Garay said, smiling.

After Weiss did so and Garay played it, he couldn't get the odd tune out of his head for days afterward. Recorded almost like a Leon Russell–style boogie-woogie number on piano with a female vocalist singing about a powerfully manipulative woman who always gets her way, Garay nonetheless liked the melody and loved the lyrics. He felt sure it could be a hit if reworked. But how?

Strumming the song's chords on his acoustic guitar for several days afterward, Garay gradually began to reduce the tempo, taking it from upbeat down to slinky. He then approached Bill Cuomo, Carnes's keyboardist, about creating some kind of unique arrangement that would help bring it to life.

"Come up with a riff that can play under this song," Garay directed.

Cuomo, leaning heavily on the use of a then cutting-edge Sequential Circuits Prophet-5 synthesizer, promptly obliged in abundance by crafting a catchy, syncopated blend of breathy synth pads (sounds) on the intro, verses, and chorus that blew Garay away. All of a sudden the peculiar-yet-riveting little song written by Donna Weiss and Jackie DeShannon was contemporary and cool. But there was to be one more crucial element soon added.

During the three weeks of woodshedding for *Mistaken Identity* at nearby Leeds Rehearsal Studios in North Hollywood, a popular spot used by many big-time producers and musicians looking to polish their material without spending a fortune on daily recording studio rental rates, Garay, Carnes, and their group of players worked hard at shaping all the songs, perhaps none more diligently than Craig Krampf. Brought in by Garay to be the album's drummer, Krampf kept fooling around on almost every song with a new contraption called a Synare. A precursor of today's highly evolved electronic drum kits that look, sound, and play remarkably like their traditional acoustic cousins, the comparatively primitive Synare consisted of a series of hard rubber pads connected to a sound-producing "brain" unit. Striking a corresponding pad with a drum stick would then yield whatever sound had been assigned.

In particular, the big selling point of the Synare had to do with the sophisticated (for its time) built-in waveform oscillator that generated sawtooth, pulse, and white noise impulses that would bend and shape anything fed through them like so much sonic Silly Putty. The results often could be downright bizarre, depending on how far the programmer/drummer wanted to take it. And although the Synare perfectly captured where so much of popular music was headed and, for that matter, had already gone (the sound of the whip cracking on Devo's "Whip It" and the alternating *thwack* on Gary Numan's "Cars" are good examples), a bunch of futuristic clatter wasn't remotely what Val Garay wanted to hear.

"If you play that thing one more time I'm going to cut off both your arms," a fed-up Garay shouted during one session. But the incorrigible Krampf persisted, slyly squeezing in his new toy whenever possible until yet another rebuke came his way. And when it came time to rehearse the Weiss/DeShannon song, by the second verse Krampf couldn't help himself—he was at it again.

Only this time around Garay loved it.

Pounding out a thin, metallic, *whap-whap whap, whap-whap whap* pattern, almost like the sound of someone slapping on a screen door to be let in, it provided an unexpectedly powerful counterpoint to both the song's melody and Carnes's vocals.

"Man, I want to marry you," an overjoyed Garay kiddingly gushed.

Garay considered Krampf's improvised effect to be possibly the most perfectly placed piece of percussion he had ever heard. But then again, that was also a producer's job—a good producer anyway. Having an open mind and a keen ear for just the right contribution could sometimes make all the difference.

Back at Record One after all the rehearsing, and now with Waddy Wachtel sitting in, it was finally time to record Garay's favorite track, the one Cuomo and Krampf had made that much better. With all the musicians in the tracking room and Carnes positioned in a vocal booth adjoining the control room while singing into the same Neumann U 67 mic Garay had been favoring for the better part of the past decade (going back to Linda Ronstadt on "You're No Good" in 1974), the first take took everyone's breath away.

Singing lines such as, "She's precocious / And she knows just what it takes to make a pro blush / All the boys think she's a spy / She's got Bette Davis Eyes,'" Carnes leaned into "Bette Davis Eyes" with her seductive, sultry best. For good measure, after playing a steady pattern of rhythmic eighth-notes throughout the song on his Les Paul, Wachtel tossed in some guitar work toward the end that sounded like dogs barking.

After asking everyone to give the song a couple more passes just to see if they could do even better, Garay realized after take three that the first one had been the keeper. As did everyone else in the room, including Waddy Wachtel.

As some of the musicians, including Carnes and Wachtel, then walked into the control room to hear the playback, Wachtel turned to Garay and said, "Val, this is a smash. I'll bet you anything. I'll bet you a couple of grams this is a fucking smash hit."

And it was. Except more so than Waddy Wachtel could have ever imagined.

"Bette Davis Eyes" flew up the charts upon its release in March of 1981, spending an astounding nine weeks at number one and becoming Billboard's biggest-selling song of the year (and eventually the second biggest seller for the entire decade of the eighties). From there, during the nationally televised Grammy Awards show the following year, Garay sat in the audience and watched as Kenny Loggins—who had finally become the solo star he had always wanted to be on the heels of such hits as "Whenever I Call You Friend" with Stevie Nicks and "I'm Alright" from the film *Caddyshack*—announced from the stage that "Bette Davis Eyes" was now the Record of the Year as well.

But as much as "Bette Davis Eyes" delighted millions of listeners during the early eighties, it also demonstrated that, with few exceptions, the days of album rock being the most popular genre in the land were over, making Bob Dylan's lyrics "He not busy being born is busy dying" from his landmark song "It's Alright, Ma (I'm Only Bleeding)" in 1965 especially prophetic in regard to the rock bands of the seventies who were still left on the scene.

BY THE EARLY SUMMER OF 1985 JAMES PANKOW HAD FINALLY taken all he could. The band Chicago's accomplished trombonist, songwriter, horn arranger, and die-hard loyalist was in the middle of a tense meeting with his fellow bandmates to discuss the future of Chicago's lead singer/bassist, Peter Cetera. And it wasn't going well.

Having just completed a huge spring tour in support of *Chicago 17*, their multiplatinum comeback LP, the group was back on top of the charts after a long slide. Once the hottest band in the land with five straight number-one albums back in the seventies, the combination of the tragic death of their guitarist, Terry Kath, along with the departure of James Guercio as their longtime hit-making producer and manager, not to mention the American public's changing music tastes, had left the septet (and sometimes octet) adrift.

But just when Chicago needed it most, along came the producer, songwriter, and pianist extraordinaire David Foster. Hooking up with the band through the combined efforts of Chicago's drummer, Danny Seraphine, and the Grammy-winning Bill Champlin—the group's recently hired, gravelly voiced singer, songwriter, keyboardist, and sometimes guitarist who had been brought in to help fill Kath's immense void—the Canadian-born Foster immediately made his presence felt.

Chicago 16, recorded in early 1982 for Full Moon/Warner Bros. Records at several Los Angeles–area studios, including Davlen in North Hollywood and the Record Plant West's new location in Hollywood just off Santa Monica Boulevard, miraculously served to resurrect the career of a band who had sorely lost its way. The admitted control freak Foster was a whirlwind of direction and activity while also cowriting eight out of the ten songs. Yet in doing so he additionally chose to radically alter the band's traditional sound by placing a distinct emphasis on adding layers of synthesizers, precision drumming, and plenty of strings. Foster even had the courage to bring in outside session musicians, including three from Toto, to augment his aural vision, something the once-mighty Chicago would have never tolerated in the past. Further, within all the sonic rearranging Foster elected to decrease the use of Chicago's signature three-piece horn section, something that pleased no one in the band except for Peter Cetera.

With a hit record on their hands, however, for the first time in years (*Chicago 16* climbed to number nine on the Billboard 200), Chicago's members for the most part looked the other way as Foster ran the show. They had done the same with James Guercio as their producer for over a decade—the band was used to being told what to do in the studio. Plus, on tour there were still all their older hits to be played too, providing lots of room for the three horns and Robert Lamm's Hammond B3 organ to still shine.

But the bigger issue with *Chicago 16* seemed rather benign at first. The adult contemporary sound Foster had implemented suited Cetera perfectly, letting him be the love-song balladeer he had always aspired to be. Which in and of itself wasn't a big deal to the other members—they had always been an unusually team-oriented band. If syrupy power ballads were the order of the day, then they would just have to suck it up and go with the flow. Whatever it took to be on the radio and sell records again. Except that as Cetera's prominence grew as Chicago's emerging front man, in the view of some of his bandmates so did his ego, which fostered a brewing resentment. To them it felt like the group had suddenly become "Peter Cetera and Chicago."

Having both cowritten and sung the album's huge breakout single, "Hard to Say I'm Sorry"—only the second number-one hit in Chicago's illustrious gold-record-filled history following Cetera's own "If You Leave Me Now" back in 1976—the pendulum of intraband power had begun to swing sharply in Peter Cetera's direction. Especially as he had also quickly developed a close working relationship with Foster, who clearly saw the high-tenor Cetera as the voice and face of Chicago going forward.

Three years later, though, by the spring of 1985, after Chicago had released the Record Plant–recorded *Chicago 17* in 1984 to even greater sales and acclaim than its predecessor (with no fewer than four *more* Cetera-sung singles becoming chart-busting hits), Chicago's unity was put to the ultimate test. Cetera made it clear that he wanted to now record a solo album and would also like to cut back on touring. He was exhausted too—surely the band could understand. Phil Collins got to come and go from Genesis as he pleased. Why couldn't Cetera have the same opportunity?

But the rest of the guys in Chicago didn't understand. They were as big now as they had been in the seventies, the grateful recipients of something few musicians ever get to experience: a second chance at being on the top of the world. To think of suddenly slamming the brakes on their hard-won momentum by taking a bunch of time off was ludicrous. Especially after several in the group had willingly sacrificed their input and roles. If it was going to be a Cetera-dominated band, well, then, okay, they could deal with that on a musical level— for now anyway. But he didn't get to call *all* the shots. Chicago was still a democracy and a brotherhood. And one of the siblings was in dire need of some tough love. Which is why the meeting had been called in the offices of HK Management. It was time to clear the air.

As Peter Cetera and the other band members each had their say during the hour-long conclave, the frustration in the room was palpable. Though hopes were high going in, by the end nothing had changed. Cetera remained unwilling to make an exclusive commitment to Chicago. Either they let him do it his way . . . or not.

After Cetera left, the other six hashed it all out. Maybe it really was time to do the previously unthinkable, some offered: find a new bass player and lead singer. Chicago *had* to continue, one way or another. Millions of dollars and a virtually unprecedented career rebirth were at stake. As the discussion continued, James Pankow, for one, felt himself get more and more angry. Who did Cetera think he was?

Able to take no more, Pankow suddenly stood up, spun around, and slammed his fist into the wall. As the plasterboard turned to powder and showered into the air, his bandmates looked on, stunned. But Pankow had made his point, and the others were in agreement: Peter Cetera would be given the chance to sign a deal with the band that would include him agreeing to go back out on tour with Chicago and put any ideas about a solo album to the side for the time being. Otherwise, it was time to move on.

But when Cetera received a phone call from the group's management providing the details of the proposed contract, Cetera told them that Chicago would just have to look for another bass player. In Cetera's view the band had forced his hand. He didn't want to leave, but he was going to do a solo album. Period.

Which Cetera soon did, with 1986's *Solitude/Solitaire*. Containing the worldwide smashes "The Glory of Love" from the blockbuster film *The Karate Kid* and "The Next Time I Fall," a duet with Amy Grant, it ensconced Cetera as an adult contemporary star. Chicago would also go on to postsplit success, at least for a while. They brought in Jason Scheff (the son of Elvis's bassist Jerry Scheff), a young, gifted bass player with a tenor voice and sense of phrasing that uncannily resembled Cetera. And for another few years the hits would continue, although the band was never quite at the same level and certainly produced nothing that sounded like the hard-driving rock/jazz/blues they used to play. But by the end of the decade even the uncommonly resilient Chicago, who had weathered everything thrown at them for almost a quarter-century, would start to feel the career-altering effects of popular music taking perhaps its biggest and most permanent left turn yet.

IN THE SPRING OF 1990, WHEN THE DRUMMER TRIS IMBODEN'S home phone rang, he couldn't have known that the incoming call would be nothing short of a lifesaver. Having been a stalwart in the Los Angeles recording studio world for the better part of two decades, Imboden had come to prominence in the late seventies as the newly solo Kenny Loggins's main drummer. Starting in 1978 with *Nightwatch*, the second Loggins LP after Kenny's split from his longtime musical partner, Jim Messina, the cheerful Imboden, a veritable groove machine, played on hit single after hit single for his new boss. On million-sellers from "This Is It" to "I'm Alright" to "Heart to Heart," Imboden sat behind the kit both in the studio and on tour while watching Loggins steadily become a star. But it was one song in particular that pushed Loggins over the top.

Three years after Loggins's success in writing and singing the song "I'm Alright" for 1981's *Caddyshack*, the producers of a new film about a rebellious high school dancer asked Loggins to once again write and sing a song for a theatrical release. Only this time it was to be the title tune.

With the perfectionist Loggins instructing his band to practice his evolving composition during the sound check each afternoon before every concert, after a month all the musicians (outside of Loggins) had become sick of it. When the day finally came for recording Loggins's handiwork in late 1983 at the Record Plant in L.A., after just two takes the new movie theme song was done and in the can—the band knew it that well. And still hated it. They figured the simplistic little ditty would have a short shelf life.

"At least that's the last time we'll ever have to play that piece-of-shit song again," a laughing Tris Imboden said to his bandmate, the bassist Nathan East, as the two walked out to their cars afterward.

Except the joke was on Imboden.

Instead of becoming a throwaway, 1984's "Footloose" went straight to number one and became the biggest smash of Loggins's lengthy solo career, with his band subsequently resigning themselves to playing it nightly thereafter.

But as the eighties came to a close, even the superstar Loggins began losing audience share. The hits had evaporated, ultimately leaving Tris Imboden looking for work. That's why the phone call he received out of the blue from Chicago's Bill Champlin came at such a welcome time. The band was replacing their old drummer.

"How would you like to join Chicago?" Champlin asked, getting right to the point.

"Are you kidding me?" Imboden gasped. "Hell, yes!"

After the departure of Peter Cetera in 1985, Chicago had soldiered on, surprising many by scoring six more Billboard Top Forty hits by the end of the decade. The band seemed to be the exception to the sharp decline in popularity among most album-rock bands by the late eighties. Yes, Chicago had changed their sound along the way too—if you closed your eyes, you might not even know it was the same bunch of players. 1988's "What Kind of Man Would I Be?" was a long way from 1970's "25 or 6 to 4" (which Chicago ironically remade during this later period to little notice). But success is success, especially in the music business. It's taken where it's found. Unfortunately for Tris Imboden, however, he joined his dream band precisely at the wrong time.

By 1991, a year into Imboden's new position, Chicago's longtime album-rock competitors such as the Doobie Brothers, Santana, REO Speedwagon, Heart, and even the seemingly imperishable Fleetwood Mac had all dropped off the charts for good. Carole King was gone. Ronstadt and Benatar too. Chicago appeared to be one of the few from the old days in the L.A. studios still standing. Until even they weren't.

Despite the band's tried-and-true dependence in later years on a slew of Diane Warren–penned songs (she had become a certifiable hit-writing juggernaut for dozens of artists in the eighties), *Chicago Twenty 1*, released in 1991, contained no hit singles and could do no better than sixty-six on Billboard's Top 200, making it Chicago's worst-selling album since 1980's *XIV*, back when the band was still reeling from guitarist Terry Kath's untimely death. But this time was different. There was no loss of confidence or lack of interest or direction on their part. They had stayed true to their late-eighties-style formula. Only now it was the nineties. Popular music had changed yet again. Chicago's balladry held little appeal for the millions of teens and twentysomethings who bought the majority of CDs. Those consumers hungered to hear rap and, especially, a fast-rising style of music known as the "Seattle Sound."

AS TOM PETTY BEGAN PLUNKING A CHORD PATTERN ON THE PIano in the key of F, his friend and producer, Jeff Lynne (the founder and former leader of Electric Light Orchestra), stopped what he was doing nearby, his natural musical instincts piqued.

"You played one chord too many," he said, smiling.

As Petty continued, he cut his simple, lilting riff down to three chords, then added some impromptu vocals.

"She's a good girl / Loves her mama / Loves Jesus / And America too."

Thinking it to be all in fun, just a silly little tune designed to get Lynne to laugh, Petty continued making up verses.

"It's a long day / Livin' in Reseda / There's a freeway / Runnin' through the yard."

But when Petty got to the chorus, just before he creating his next line, Lynne leaned over and said, "Free falling."

With the utter simplicity and appropriateness of the two words catching Petty by surprise, he began singing them over and over while going up an octave.

"And I'm *freeee*, free fallin'."

Within a few short minutes, when he least expected it, Petty, with Lynne's help, had just composed a future hit song about aspects of his life from back when he had left his native Florida many years before for the big time in Los Angeles. The title also reflected the state in which the album-rock world, which Petty had been a part of for so long in L.A., now found itself. In the wake of Tom Petty and the Heartbreaker's previous album, 1987's *Let Me Up I've Had Enough*, having been the band's poorest-charting effort since 1978, Petty, by 1988, had decided to cut a solo LP instead as his next musical venture. And rather than record the whole thing (*Full Moon Fever*) at Sound City as he had done so many times before, Petty elected to utilize a variety of studios around town, including—tellingly—his bandmate Mike Campbell's well-equipped garage facility where Petty wrote and ultimately recorded "Free Fallin'."

By this time, in the late eighties, high-end recording gear had become far more affordable, for the first time allowing many professional musicians the luxury of building their own studios at home. Which left places like Sound City on the outside looking in. Rather than changing with the times and investing in digital equipment, the Sound City owners had chosen to stick with what they knew: racks of increasingly obsolete analog gear. Their refusal to switch to digital left them uncompetitive in relation to premier studios such as the Record Plant, the Village Recorder, and Sunset Sound just as analog tape machines and consoles were now also being sold by the likes of Guitar Center, which opened in 1985, and the venerable West L.A. Music, which had been around since the sixties. If an act wanted digital recording capabilities, they could go to one of the big studios in town. If they wanted analog, well, there were plenty of ever-more affordable choices, including just setting things up in their own garage.

Keith Olsen, however, had seen digital recording's value early on. He had already been integrating its use into his studio, Goodnight LA, for some time. Sound City, his next-door neighbor, had not. Excruciatingly slow though it was in its earliest incarnations, the editing options digital provided were worth it alone, in some cases able to shave hours, if not days, from a project's timeline. Instead of manually cutting and splicing two-inch magnetic tape every time an edit needed to happen as he had done since the sixties, Olsen could now simply make the corrections on a computer screen with the audio wave forms for each track right in front of him. For a natural-born tinkerer and techie like Olsen, digital's possibilities were a gift from the heavens. And as he got better and better at it, he became the man to talk to.

Further, from Olsen's vantage point as one of the top record producers of his era, he knew all along he was going to have to go after as many genres as he could if he wanted to stay relevant as the eighties headed toward the nineties. He in no way wanted to be pigeon-holed—that was a quick way to see a career disappear.

By then the once all-inclusive Top Forty–style of radio programming that had done its best to offer something for everyone was but a fond memory. In its place had come a mind-numbing mélange of genre-specific formats (and subformats), all fighting for their slice of people's attention. With AM radio mostly having ceded its airwaves to news, talk, and sports during the eighties, FM was now the wide-ranging musical home to stations that featured oldies, classic rock, adult contemporary, active rock, adult album alternative, mainstream rock, urban, and a dizzying array of other niches, including several country formats. Gone were the days of hearing Johnny Cash followed by Led Zeppelin followed by Joni Mitchell all on one Top Forty station. Though Top Forty was still around too, it had long since changed by the mid-eighties, evolving into a tightly scripted "contemporary hit radio" showcase for the kind of pop music that dominated MTV, featuring acts such as Madonna, Lionel Ritchie, Culture Club, and Bananarama. But other forms of music were still around as well, if in rapidly changing forms.

With heavy metal and glam rock more or less merging in the mid- to late eighties to create the red-hot genre of so-called hair metal,

Olsen decided to go with that particular trend and find some of his own clients with whom to work. Van Halen had basically started the whole thing in 1978, with Dio and, especially, Guns N' Roses, putting their own mammoth imprints on the genre by the mid-eighties. And from there Mötley Crüe, Poison, Quiet Riot, Ratt, and a swarm of others featuring preposterously teased hair and spandex leggings took the visuals to almost a comic-book level. In their own theatrical way these bands were all trying to pick up where the hard rock Led Zeppelin, Black Sabbath, and Deep Purple left off in the late seventies, with more than a dash of the flashiness of David Bowie, T. Rex, and Mott the Hoople mixed in for good measure.

Subsequently producing platinum albums for premier metal acts such as Whitesnake, Ozzy Osbourne, and the Scorpions as the decade came to a close, Olsen made the transition as well as anyone in the business. But as the eighties became the nineties, hair metal finally began falling out of favor too. Just like always, popular music was moving on to reflect the tastes of the younger generation.

As an almost direct reaction to the onslaught of all the over-the-top glitz that hair metal bands had thrown in people's faces, a stripped-down, punk-influenced genre known first as the Seattle Sound then as "grunge" began gaining traction by the beginning of the nineties. Grunge featured bands such as Soundgarden, Pearl Jam, Mother Love Bone, Alice in Chains, Mudhoney, and Screaming Trees that wore their disillusionment on their stereotypically plaid flannel shirt sleeves by proffering a frenetic, often three-chord-driven, highly distorted sound aimed at eliminating all subtlety and any questions about their disaffected, glowering intentions—they were pretty much anti-everything.

DURING THE SPRING OF 1991, HAVING JUST COME OFF OF PRO-
ducing what would be the Scorpions' last big album, *Crazy World*,
featuring the worldwide smash "Winds of Change," which had so
perfectly mirrored the recent fall of the Berlin Wall and the collapse
of the Soviet Union, Keith Olsen was sitting in his office one day at
Goodnight LA when his receptionist, Victoria Seeger, stuck her head
inside his door.

"Keith, there's a Butch Vig here that would like to see you."

Vig, an exceedingly intelligent, mild-mannered son of a physician,
had grown up fascinated with music. His mother, a free-thinking
teacher who loved practically every genre, frequently brought home
records ranging from Frank Sinatra to the *Camelot* soundtrack to the
latest Top Forty rock-and-roll hits played on the local AM radio station. Though a fan of British Invasion bands such as the Beatles and
Herman's Hermits along with their American "answer" Paul Revere
and the Raiders, it was particularly while watching the Who's manic
Keith Moon and his exploding drums during a now-famous telecast
of the *Smothers Brothers Comedy Hour* in 1968 that led Vig to desperately want a kit of his own.

Subsequently playing drums in various pop-rock bands with names
like the Rat Finks and Eclipse throughout his grade school, junior
high, and high school years in and around his hometown of tiny Vir-
oqua, Wisconsin, Butch Vig graduated, after several stops and starts,
from the nearby (two hours away) University of Wisconsin-Madison
in the early eighties with a degree in communication arts and with
only one thought on his mind: playing more music.

After pairing up with a close friend and fellow musician, Steve
Marker, the two opened a fledgling recording facility in Madison
called Smart Studios with a tiny amount of basic gear, including a
twelve-channel mixing board, a Space Echo unit, and a used compres-
sor from a garage sale. Catering to the needs of local bands and those

who might be passing through on the concert trail, Smart Studios gradually became known by the mid- to late eighties as *the* place to lay down some tracks in the greater Madison area and, for that matter, the entire upper Midwest.

With Vig's reputation for especially bringing out the best in up-and-coming alternative-rock bands such as Killdozer, Tad, and the Smashing Pumpkins, the Sub Pop record label in Seattle eventually approached him about producing a three-piece band they had under contract called Nirvana. Consisting of the charismatic Kurt Cobain on guitar and vocals (and as chief songwriter) along with Chad Channing on drums (soon to be replaced by Dave Grohl) and Krist Novoselic on bass, Nirvana traveled to Madison and cut most of an album with Vig at Smart Studios.

But while waiting several months to then hear back about mixing the record, Vig got a call from Novoselic telling him the band had signed a new deal with Geffen Records and wanted Vig to join them in Los Angeles to produce it. Agreeing to be their man, Vig then flew to California and, with a tiny budget in hand from Geffen of only $65,000 to complete the entire project, he and the band ended up at the by-then mostly empty, exceedingly affordable Sound City, which cost only six hundred bucks a day.

While spending a little over two weeks in the studio with Nirvana, Vig coaxed and cajoled one memorable performance after another out of Cobain, Novoselic, and Grohl on songs such as "Lithium," "Come as You Are," and "Smells Like Teen Spirit." Sound City's reputation for making drum sounds come alive especially pleased both Vig and Grohl, who knew how important a solid bottom end was to any good recording.

Toward the end of cutting the album, however, as Vig found himself in need of possibly adding some percussion effects, he popped next door to talk with Keith Olsen. Vig, being a longtime student of the recording industry in terms of the major producers and engineers, was well aware of the living legend working right next door at Goodnight LA, who just so happened to have been responsible for the Neve mixing console Vig had been using—and loving—inside Sound City's Studio A.

"So who's the guy I've heard about that you've been using to create computer-generated percussion loops?" Vig asked Olsen during their sit-down.

After giving Vig the name and contact information for Eric Persing, a guy who could twist and turn various sounds into a digitally rendered rhythm track that could then be dropped neatly (if slowly) into a song, the two chit-chatted for a bit and then Vig was on his way, back to finishing the Nirvana project next door. And at that moment, without either of them realizing it, the torch had been passed.

Nirvana's album *Nevermind* would come out later in the year to rave reviews and stratospheric sales, becoming not only the biggest music story of 1991 but also the most influential LP of the nineties. Following its multiplatinum success Butch Vig, just like Olsen before him on the heels of the breakout success of the *Fleetwood Mac* album in 1975, would go on to dizzying heights as one of the most sought-after producers in popular music (as well as one of the founding members of the multiplatinum alternative band Garbage).

But for Keith Olsen, along with his friend Waddy Wachtel—and virtually every other album-rock practitioner who made it big in the seventies and eighties—the arrival of Nirvana and the huge grunge-rock scene that followed effectively shut their door for good. Olsen and Wachtel's hit-making days were over. For them the seventies and eighties had been the musical gift that kept on giving. That golden era of album rock in the Los Angeles studios had become bigger than they could have dreamed. Olsen's ocean-front home in Malibu and the Lamborghini Jalpa and Ferrari Mondial in his garage, along with

Wachtel's horse property, were gratefully earned reminders of all that had come their way.

And though both Olsen and Wachtel were immensely talented, it was more than that. The Los Angeles–based pair had also been in the right place at the right time. Album rock or classic rock or whatever anyone wants to call it was different from anything before or since. It has reached listeners and endured like no other musical genre. Songs that Olsen and Wachtel helped create such as "Rhiannon," "Double Vision," and "Werewolves of London" are heavily played to this day, decades after release.

So why does this style of music from so long ago still matter so much to so many? Furthermore, how were the septuagenarian classic rockers Bob Dylan, Paul McCartney, the Rolling Stones, Roger Waters, the Who, and Neil Young able to headline a sold-out series of concerts before hundreds of thousands of rabid fans in California at Desert Trip 2016? The answer boils down to one element: the songs.

Everybody who enjoys music has their own favorite recordings, those that came along during key points in life. Maybe during a high school prom or as part of a wedding or at a time of despair when only the lyrics of a cherished song could bring solace. Of course, the forties had some of these. The fifties too. Except those were mostly short and sweet love and/or novelty songs. "Que Sera, Sera (Whatever Will Be, Will Be)" "Oh! My Pa-Pa (O Mein Papa)," and even Elvis's "Hound Dog," as cool sounding as it was, could only take a person so far. Even through the bulk of the sixties most rock and roll hewed toward brevity and simplicity. It took the always forward-looking Beatles until 1967 before they came out with the transformative "Strawberry Fields Forever" and "A Day in the Life," which were nothing like anyone had heard before. Yet true sophistication within popular music really only began to develop across the board in the late sixties, when the format of album rock started to take hold.

Free Fallin'

Without a two- or three-minute time constraint requirement as with most singles, by the dawn of the seventies especially, record labels were now giving their rock musicians carte blanche to explore the human condition in full-blown sonic detail, to create miniature worlds and metaphorical imaging that had the capacity to resonate deeply and make people think and feel. It didn't matter the length of the tune—it just needed to be good, whether it trucked in at five minutes or eight, which was a revelation. Suddenly the palate was wide and the color choices were bounteous. Rock songs began featuring actual movements and layers, complex elements that occasionally even rivaled the works of the great classical composers. Sometimes it was the lyrics, sometimes it was the melody, and sometimes it was the arrangement that mattered most to listeners. Usually, however, it was the deftly intertwined combination of all three.

Whatever the precise components of the equation, songs created during the album-rock era, especially those coming out of the Los Angles studios, brought a previously unheard level of human emotion, storytelling, and expansive musicality to the masses. Who can't help but sing along with and probably relate to Los Angeles–recorded favorites such as "The World Is a Ghetto" by War or "Don't Come Around Here No More" by Tom Petty and the Heartbreakers or "Let Me Take You Home Tonight" by Boston? Yes, they have by now become vastly overplayed on the radio, both terrestrial and satellite. But that's precisely the point. Forty years on, these cuts and hundreds more album-rock tracks just like them from the seventies through the early to mid-eighties are evergreens extraordinaire for a good reason: song for song, the quality and depth of artistry contained within them is as good as it gets. And that has never happened before or since on such a massive—and massively satisfying—scale.

EPILOGUE

WHILE CLASSIC ROCK'S GLORY YEARS AND THOSE OF THE GREAT recording studios in Los Angeles came and went with remarkable speed, many of the artists who cut their masterworks in that city from the early seventies through the mid-eighties are astonishingly not only still around but also thriving. Though most haven't been anywhere near the singles charts since their heydays back when Nixon, Ford, Carter, and finally Reagan took turns occupying the Oval Office, an awful lot of these bands and solo artists are on tour every summer to this very day, playing the FM album-rock style of music that just doesn't seem to want to go away. Chicago is still out there. So is REO Speedwagon. And Fleetwood Mac. Plus Kenny Loggins and Jim Messina, sometimes even together. Eddie Money, Boston, America, Pat Benatar, Foreigner, Heart, Rick Springfield, Steely Dan, and Santana too. The list only goes on from there.

During the dozens upon dozens of interviews I conducted for *Goodnight, L.A.*, almost every musician, producer, and engineer I spoke with related how astounded and grateful they remain that the songs they created so long ago inside the walls of shrine-like, still-operating places such as the Village Recorder, Sunset Sound, the Record Plant, and the Sound Factory (plus, of course, Sound City and Goodnight LA, among other now-defunct facilities) have so ably stood the test of time. It is hardly just a bunch of fifty-, sixty-, and seventy-year-old die-hards devotedly making their annual pilgrimages to classic-rock concerts these days either. It's also the children of those fans. And the children's children. To create such enduring music, something really *must* have been in the air, to paraphrase the old Thunderclap Newman song. If nothing else, classic rock certainly has legs.

Keith Olsen and Waddy Wachtel are still very much alive, well, and active too. Keith continues to provide his world-class production skills on various recording projects in his private, state-of-the-art studio for mostly up-and-comers who are thrilled to be working with a legend. That always was Keith's best skill: taking someone's music and making it bigger and better and almost always more successful. As for Waddy, he hasn't slowed down a lick either (guitar pun intended). Closing in on the age of seventy, he is a first-call touring and recording guitarist (and band leader) for many of his superstar pals and peers, ranging from Stevie Nicks to Joe Walsh to Keith Richards.

ACKNOWLEDGMENTS

Thank you for the interviews: Mark Andes, Peter Asher, Kevin Beamish, Michele Botts, John Boylan, Merel Bregante, Harold Ray Brown, Jimmy Buffett, Ken Caillat, Jonathan Cain, Jorge Calderón, Bill Champlin, Paul Cowsill, Kevin Cronin, Tim Danesi, Richard Dashut, Dave DeVore, Denny Dias, Craig Doerge, Neal Doughty, Bill Drescher, Walter Egan, Les Emmerson, Steve Escallier, Don Felder, Jay Ferguson, Brian Foraker, John Fischbach, Val Garay, John Good, Lou Gramm, James Guercio, Bruce Hall, Barry Hansen (AKA Dr. Demento), Gary "Hoppy" Hodges, Neil Hopper, Lyle Ireland, Tris Imboden, Tom Keenan, Danny Kortchmar, John Kosh, Mike Love, Stuart Margolin, John McFee, Jim Messina, Chris Minto, Eddie Money, Shivaun O'Brien, Keith Olsen, Michael Omartian, Lee Oskar, James Pankow, Dave Plenn, Judi Pulver, Linda Ronstadt, Marv Ross, Rindy Ross, Michel Rubini, Paula Salvatore, Duane Scott, Howard Scott, Victoria Seeger, Bob Siebenberg, Patrick Simmons, Lee Sklar, Rick Springfield, Bill Szymczyk, Wayne Tarnowski, Butch Vig, Waddy Wachtel, Tom Werman, Ann Wilson, Edgar Winter, and Shelly Yakus.

Acknowledgments

Special thanks to: Heather, Brenden, and Eddy at Circle Triangle Square, Bart Day, Ben Engen, Terry Finley, Ann Bieber Gregory, John Kosh, Josephine Mariea, Louise Palanker, Alan Rommelfanger, Cisca Schreefel, Susan Shearer, and Dana Spector.

Supreme thanks to: Helen Zimmermann, my trusted literary agent and unerring voice of reason; Ben Schafer, my fantastic editor at Da Capo; and Carl Lennertz, my irreplaceable musical sounding board.

And to Valerie, for everything.

SOURCE NOTES

ONE: TALK, TALK

Author Interviews

Mark Andes, October 3, 2013; Jorge Calderón, August 13, 2013; Bill Drescher, June 2, 2013; Jay Ferguson, October 20, 2013; Barry Hansen (AKA Dr. Demento), October 28, 2013; Gary "Hoppy" Hodges, August 16, 2013; Mike Love, November 2, 2016; Keith Olsen, April 12, 2013, April 13, 2013, May 10, 2013, May 29, 2013, June 12, 2013, June 27, 2013, July 24, 2013, and August 15, 2013; Judi Pulver, October 21, 2013; Waddy Wachtel, October 17, 2013.

Articles

Nelson, Paul. "Janis: The Judy Garland of Rock and Roll?" *Rolling Stone*, March 15, 1969.

Books

Bugliosi, Vincent. *Helter Skelter: The True Stories of the Manson Murders*. New York: W. W. Norton and Company, 1974.

Whitburn, Joel. *Billboard Hot 100 Charts: The Sixties*. Menomonee Falls, WI: Record Research, 1990.

———. *Billboard's Top Pop Albums 1955–2001*. Menomonee Falls, WI: Record Research, 2002.

Other

Spirit. CD liner notes. *Twelve Dreams of Dr. Sardonicus*. Sony Music Entertainment, 1996 (original vinyl LP released in 1970 on Epic Records).

TWO: COLOUR MY WORLD

Author Interviews

Paul Cowsill, July 29, 2013; James Guercio, September 5, 2015; James Pankow, November 19, 2014; Waddy Wachtel, October 17, 2013.

Articles

Duncan, Robert. "Chicago Is Revolting." *Creem*, February, 1976.

Books

Jacobs, Ron. *KHJ: Inside Boss Radio*. Stafford, TX: Zapoleon Publishing, 2002.

Whitburn, Joel. *Billboard Hot 100 Charts: The Seventies*. Menomonee Falls, WI: Record Research, 1990.

———. *Billboard Hot 100 Charts: The Sixties*. Menomonee Falls, WI: Record Research, 1990.

Audio

Lamm, Robert. Audio interview. *In the Studio with Redbeard*. www.inthestudio.net/online-only-interviews/chicago-5-6-7-robert-lamm.

American Top 40 (various 1970s episodes). Author's personal collection.

Video

Family Band: The Cowsills Story. DVD documentary. Palcorp, 2013.

Other

Chicago Transit Authority. CD liner notes. *Chicago Transit Authority*. Rhino Records, 2002 (original vinyl LP released in 1969 on Columbia Records).

Chicago. CD liner notes. *Chicago*. Rhino Records, 2002 (original vinyl LP released in 1970 on Columbia Records).

Source Notes

THREE: CRYING IN THE NIGHT

Author Interviews

Jorge Calderón, August 16, 2013; Paul Cowsill, July 29, 2013; Richard Dashut, August 28, 2013, and July 8, 2014; John Fischbach, September 6, 2015; Keith Olsen, April 12, 2013, April 13, 2013, May 10, 2013, May 29, 2013, June 12, 2013, June 27, 2013, July 24, 2013, and August 15, 2013; Judi Pulver, October 21, 2013; Waddy Wachtel, October 17, 2013.

Books

Whitburn, Joel. *Billboard Hot 100 Charts: The Seventies*. Menomonee Falls, WI: Record Research, 1990.

———. *Billboard Hot 100 Charts: The Sixties*. Menomonee Falls, WI: Record Research, 1990.

———. *Billboard's Top Pop Albums 1955–2001*. Menomonee Falls, WI: Record Research, 2002.

Video

Family Band: The Cowsills Story. DVD documentary. Palcorp, 2013.

FOUR: FROZEN LOVE

Author Interviews

Jorge Calderón, August 16, 2013; Ken Caillat, August 7, 2013; Richard Dashut, August 28, 2013, and July 8, 2014; Dave DeVore, June 6, 2013; Keith Olsen, April 12, 2013, April 13, 2013, May 10, 2013, May 29, 2013, June 12, 2013, June 27, 2013, July 24, 2013, and August 15, 2013; Waddy Wachtel, October 17, 2013.

Articles

Brantley, Ben. "A Songwriter Who Found Her Voice." *New York Times*, January 12, 2014.

Books

Whitburn, Joel. *Billboard Hot 100 Charts: The Seventies*. Menomonee Falls, WI: Record Research, 1990.

———. *Billboard's Top Pop Albums 1955–2001*. Menomonee Falls, WI: Record Research, 2002.

Other

Fleetwood Mac. CD liner notes. *25 Years: The Chain*. Warner Bros. Records, 2002.

FIVE: ONLY LOVE IS REAL

Author Interviews

Merel Bregante, December 15, 2015; Richard Dashut, August 28, 2013 and July 8, 2014; Dave DeVore, June 6, 2013; Craig Doerge, July 1, 2015; Danny Kortchmar, July 15, 2015; Keith Olsen, April 12, 2013, April 13, 2013, May 10, 2013, May 29, 2013, June 12, 2013, June 27, 2013, July 24, 2013, and August 15, 2013; Jim Messina, October 20, 2015, and November 21, 2015; Lee Sklar, July 22, 2015; Waddy Wachtel, October 17, 2013.

Articles

Freedland, Nat. "Reddy Close Call Halts One-Niters." *Billboard*, October 20, 1973.

Nolan, Tom. "There's Gold in the Middle of the Road." *Rolling Stone*, February 27, 1975.

Books

Whitburn, Joel. *Billboard Hot 100 Charts: The Seventies*. Menomonee Falls, WI: Record Research, 1990.

———. *Billboard's Top Pop Albums 1955–2001*. Menomonee Falls, WI: Record Research, 2002.

Other

Fleetwood Mac. CD liner notes. *25 Years: The Chain*. Warner Bros. Records, 2002.

SIX: THE TIME HAS COME

Author Interviews

Paul Cowsill, July 29, 2013; Richard Dashut, August 28, 2013, and July 8, 2014; Dave DeVore, June 6, 2013; Craig Doerge, July 1, 2015; Danny Kortchmar, July 15, 2015; Keith Olsen, April

12, 2013, April 13, 2013, May 10, 2013, May 29, 2013, June 12, 2013, June 27, 2013, July 24, 2013, and August 15, 2013; Lee Sklar, July 22, 2015; Waddy Wachtel, October 17, 2013.

Books

Whitburn, Joel. *Billboard Hot 100 Charts: The Seventies*. Menomonee Falls, WI: Record Research, 1990.

———. *Billboard's Top Pop Albums 1955–2001*. Menomonee Falls, WI: Record Research, 2002.

Video

Family Band: The Cowsills Story. DVD documentary. Palcorp, 2013.

Other

Fleetwood Mac. CD liner notes. *25 Years: The Chain*. Warner Bros. Records, 2002.

SEVEN: THAT'LL BE THE DAY

Author Interviews

Peter Asher, December 14, 2012; John Boylan, July 31, 2013; Ken Caillat, August 7, 2013; Richard Dashut, August 28, 2013, and July 8, 2014; Walter Egan, July 9, 2013; Val Garay, April 18, 2013, June 17, 2013, August 4, 2013, September 22, 2013, and July 9, 2015; Keith Olsen, April 12, 2013, April 13, 2013, May 10, 2013, May 29, 2013, June 12, 2013, June 27, 2013, July 24, 2013, and August 15, 2013; Linda Ronstadt, September 8, 2011; Waddy Wachtel, October 17, 2013.

Books

Whitburn, Joel. *Billboard Hot 100 Charts: The Seventies*. Menomonee Falls, WI: Record Research, 1990.

———. *Billboard's Top Pop Albums 1955–2001*. Menomonee Falls, WI: Record Research, 2002.

Video

Classic Albums: Rumours. DVD documentary. Rhino Home Video, 1997.

Other

Fleetwood Mac. CD liner notes. *25 Years: The Chain*. Warner Bros. Records, 2002.

Gold, Andrew. Unreleased interview by Mike Botts, 2002. From author's personal collection.

EIGHT: ANGRY EYES

Author Interviews

Merel Bregante, December 15, 2015; Dave DeVore, June 6, 2013; Keith Olsen, April 12, 2013, April 13, 2013, May 10, 2013, May 29, 2013, June 12, 2013, June 27, 2013, July 24, 2013, and August 15, 2013; Jim Messina, October 20, 2015, and November 21, 2015.

Articles

Fong-Torres, Ben. "Clive Davis Ousted; Payola Coverup Charged." *Rolling Stone*, July 5, 1973.

Wenner, Jann. "The End of the Middle of the Road." *Rolling Stone*, July 29, 1976.

Books

Whitburn, Joel. *Billboard Hot 100 Charts: The Seventies*. Menomonee Falls, WI: Record Research, 1990.

———. *Billboard's Top Pop Albums 1955–2001*. Menomonee Falls, WI: Record Research, 2002.

Other

Buckmaster, Paul. Interview with Southern California Public Radio, May 16, 2016. www.scpr.org/programs/the-frame/2016/05/16 /48900/inside-the-rock-star-s-studio-with-music-arranger.

Grateful Dead. CD liner notes. *Terrapin Station*. Grateful Dead/Rhino Records, 2006 (original vinyl LP released in 1977 on Arista).

NINE: BABY, WHAT A BIG SURPRISE

Author Interviews

John Boylan, July 31, 2013; Bill Champlin, June 13, 2013; James Guercio, September 5, 2015; James Pankow, November 19, 2014; Wayne Tarnowski, April 28, 2016; Tom Werman, August 13, 2013.

Articles

Baird, Jock. "Tom Scholz's Battle for Boston." *Musician*, January, 1987.

Books

Whitburn, Joel. *Billboard Hot 100 Charts: The Seventies*. Menomonee Falls, WI: Record Research, 1990.

———. *Billboard's Top Pop Albums 1955–2001*. Menomonee Falls, WI: Record Research, 2002.

Audio

Lamm, Robert. Interview. *In the Studio with Redbeard*. www.inthe studio.net/online-only-interviews/chicago-5-6-7-robert-lamm.

Other

Watertown, Massachusetts official Website. www.ci.watertown.ma .us/index.aspx?NID = 199.

Chicago, and William James Ruhlman. CD liner notes. *Group Portrait*. Columbia Records, 1991.

Chicago. CD liner notes. *Chicago X*. Rhino Records, 2002 (original vinyl LP released in 1976 on Columbia Records).

Chicago. CD liner notes. *Chicago XI*. Rhino Records, 2002 (original vinyl LP released in 1977 on Columbia Records).

The Secret Life of Scientists & Engineers: Tom Scholz. PBS/Nova online. https://opb.pbslearningmedia.org/resource/nvslos-sci-tomscholz /wgbh-nova-secret-life-of-scientists-and-engineers-tomscholz /#.WMZA0BSwKlI.

TEN: FOOTLOOSE AND FANCY-FREE

Author Interviews

Jorge Calderón, August 16, 2013; Don Felder, March 3, 2015, and March 5, 2015; Danny Kortchmar, July 15, 2015; John Kosh, July 12, 2012; Bill Szymczyk, March 30, 2015; Waddy Wachtel, October 17, 2013.

Articles

Werbin, Stuart. "From Gasoline Alley to Park Avenue." *Rolling Stone*, June 21, 1973.

Books

Whitburn, Joel. *Billboard Hot 100 Charts: The Seventies*. Menomonee Falls, WI: Record Research, 1990.

———. *Billboard's Top Pop Albums 1955–2001*. Menomonee Falls, WI: Record Research, 2002.

Video

History of the Eagles: The Story of an American Band. DVD documentary. Capitol Records, 2013.

ELEVEN: MEXICAN REGGAE

Author Interviews

Don Felder, March 3, 2015 and March 5, 2015; John Kosh, July 12, 2012; Linda Ronstadt, September 8, 2011; Bill Szymczyk, March 30, 2015.

Articles

Herold, Ann. "One Spanish Colonial Revival Architect Launched California Style." *Los Angeles Times*, February 2, 2006.

Books

Flory, J. Kelly. *American Cars, 1946–1959: Every Model, Year by Year*. Jefferson, NC: McFarland, 2008.

Whitburn, Joel. *Billboard Hot 100 Charts: The Seventies*. Menomonee Falls, WI: Record Research, 1990.

———. *Billboard's Top Pop Albums 1955–2001*. Menomonee Falls, WI: Record Research, 2002.

Video

History of the Eagles: The Story of an American Band. DVD documentary. Capitol Records, 2013.

TWELVE: DAMN THE TORPEDOES

Author Interviews

Keith Olsen, April 12, 2013, April 13, 2013, May 10, 2013, May 29, 2013, June 12, 2013, June 27, 2013, July 24, 2013, and August 15, 2013; Shelly Yakus, March 12, 2014, and March 14, 2014.

Source Notes

Articles

Gilmore, Mikal. "Tom Petty's Real-Life Nightmares." *Rolling Stone*, February 21, 1980.

"The 10 Wildest Led Zeppelin Legends, Fact-Checked." *Rolling Stone*, November 21, 2012. www.rollingstone.com/music/lists/the-10-wildest-led-zeppelin-legends-fact-checked-20121121/led-zeppelin-once-defiled-a-groupie-with-a-mud-shark-19691231.

Books

Dannen, Fredric. *Hit Men: Power Brokers and Fast Money Inside the Music Business*. New York: Crown, 1990.

Knoedelseder, William. *Stiffed: A True Story of MCA, the Music Business, and the Mafia*. New York: Harper Collins, 1993.

Whitburn, Joel. *Billboard Hot 100 Charts: The Seventies*. Menomonee Falls, WI: Record Research, 1990.

———. *Billboard's Top Pop Albums 1955–2001*. Menomonee Falls, WI: Record Research, 2002.

Video

Bogdanovich, Peter. *Tom Petty and the Heartbreakers: Runnin' Down a Dream*. DVD documentary. Warner Bros., 2007.

Classic Albums: Damn the Torpedoes. DVD documentary. Eagle Rock Entertainment, 2010.

THIRTEEN: WINNING

Author Interviews

Richard Dashut, August 28, 2013, and July 8, 2014; Lou Gramm, May 31, 2003; Mike Love, November 2, 2016; Chris Minto, June 3, 2013, and June 19, 2013; Keith Olsen, April 12, 2013, April 13, 2013, May 10, 2013, May 29, 2013, June 12, 2013, June 27, 2013, July 24, 2013, and August 15, 2013.

Articles

"120 Workers Cut at CBS Records." *New York Times*, August 11, 1979.

Harrison, Ed. "Warner Bros. Pink Slips 55 in 'Streamlining' Move." *Billboard*, December 1, 1979.

Kilgannon, Corey. "Sri Chinmoy, Athletic Spiritual Leader, Dies at 76." *New York Times*, October 13, 2007.

Sawyers, Arlena. "1979 Oil Shock Meant Recession for U.S., Depression for Autos." *Automotive News*, October 13, 2013.

Sciafani, Tony. "When 'Disco Sucks!' Echoed Around the World." MSNBC/*Today* (Show) Music, July 10, 2009. www.today.com /id/31832616/ns/today-today_entertainment/t/when-disco -sucks-echoed-around-world/#.WMezMBSwKlI.

Tschmuck, Peter. "The Recession in the Music Business: A Cause Analysis." *International Journal of Music Business Research*, March 2010.

Wake, Matt. "A&R Legend John Kalodner Talks Aerosmith and Why Rock Won't Reach the Masses Again." *LA Weekly*, June 13, 2016.

White, Timothy. "Carlos Santana: A Portrait of the Artist." *Billboard*, December 7, 1996.

Books

Dahl, Steve, and Dave Hoekstra. *Disco Demolition Night: The Night Disco Died*. Chicago: Curbside Splendor Publishing, 2016.

Dannen, Fredric. *Hit Men: Power Brokers and Fast Money Inside the Music Business*. New York: Crown, 1990.

DiMartino, Dave. *Pop Music's Performer-Composers, from A to Zevon*. New York: Billboard Books, 1994.

Whitburn, Joel. *Billboard Hot 100 Charts: The Eighties*. Menomonee Falls, WI: Record Research, 1995.

———. *Billboard Hot 100 Charts: The Seventies*. Menomonee Falls, WI: Record Research, 1990.

———. *Billboard's Top Pop Albums 1955–2001*. Menomonee Falls, WI: Record Research, 2002.

Audio

Gramm, Lou, and Mick Jones. Interviews on *In the Studio with Redbeard*. www.inthestudio.net/redbeards-blog/foreigner-double -vision-35th-anniversary-mick-jones-lou-gramm.

Source Notes

FOURTEEN: VIDEO KILLED THE RADIO STAR

Author Interviews

Kevin Beamish, August 6, 2013; John Boylan, July 31, 2013; Kevin Cronin, October 2, 2014; Neal Doughty, October 1, 2014; Bill Drescher, June 2, 2013; Bruce Hall, September 30, 2014; Chris Minto, June 3, 2013, and June 19, 2013; Keith Olsen, April 12, 2013, April 13, 2013, May 10, 2013, May 29, 2013, June 12, 2013, June 27, 2013, July 24, 2013, and August 15, 2013; Rick Springfield, October 3, 2013.

Articles

Pond, Steven. "Pat Benatar: This Year's Model." *Rolling Stone*, October 16, 1980.

Books

Marks, Craig, and Rob Tannenbaum. *I Want My MTV: The Uncensored Story of the Music Video Revolution.* New York: Dutton, 2011.

Whitburn, Joel. *Billboard Hot 100 Charts: The Eighties.* Menomonee Falls, WI: Record Research, 1995.

———. *Billboard Hot 100 Charts: The Seventies.* Menomonee Falls, WI: Record Research, 1990.

———. *Billboard's Top Pop Albums 1955–2001.* Menomonee Falls, WI: Record Research, 2002.

FIFTEEN: FREE FALLIN'

Author Interviews

Bill Champlin, June 13, 2013; Val Garay, April 18, 2013, June 17, 2013, August 4, 2013, September 22, 2013, and July 9, 2015; Tris Imboden, January 5, 2016; Shivaun O'Brien, June 4, 2013; Keith Olsen, April 12, 2013, April 13, 2013, May 10, 2013, May 29, 2013, June 12, 2013, June 27, 2013, July 24, 2013, and August 15, 2013; James Pankow, November 19, 2014; Paula Salvatore, August 7, 2013; Victoria Seeger, November 6, 2013; Butch Vig, June 3, 2013; Waddy Wachtel, October 17, 2013.

Source Notes

Articles

Applefield Olson, Cathy. "Tom Petty Originally Wrote 'Free Fallin' Just to Make Jeff Lynne Laugh." *Billboard*, June 7, 2016.

Hajdu, David. "The Who on 'The Smothers Brothers Comedy Hour.'" *New Republic*, February 11, 2010.

Sullivan, Caroline. "Diane Warren: I've Never Been in Love." *Guardian*, May 13, 2009.

Books

Whitburn, Joel. *Billboard Hot 100 Charts: The Eighties*. Menomonee Falls, WI: Record Research, 1995.

———. *Billboard Hot 100 Charts: The Nineties*. Menomonee Falls, WI: Record Research, 2000.

———. *Billboard's Top Pop Albums 1955–2001*. Menomonee Falls, WI: Record Research, 2002.

Video

Classic Albums: Nevermind. DVD documentary. Eagle Rock Entertainment, 2004.

Bogdanovich, Peter. *Tom Petty and the Heartbreakers: Runnin' Down a Dream*. DVD documentary. Warner Bros., 2007.

Other

Chicago. CD liner notes. *Chicago 16*. Rhino Records, 2006 (original vinyl LP released in 1982 on Full Moon/Warner Bros.).

Chicago. CD liner notes. *Chicago 17*. Rhino Records, 2006 (original vinyl LP released in 1984 on Full Moon/Warner Bros.).

INDEX

Index

Index

Index

Index